East European Monographs, No. DCCXI

ISBN: 978-0-88033-609-3
Library of Congress Control Number: 2007935634

Printed in the United States of America

BOSNIA AND HERZEGOVINA: IDENTITY, NATIONALIST LANDSCAPES AND THE FUTURE OF THE STATE

Steven Oluić

2007
East European Monographs, Boulder, Colorado
Distributed by Columbia University Press, New York

CONTENTS

Acknowledgements

There are many people that I would like to thank for their support and friendship over the past three years. I apologize in advance to those that I may have inadvertently left out, it certainly wasn't intentional. First of all, I would like to express my gratitude to Dr. Dave Kaplan, my advisor and dear friend. His guidance, enthusiasm and support were instrumental to me in completing the dissertation within three years. My heartfelt for all you have done.

I wish to also thank Dr. Jim Tyner for his role as a committee member and valued friend. His efforts certainly exceeded what is normally expected of a committee member and for that I am forever grateful. Jim's insights, genuine interest in my work and academic direction have led me to look at and understand the world in an entirely new way and for that I will be eternally indebted. I will miss the scholarly discussions while enjoying refreshment at various Kent establishments.

Dr. Vic Papacosma, my cognate committee member, has been a true friend and mentor. His knowledge of the Balkans and encouragement during those "low times" helped me succeed. Scholars such as Vic are hard to come by these days and I consider myself truly fortunate to count him as one of my educators. I will miss our lunchtime discussions.

To Dr. Shawn Banasick, I thank you for your role as committee member and working in the background to help me complete my studies. Your quiet support and academic input were helpful.

There are so many individuals that assisted in my field research that I am sure someone will be missed. Nonetheless I will start by thanking His Excellency Dr. Igor Davidović, the Bosnian Ambassador to the US, for his assistance in assisting me in coordinating my research trips to Bosnia. I would also like to thank MAJ Dave Galles, LTC Randy Everett, MSgt Craig Sweeney, and Dalibor Šmit of the Office of Defense Cooperation, European Command, in Sarajevo, Bosnia. In some respects you were the headquarters and safety net during my research travels across Bosnia. The use of your office and equipment are tremendously appreciated.

My fieldwork in the Banja Luka region would have been impossible without the outstanding support of the International Orthodox Christian Charity (IOCC) non-governmental organization. Ms. Tina Wolfe's efforts were simply stupendous and the success of my research can be directly attributed to her efforts in assisting my daily trips scouring the countryside for nationalist iconography and in conducting surveys and interviews. Mike Montgomery of the Office of the High Representative in Tuzla is due a big thank you for supporting my research travel in Bosnia and by answering so many of my questions from the US via email. Vedrana Dimitrijevic, of the

OSCE, graciously volunteered her time and advice in support of my research travels and coordination. I am sincerely indebted to all of you.

Both Rado Djurdjevic and Nikolina Obradovic of the OHR, have been, and continue to be, extremely helpful in my research interests. Their knowledge and regional expertise allowed me to focus my research time during my Bosnian travels instead of combing the countryside trying to discover "something." I would also like to thank Dr. Draško Marinković of the University of Banja Luka, Sanja Klajić, and the staff of the Hotel Firenca for their kindness and support while in Banja Luka.

To my many translators, or as they prefer, interpreters - hvala! Ažur, Maria, Siniša, and especially Vlado, all of you made my long days much less tedious and much more productive and joyous. I could not have completed the surveys and interviews without their sincere desire to provide me with their best effort. I am eternally grateful and look forward to seeing them again in the future.

To the people of Bosnia and those who I was lucky enough to interview and survey, thank you. Your warmth and welcoming demeanor made my trips to Bosnia worthwhile. I pray that permanent peace and prosperity comes to you in the near future.

To my family - my wife Gisela, my son Thomas, my daughters Sophia and Julia, thanks for always being there and supporting me when my "mojo" was running on empty or when I was dealing with one of the numerous crises I inevitably encounter. My wife's never ending encouragement and support merits my deepest thanks. My family makes my life worth living. I could not have completed this dissertation without your everlasting and unconditional love, warmth and support. And it is to my family that I dedicate this dissertation.

CHAPTER I

INTRODUCTION

"The opening of Mostar's bridge in July [2004] symbolized the extraordinary progress in knitting together communities so recently torn apart by war."

Lord Paddy Ashdown, HR, July 2004

In 1995 the Dayton Peace Accords (DPA) ended the fighting in Bosnia. The resultant Bosnia and Herzegovina was formed of two entities; one Serb, the Republika Srpska, the other an amalgamation of Bosnian Muslims (Bosniaks) and Bosnian Croats within cantons and named the Federation. My research investigates and reports on how Bosnia's three major ethnic groups – the Bosniaks, the Croats and the Serbs - affect Bosnia's development as a unitary, sovereign state and the creation of a common Bosnian identity.

Primary Research Questions

1. Does the Bosnian landscape reflect the impression of a sovereign and unitary Bosnian and Heregovinian state or an amalgamation of separate national spaces?
2. How do Bosnia's Muslims, Serbs and Croats characterize and understand their ethnic identity and how does this foster or inhibit the development of Bosnia and Herzegovina as an identity and a state.

Statement of the Problem

The Bosniaks, Croats and Serbs envisage their identities as being distinct and separate – there is neither a prevailing common Bosnian identity nor are the Croats and Serbs willing to subsume their identity within a greater Bosnian one. Both the Croats and Serbs fought a savage war for separately desired unions with Croatia and Serbia proper, and the Bosniaks for an independent state within the boundaries of the former Yugoslavian Republic of Bosnia. It appears that rapprochement between the national groups is far off.

The Dayton Peace Accords ended the fighting and compelled compliance to the notion of a Bosnian state; however, it divided Bosnia into two entities in an attempt to accommodate the territorial and nationalist goals of the Bosnian Serbs and divided the Federation into cantons to accommodate the Bosnian Croats. The Inter Entity Boundary Line (IEBL) is a dominant feature on the Bosnian landscape separating the entities both politically and physically. Both entities see the IEBL in stark contrast to one another. For the Bosniaks the IEBL is an obstacle to true statehood, providing the Serbs with a pseudo-state. For the Bosnian Serbs, the IEBL clearly represents the boundary of their national territory and a symbol of national security mandatory within the framework of Bosnia.

The roles played by national and political actors from state to local levels and the manifestation of nationalist symbols across the landscape indicate that Bosnia has a long way to go in achieving true statehood. The three national groups have developed asymmetrical spatial identities and have altered the cultural landscape, blatantly challenging the notion of a unified state and common Bosnian identity. Under the auspices of the Dayton Peace Accords, both the Croats and Serbs envision separate territorial legitimacy and identity: one at cantonal or municipal levels and the other at the entity level. The Bosniaks, however, see territorial legitimacy and their identity as being congruent with the entire territory of Bosnia and Herzegovina.

Significance of the Study

Recent discussion among foreign policy and political elites indicates a relatively common consensus that the existing situation in Bosnia and the Dayton Peace Accords has been a success. This model should be considered a success in the management of inter-ethnic hostilities, volatile nationalism and in state building. Its adaptation to other regions such as Kosovo and even to Afghanistan and Iraq is openly advocated. My research sheds light on how successful the International Community, namely NATO and the UN, has been in developing this premise of Bosnia as a success story.

The concept of creating, or imagining "nations" as purely social constructions is popular in academia and has been used extensively to explain nationalism in many contexts over the last 30 plus years. From such an instrumentalist approach it follows that a distinct Bosnian identity will emerge, subsuming current Bosniak, Croat, and Serb ethnic identity and nationalisms. I contend that national identity and nationalism cannot be only comprehended through any universal approach such as the instrumentalism or primordialism, but are better understood within the ethno-symbolic approach of Smith (1998). However I do contend that primordialism does play a major role in the way the people understand identity and must be included with Smith's (1998) approach. I also argue that the characteristics of national identity and concomitant nationalism are neither easily created nor manipulated, leading to a dilemma that perhaps a common Bosnian identity is unachievable and Bosnia's political future as a state is bleak.

Objectives of the Study

My research objectives are ambitious. First, I plan to increase the understanding of how Bosnia's ethnic groups envision their national identity and the transmission of that identity within contemporary theoretical approaches of identity formation. I will capture the attitudes and feelings towards the notion of a Bosnian identity and also the Dayton Peace Accords mandated constitution and state structure.

Second, I intend to illuminate the contemporary realities and impacts of nationalism and nationalist politics, as manifested on the landscape, on Bosnia. The cultural landscape of Bosnia includes significant national and nationalist symbology which correlates well with ethnic group and nationalist attitudes within the entities and can serve as indicators of the success or failure of Bosnia as a functional sovereign state and the development of a Bosnian identity.

Last, I intend to challenge the notion of Bosnia's successes by using questionnaire and interview data that contradicts Paddy Ashdown's judgment cited above. This quote is illustrative of the current discourse among foreign policy elites and international community constructions of Bosnia and Herzegovina as a success story of ethnic reconciliation and state building and that it is a useful model for future interventions elsewhere worldwide.

My dissertation will realistically reflect the perceptions and attitudes of selected actors and the Bosnian public at large towards the development of the entities as nation-based statelets within the Dayton Peace Accords framework of pseudo-state Bosnia, or as integral members Bosnia itself. It will provide a better understanding of the levels of antagonistic national sentiment regarding the entity versus the state or even the canton versus the entity within the Federation.

Organization of the Dissertation

This dissertation is organized in nine chapters beginning with this first chapter, the Introduction. Chapter II is my research framework, addressing the concepts national and spatial identity, theories of nationalism, concepts of landscape, boundaries, nations and states. Chapter III outlines the methodology used, which is a combination of qualitative and quantitative methods. The chapter overviews the methods to obtain data and analysis used for findings. Chapter IV provides an abbreviated historical background necessary to understand the dynamics and current history of Bosnia.

It is in Chapters VI, VII, VIII, and IX I present the main findings of my research. Chapters VI and VII engage the aspects of ethnic and national identity, and the notion of territoriality in contemporary Bosnia. Chapter VIII presents the observations and understandings of the nationalist landscape in contemporary Bosnia. Chapter IX presents the findings from the questionnaire survey conducted. Chapter X, the conclusion, identifies the main findings of the research and discusses the implications affecting Bosnia and Herzegovina.

CHAPTER II

RESEARCH FRAMEWORK

"If I could convince both sides to stop killing their own people for CNN, perhaps we could have a ceasefire."

Major-General Lewis MacKenzie, 1992

National Identity

The concept of "nation" has been the focus of great interest for many scholars and researchers especially since the fall of the Berlin Wall. What exactly constitutes a nation? Common language, race, territory, religion, economic life and culture are some key characteristics used by scholars in an attempt to define the nation. While nation and ethnicity are not coterminous - attaching territory and political goals to an ethnic group sets the concept of nation apart from ethnicity. I use the terms ethnic group and nation interchangeably in this section.

Bosniaks, Croats and Serbs possess the hallmarks of national identity – religion, language, geography or location, and state (Seton-Watson, 1997). To varying degrees they share three of the four hallmarks in common. Language is not a significant factor of difference in Bosnia as it is, for example, in Belgium between the Walloons and Flemish. Religion is the crucial characteristic and difference that clearly separates the three national groups in Bosnia.

The concept of "nation" arises in tying territory to the aspect of ethnicity. A useful definition of nation is provided by Konstantin Symmons-Symonolowicz (White, 2000, 16) where he defines nation as:

> A territorially-based community of human beings sharing a distinct variant of modern culture, bound together by a strong sentiment of unity and solidarity, marked by a clear historically-rooted consciousness of

national identity, and possessing, or striving to possess, a genuine political self-government.

These descriptions of national identity and nation will serve as the basis for my research involving the national groups of Bosnia and Herzegovina.

I draw on the extensive literature within the realm of scholarship on nations and nationalism to develop a theoretical approach to answer my guiding research questions. Within this body of literature lie several key theoretical approaches to the study of ethnic or national identity and nationalism. The two major approaches are (1) primordialism and (2) instrumentalism (or circumstantialism) (Bonus, 2000, Conversi, 1995, Gil-White, 1999). However there are other approaches that have gained in stature over the past several years. Anthony Smith (1998) and John Hutchinson present an ethno-symbolic approach that bridges, in some part, the large divide between primordialists and instrumentalists. More recently, scholars such as Billig (1995) and Edensor (2002) promote the concept that the everyday or popular culture is as important in developing national identity as are the elite of high cultures discussed in the other approaches. Their approach intimates that national identity is grounded in the everyday mundane details of social interaction, habits, routines and practical knowledge which serve as a basis of identity (Edensor, 2002, 24). My theoretical approach to the study of national identity and nationalism draws heavily upon Smith's ethno-symbolism as a way to incorporate the idea of instrumentalism with primordialism (Anderson, 1983, Armstrong, 1982, Geertz, 1963, Grosby, 1994).

Primordialists view identity as a sense or sentiment of belonging to a group based on some original ancestry, culture and homeland. Such an approach stresses the essential commonalities that unite the group and the indescribable and consuming qualities of *a priori* human attachments (Eller and Coughlin, 1993). Clifford Geertz (1963) typically characterizes the proponents of primordialism's views as that in which one is bound to one's kin by religion, language, or social practices. He asserts that these characteristics and practices have an ineffable, and at times overpowering, coerciveness on nations and their ties (Geertz, 1963).

Much is attributed to sentiment and the emotional strength of ethnic (or national) bonds. Steven Grosby (1994) argues that this primordial concept of ethnicity can drive humans to sacrifice themselves for their family and their nation. Francisco Gil-White's (1999) research indicates a very real perception of "ethnic membership" at the individual level based upon common biological ancestry. This perception, feeling or sentiment is very real and influences behavior and actions on members of an ethnic group. The historical past and ancestry determines one's identity – an outlook shared by many (Casares, 2003). Certainly in the former Yugoslavia, the ties of religion and notions of common heritage served to bind the successor-state national groups together as civil war erupted in 1992. Indeed, even an authoritarian communist state was unsuccessful in subsuming ethnic identities within common Yugoslav citizenship.

Instrumentalists, on the other hand, distinguish certain actors as manipulating groups in pursuit of common goals or interests and which can be seen as a modern phenomenon (Hutchinson, 1996, Gellner, 1983, Anderson, 1983). An ethnic or national identity is constructed to support social, political, and cultural interests and/or goals by key actors or elites, such as political leaders, academicians, or military officers (Hall, 1992). E. J. Hobsbawm (1996) goes further by asserting that the nation is a product of invented tradition. Primordial ties have little credibility from this perspective, as here identity is created and not an assumed given. Slobodan Milošević, Franjo Tudjman and Alija Izetbegović can all be attributed with instigating the renewed sense of national identity among the Serbs, Croats and Bosniaks, respectively, at the cost of any idea of a Yugoslav nation and state (Denitch, 1996). In spite of their differences, both approaches do agree to some extent that common descent is a crucial factor in ethnic group formation (Gil-White, 1999).

Although both the primordialist and instrumentalist approaches have aspects applicable to identity in Bosnia-Herzegovina, alternative views outside of these are also appropriate. The ethno-symbolic approach of Anthony Smith

(1998) provides an effective model by considering the issue(s) between an ethnic group that has been able to maintain an identity for centuries and one that is simply a construct of nationalist or elite manipulations. He stresses the symbolic legacy of ethnic identities, and seeks to show how modern nationalism rediscovers and reinterprets the symbols, myths, memories, traditions and values of their national histories, especially in times of change (Smith, 1998). A key ethno-symbolic approach argument is that modern nations and nationalism are grounded in pre-existing ethnic ties and that the nationalist mobilization is based on this legacy. As Billig (1995, 26) even writes, "Some identities have existed previously and a general sense of community was not entirely invented in the eighteenth century" as Anderson (1983), Gellner (1983) and others would write.

John Armstrong (1982) uses both the Armenian and Jewish ethnic groups to illustrate the power of "sacral myths" and distinctive religions, with their ecclesiastical institutions, in maintaining identity through time and as diasporas. Anthony Smith (1998, 192) writes how he saw "clusters of myths, symbols, memories, values and traditions, emerging from shared experiences of several generations of cohabitating populations, as the defining cultural elements from which ethnic groups emerged." He also argues that ethnic persistence (as opposed to a new construct) can be traced to an ethnic group's history and values represented by symbols and the use of myths to give meaning to their history and values (Smith, 1998). By incorporating this age old sense of self (primordialism) with current nationalist activity (instrumentalism) the two major theoretical approaches to identity are bridged within this ethno-symbolic theoretical framework. Smith notes that nations rely on a preexisting texture of myths, memories, values, and symbols as a basis for their identity, and so history is critically important to understanding national identities (Conversi 1995, Smith 1998).

Spatial Identity

Nation as opposed to ethnic group specifically connotes the tie of people to territory. Kaplan (1994) writes that the degree of correspondence between the spatial identities of national groups helps to account for a group's conception of its national identity, the relations between the groups, and the possible zones of conflict. Current political arrangements in Bosnia essentially leave the Bosniaks in control of the state apparatus, due in no small part to the International Community's support during and after the civil war. And although multiple nations - the Bosniaks, Croats, and Serbs coexist to some degree in Bosnia - the politically dominant group will come to control, or in this case, may attempt to control and submerge the identities of the others by their use of institutions available to them. The United Nations Office of the High Commissioner and NATO forces have aligned with the interests of the Bosniaks and have caused fear and consternation by the non-Muslim nations. In essence, the Bosniak's spatial identity covers the entire Bosnian state.

Some scholars view spatial identity differently and surmise that borders are becoming less important to the notion of one's identity. Jukarainen (1999) writes that future spatial identities will rely less on strict borders and who the "we" happen to be. This assertion may be applicable to the French-Spanish Catalan borderland or the Alsace region, but it is hard if not incomprehensible to overlay this notion on the reality of a Bosnia where new spatial identities have been formed, strict new borders are present, and the "we" carries great significance.

Nationalism

Nationalism, the political ideology linking nation and territory, is a relatively modern phenomenon in social theory and human history (Gellner 1983; Hall 1995; Kedourie 1960; Seton-Watson 1977). Outside the discussion of common religion, language and shared histories, the power of the nationalist idea - that a people of a common culture should be ruled by their own and within their territory - is historically novel according to Hall (1995). This position is contentious and must be studied contextually when observing the Balkan national struggles to free themselves of Hapsburg or Ottoman rule.

There is no one universal or essential theory of nationalism. In fact, when looking at the former Yugoslavia various theories may be applicable. As with the theoretical approaches to national identity, theories of nationalism have been traditionally categorized into either primordialist or instrumentalist (Conversi, 1995, Hall, 1998, Smith 1995). Both categories envisage nations as being fundamental, basic units of social cohesion, and as a universal attribute of humanity.

Primordialist nationalism, sometimes called "organic nationalism" pictures a spontaneous process stemming from a naturally given sense of nationhood (Conversi, 1995). In this view, the world has always consisted of nations which are the bedrock of history and chief actors in the historical drama (Smith, 1998). Although there are many criticisms of this approach such as how can we ever truly "know" this attachment to kin or trace one's ties back to a nation's beginnings, this theoretical approach incorporates the notion that a nation stems from an original core. It does not assume a biological basis but one that is historically rooted.

Clifford Geertz (1994) provides a constructive description of the foci around which primordial nationalism can develop. These are: (1) *assumed* blood ties, (2) race, (3) language, (4) region, (5) religion, and (6) custom (to include history). These foci are a useful launching point when analyzing the popular nationalist events in the former Yugoslavia. Although race and language are not applicable to all nationalist struggles in Yugoslavia, the other foci were vital in the development of what can be seen as primordial nationalist behavior at the popular level in Bosnia, Croatia and elsewhere in the Balkans.

The instrumentalist approach, associated with modernism (Smith, 1998), contends that nationalism is a product of elite manipulation and forwards that nations can be fabricated, if not outright invented. Both Eric Hobsbawm (1992), through his notion of *invented traditions*, and Benedict Anderson's *Imagined Communities* (1983), believe that nations and nationalism are constructs and cultural artifacts (Smith, 1998). Anderson (1990) writes that: (a) despite the limited bounds of an individual's activities, the nation is associated with a larger sense of communion than that of his local environment; (b) it is *imagined* as limited in geographical reach by finite, if elastic, boundaries beyond which lie other nations; (c) it is *imagined* as sovereign and thus the ideal is freedom in a sovereign state and (d) it is *imagined* as community based on a territorial relationship which subsumes other community cleavages and divisions.

The role of intellectuals as a driving force in the invention of nations and the rise of nationalism are a basic tenet of the instrumentalist approach (Breuilly 1982; Gellner 1964). Ernest Gellner (1964) condemns any notion that "nationalism is the awakening of nations to self-consciousness" and asserts that intellectuals and elites construct new entities and that modern nations have an *invented* character to them. Gellner (1983) also ties his theories of nationalism with that of the logic of industrialism and its middle class, leading to the integration of all citizens within industrial society giving rise to nationalism. However Elie Kedourie (1960) delinks the two, as industry and middle class did not necessarily exist in locations where nationalism arose. Even Hegel lends credence to the concept that nations may have had long histories prior to any state formation and therefore are not recent creations (Gellner, 1963).

Anthony Smith (1998), not an ardent proponent of either primordialism or instrumentalism, does believe in the historical longevity of the nation and ethnicity. Through this idea he bridges the instrumentalist and primordialist approaches in nationalism with his ethno-symbolic approach. Although modern "nationalism" itself (the idea of popular self rule) is only 200 years old, he asserts that ethnic identity and nations have existed for thousands of years, and nationalism can only be understood as its modern articulation (Smith, 1998).

Although the ethno-symbolic and primordialist approaches to nationalism are most relevant to my research, the discussion of nationalism in Bosnia and Herzegovina invites one aspect of the instrumentalist approach to be acknowledged. The role of national elites and institutions in the maintenance of nationalism in Bosnia today bears note and may need to be incorporated within the greater framework of my theoretical approach. In any case, both Armstrong (1982) and Smith's (1998) writings on the ethno-symbolic approach are useful in bridging salient features of primordialism and instrumentalism by utilizing the historical legacies, national myths, nationalist symbolism, and aspects of religion that are common facets of both approaches and therefore are of greatest relevance to my research.

Landscape

"Landscape denotes the interaction of people and place; a social group and its spaces, particularly the spaces to which the group belongs and from which its members derive some part of their shared identity and meaning" (Groth, 1997, 1). Inquiry into the landscapes of Bosnia is especially useful in developing the narrative of nationalism's manifestation and ethnic identity in the entities. Although Paul Groth (1997) focuses on cultural and social aspects, certain political and "national" actors and populations are using the Bosnian landscape to obstruct inter-ethnic and inter-entity political relations. The landscape is being used as a platform to telegraph nationalist symbols. As Muir (1999) writes "human agency alters the landscape which reminds us that it is a social product." Historical linkage, place names, monuments, symbols are all significant markers of national identity. Placed on the landscape they assume great importance on the national psyches of the peoples of Bosnia.

Michael Billig's (1995) perspectives in *Banal Nationalism* provide a unique approach to understanding the manifestation of nationalism on the landscape. He writes that nationalism is omnipresent, not just found among the ideologies of the separatist movements or at the peripheries of a state. Just as in America where symbols are present reminding one of nationhood, such as flags and banners of red white and blue, numerous other nations and states also manifest these symbols. Nationalism as Billig (1995) writes is not an "intermittent mood" but an endemic condition. The landscape dotted with new churches, mosques, monuments to "our" war dead, banners and flags of "our" nation not the state of BiH are all significant reminders across Bosnia that nationalism is all-pervasive in everyday lives.

Inquiry into the symbols and monuments on the landscape allows a fuller development and understanding of current nationalism in Bosnia. The war memorials that dot the Bosnian landscape have a purpose, as Mayo (1988, 68) writes memorials "can be intentionally designed to evoke, often forcefully, memories of war," or in Bosnia the control of territory.

Boundaries

Traditional political geography and boundary studies have addressed boundaries as fixations of modernity (Giddens, 1998). J.R.V. Prescott (1987), Dennis Rumley and Julian Minghi (1991) and Friedrich Ratzel (1897) are key figures in the study of the political geography of boundaries. Ratzel categorized vigorous states as those expanding spatially, thus increasing their size and boundaries. Boundaries have been interpreted in different ways. In earlier history natural boundaries (rivers, mountains, etc.) were seen as "the only real boundary" that were written and drawn in nature (Paasi, 1999). Man-made boundaries were considered arbitrary and temporal and it was not until the inter-war period that the establishment of a fixed boundary terminology was produced for the language of political geographers. Fixed meanings were produced for boundary, border, and frontier (Prescott, 1987, Rumley and Minghi, 1991).

John Agnew (2001) contends that during war or in times of conflict, borders assume a much greater importance. Indeed, rigid boundaries, territorial demarcation and borders are hallmarks of political space within Central and Eastern Europe. Bosnia and Herzegovina's formation has not followed what may be seen as "typical" of boundary-making since the end of the Cold War. Although war creates states and states create war, Bosnia is an amalgamation of mutually antagonistic inhabitants that are forced to live together by external actors in the former republic borders. The Inter Entity Boundary Line (IEBL) has assumed significant importance and its presence, both physical and political, is strongly contested between the Bosniaks and Serbs.

Boundaries, borders and territory are a critical component of the secessionist wars in Yugoslavia. Indeed Paasi (1999) writes that boundaries are not merely technical instruments exploited by sovereign bodies, but they are usually among the major constituents of national identity, since boundaries and their representations are used to connote and symbolize territoriality, often by means of specific national or social symbols. Paasi provides excellent insight to the perception of the IEBL by both parties; it is a clear symbol of Serb territory and control while at the same time an obstacle to Bosnian (read Bosniak) state level control and development.

One of the greatest characteristics of the Balkans is the notion of an elemental or timeless tie to the land – the peasant's desire to "be buried where I was born." Steven Grosby (1995) writes that territoriality existed long before modernity and it is one feature of all societies and one element of territoriality is the transcendental, primordial attachment of the nation to the land. The use of "primordial" is used not only in the context of national identity and nationalism but in also the concept of territoriality. The element of history is also a major factor in the connection between man and place. Serb participation within the confines of the IEBL is leading to a transcendental significance of that space; the RS has become a meaningful structure whereas the Federation entity is struggling for Croatian minority participation, thus detracting from the territoriality of Federation space. Territorial integrity and sovereignty are extremely important in the organization of human society; it remains a fundamental, constitutive element of modern Western society.

Boundaries are of absolute significance in Bosnia. The unencumbered movement of Bosnian Croats and Serbs across international boundaries to their respective national states of Croatia and Serbia and their concomitant borderland development stands in stark contrast to Bosnia's IEBL. In some cases the IEBL can be interpreted as a "hard" boundary between entities within the same state. The increase of cross boundary activities (and transgressions), the movement of goods, ideas, capital, and human beings has dramatically affected boundary studies across the globe (Kaplan and Häkli, 2002). These cross boundary "flows" have altered the traditional understanding of borders and boundaries and how they have impacted Bosnia. The human dimension alone is staggering with the role of ethnic diasporas, in many cases refugees and displaced persons, affecting their former homeland through subversive activities, financial assistance to various parties and even lobbying their newly found home's political leadership to act on behalf of 'their side' (Paasi, 1999).

We often witness that new boundaries and the borderlands between emerging states tend to be zones of cultural overlap and political instability (Augelli, 1980). Such a situation does not necessarily exist in BiH in spite of some commonalities among the population. Although both entities are politically immature, both exert effective and substantial control within their entity boundaries. Within this context the Serbs of the RS are most concerned with their jurisdictional and "national" control of the RS and are less interested in developing ties that would bind them ever closer to the Federation and subject them to greater control by the Bosnian state. This creates the political instability noted by Augelli (1980).

Nations and States

"The state is a legal entity, internationally recognized, whose responsibility is to organize and guarantee the welfare and security of its citizens within its territory, where it is the supreme authority, tolerating no competitor or challenge to its sovereignty and demanding obedience from its inhabitants (Mellor, 1989, 32)." Mellor's (1989) definition of the state contradicts the very notion of Bosnian statehood. Bosnia's state institutional powers are inadequate, nonexistent, or not permitted to provide for the welfare of its population except via entity institutional action. As the concept of state itself is challenged by the two entity arrangement within Bosnia, Bosnia itself does not fit into any definition of statehood. The role of the High Representative and NATO further erode the understood principles of statehood in Bosnia.

Anthony Giddens (1991) writes that the state is a critical actor because it is the institution that allows representation of a nation within its controlled territory; however this is not the case in Bosnia *per se.* The Dayton Peace Accords provides for national group representation at the entity level for the Serbs and Canton or municipality level for the Croats.

Historically, not all states existed side-by-side with nationalism. The Roman, Habsburg and Ottoman Empires are examples of states that were able to maintain the fabric of social cohesion and the loyalties of men for long durations (Kedourie, 1960). However, the current concept of "state" is under great pressure from many academic quarters today. Jukarainen (1999) sees the "state" being unceasingly challenged by the dual processes of [ethnic] fragmentation and globalization, whereas Kaplan and Häkli (2002) envisions the nation-state role as the crucial and dominant scale in European political order. Elements of both can be seen in the political dimensions of Bosnia; ethnic fragmentation on the one hand, is still a mortal threat, whereas nation-state status accorded by the DPA and international recognition provides legitimacy and acceptance in the International Community.

However when taken in context with globalization, the state is largely taken for granted as a geographical entity (Murphy, 2002). Murphy emphasizes the characteristic of the state as a political-territorial entity. Perhaps the most distinctive and fundamental feature in this modern state system is the territorial order on which it is based and the need to understand how that order is implicated in the political arrangements and understandings on which the system is based (Murphy, 2002). The notion of territoriality, the exercise of power or control over a portion of space and its contents, is closely related to the state structure (Sack, 1986). The development of the state system would be better understood by placing the political-historical arrangements and understandings within a geographic context. The fairly recent establishment of Bosnia in 1995 as an imposed state system and boundaries conveys its artificiality. The Bosnian state doesn't correspond to territorial realities, which is partitioned between two entities. Whereas many scholars tend to frame the world by difference in state government and economy, such as colonial versus non-colonial and developed versus non-developed, Murphy sees the distinctions based on territorial differences (including ethnic claim to territory) being decisive in analyzing state conflict. In many cases the source of ethnic conflict is about the territorial dreams and ambitions of nations, as was seen in the civil wars in Yugoslavia.

The recent inter-ethnic nationalist warfare and resultant Dayton Peace Accords with its stipulated entities and demarcating IEBL represent distinct geographical and territorial impacts on Bosnia. The realities of the DPA Constitution and its IEBL, perceived so differently by Bosnia's national groups would indicate that indeed the territorial differences between them may be too insurmountable without time, aid and international community presence.

CHAPTER III

METHODOLOGY

"I consider Bosnia & Herzegovina a sovereign, undivided state that should be without entities; that is, if there are entities there will always be divisions among peoples and I know that if there would ever be more war, it would be caused by the mere existence of entities."

Survey Respondent, Bosanski Petrovac, 2004

I used elements of both qualitative and quantitative methods in conducting my research and gathering data to answer my guiding research questions. Through the methods outlined below I addressed how the concept and understanding of national identity, nationalism as it is symbolically manifested on the landscape and national territoriality impact Bosnia and Herzegovina.

The primary methods I used to obtain, analyze and present data are: (1) visual observation (2) survey questionnaires and (3) interview and discussions. These methods are synchronized and overlap one another, each building upon the other to provide a fuller and richer understanding in answering my guiding research questions.

Study Area

My study area encompasses the state of Bosnia and Herzegovina. The municipalities I traveled are highlighted in the map below, Figure One.

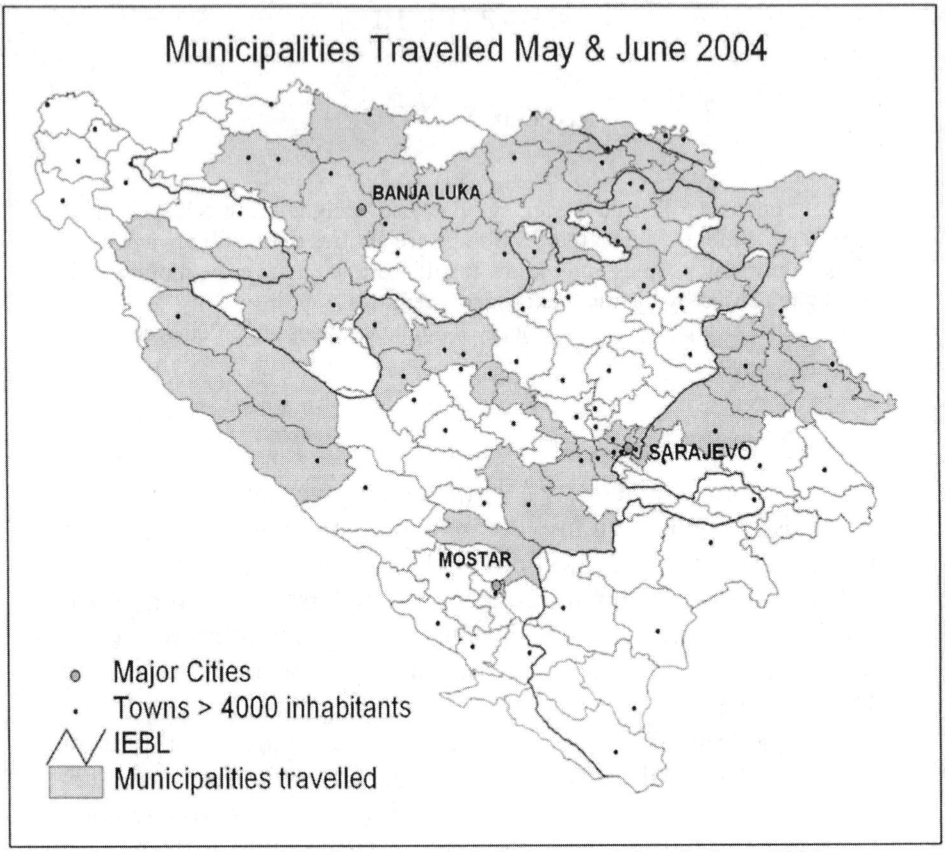

Figure 1 – Map of municipalities traveled during my May & June 2004 fieldwork.

Coordination and Planning Visit to Bosnia - July 2003

I conducted a reconnaissance of my tentative research area in July 2003. The goals of this initial visit were to:

a. Visit various government, NGO and military organizations and develop a list of contacts that would support my up front planning, coordination and research efforts during my 2004 field research.

b. Determine which areas appeared to provide the best opportunities to conduct my survey and whether or not the landscape possessed the nationalist symbolism that frames much of this research.

c. Ascertain whether the travel routes were conducive to frequent stops to photograph the landscape and to develop a feasible travel timeline for my 2004 trip.

<u>Fieldwork Data and Landscape Observation Methods</u>

A significant portion of my research analyzes the manifestation of nationalism on the landscape and national spatial identity. Therefore I accumulated data based on visual methodology - observations and digital photographs. Coupling this method with opportunistic conversations, interviews and survey questionnaires, I was able to develop a much better appreciation of the meanings of the nationalist landscapes and implications for Bosnia.

Observation of the landscape, its documentation, analysis and interpretation is the critical component of my field research. During my 23 May to 16 June 2004, or 25 days, field research I was able to take 1246 digital images. According to Kearns (2000), observation allows the researcher to achieve his/her [research] purpose by: counting, complementing and contextualizing [objects of research]. Observation permits a contextual understanding and interpretation of a particular time and place through direct experience (Kearns, 2000). Interpreting images does not involve claims to any essential "truth" (Rose, 2001). This interpretation unfolds the meanings inherent in my observation of the nationalist landscapes.

This approach in my qualitative research is typical of J.B. Jackson's (1984) essays on cultural landscape – an approach that seeks to study explanation that every landscape is a code, and which captures meaning and emotions in the vernacular landscape (Meinig, 1979). Additionally, Peter Jackson's (1983) work in depicting landscape as a reflection or recipient of a given culture further provides a mechanism to interpreting the nationalist landscape.

Photos of symbols (nationalist monuments, graffiti, and churches/mosques), the re-naming of place, and the construction of distinctly national structures are valuable data when coupled with the opportunity interviews and questionnaire survey in gaining insights into the impacts of nationalism and identity. Comparison and contrast at various scales (municipal, cantonal, entity) within the Bosnian state allowed me to note any scalar or regional differences among the population.

As noted by Holdsworth (1997) visual information alone cannot fully explain questions of human geography. The landscape is a phenomenal resource of relics, visual cues, and even evidence of social (including nationalism) or economic forces at work in Bosnia. Envisioning the landscape is limited solely when focusing on the visual at the expense of other methods. It should not be considered the quickest or most reliable route into inquiry (Holdsworth, 1997). Indeed, coupling the information gleaned from survey questionnaires and interviews with my observations provide a better understanding of not only the landscape in and of itself, but the processes behind it and the resultant impacts.

Signs, monuments, ethno-symbolism are omnipresent in Bosnia and provide excellent sources of information to decipher meaning(s), possible intent and desire on the part of the various national groups regarding the state of BiH. Given my prior trips to Bosnia, comparative aspects of place, before and after, are essential in delineating the direction and current status of nationalism within Bosnia. Some categorical examples I found on the landscape are:

(1) Increased national identity.
- New churches / mosques, new monuments (war or national hero).
- Changing place names – streets, town names, etc.
- Resurrection of symbols of the past (revisionism).

(2) Strengthening of boundaries.
- Indicators on the IEBL (signs and nationalist symbology).
- Refugee return status noted by new construction.
- Status of IEBL minefields (a physical barrier) that limit freedom of movement.

(3) Attempts to create state identity at entity and/or cantonal level

- Manifestation of nationalist symbolism (flags, pictures, posters) at political levels; lack of state level symbolism
- Institutional disregard for federal authority

As mentioned, during my fieldwork I photographed the physical aspects of the symbolic landscape and recorded my observations and impressions within the context of the recent civil war and related nationalisms in Bosnia. Concurrent with this I conducted opportunity interviews, recording these discussions concerning the landscape's (or symbol's) representation to the interviewee. The most noticeable and generally acknowledged symbol for all interviewees/discussants was (and is) the Inter Entity Boundary Line.[1] I was able to gain insights into the meaning of the symbols on the landscape at the local level – my primary level of research.

<u>Observation Analysis</u>

Within the framework of observation as a method, I have used the approach to "landscape as text" (or representations) as a mechanism to analyze and interpret the nationalist symbolic landscape of Bosnia within an overall narrative of the nationalist landscape in Bosnia. This approach offers some advantage in analyzing and interpreting the landscape. As noted by Cosgrove (1984) and Muir (1999) not only can the history of a region be understood by its landscape, so can its politics. Scholars, such as Duncan (1994), claim that political analysis is central to and therefore should be included into landscape interpretation. The nationalist representations on the landscape impact the populace through the meanings the landscape conveys and therefore influences all aspects of a society or national group in the region.

Narratives developed through the process of observation do have some limitations as they are subjective by their very nature. However, nationalist imagery in Bosnia is not a subtle method or easily missed and lends itself to interpretation when coupled with more methods. The use of nationalist symbols by all parties was an intrinsic part of their warfare and part of their identity. They are simply commonly understood codes that were strengthened and radicalized in the last war. Most of these symbols have been used before in times of conflict – especially in the Second World War. As such this data is extremely conducive to teasing out meanings and messages. The symbol of one group is in most cases a provocation to another. By noting prevalence, apparent rate of construction or overt action (such as in renaming of place), it is possible to capture the meanings inherent across the Bosnian landscape(s).

Observation of the landscape, based upon where I was, allowed for the categorization of the data. Monuments and memorials imbued with nationalist symbology certainly placed it in a category that I consider contradictory to the notion of a united Bosnia and supportive of national groups. Moreover, when noting that the nearby region lacked any Bosnian state symbology, such as state flags on local government buildings, or that nearby areas still lacked refugee returns evidenced by destroyed homes, a clearer pattern and narrative emerges.

"Reading texts" or narratives in the interpretation of representations on the landscape is certainly a facet of observation (Geertz, 1973) and complements the visual methodology, allowing me to discern the nationalist, even separatist, themes and narratives present. Ways of reading or understanding the landscape (also known as decoding) is dependent on whom, or which national group, is reading the landscape – responses in the survey and interviews captures this and complete this analysis. In any case, observation of and reading the landscape cannot be accomplished without an understanding of the history of the region and its national groups. The use of documents provides an in-depth historical and contemporary understanding of Bosnia and its people.

Survey Data, Analysis and Interviews

My survey questionnaire was designed to complement the observation of the landscape and the interviews. The objectives of the survey were to:

a. Interpret and measure the significance of the (1) Inter Entity Boundary Line (IEBL), the (2) establishment of a stronger central government in Sarajevo, and the (3) an independent Kosovo as it relates to the development of Bosnia as a state and an identity.

b. Ascertain and explore the national identity of the Bosnian population. Determine their identification with the various ethnic groups before and after the war and identify any broad trend(s) arising from the data.

c. Explore and measure the concept of primordialism in Bosnia's national groups by using aspects of Dr. Francisco Gil-White's "ethnic transmission and acquisition model" (ETAM) research.

d. Collect limited demographic data and measurements.

e. Evoke a response either in (1) written comments on the survey or (2) leading to a follow-up or opportunity interview.

Survey Execution.

I conducted the survey from 27 May to 16 June 2004. A total of 216 questionnaires were completed over the course of 25 days. Although not initially planned as a central part of my research, the flexibility and adaptability of my research design allowed me to incorporate the questionnaire survey as a major component of my fieldwork. The questionnaires quickly gained importance as I was able to obtain many more respondents and conduct a broader spatial coverage of Bosnia than I believed initially possible.

A key advantage of utilizing a survey is that researchers may be able to identify broad trends (Hoggart, 2002). Surveys are aimed at establishing general trends, and providing an empirical base for explanations and interpretations. Due to the complexity and resource demands, surveys tend to be a research method of last resort when alternative methods are not available (Sheskin, 2002 and Fowler, 1990). Every attempt should be made to obtain data by other means based on the aforementioned reasons and sources; however, for Bosnia the information is simply not available through a census office or government statistics agency. Accurate population statistics are not available from the various state and entity level governments.[2]

Since 1995 there has been insignificant geographical fieldwork and research covering extensive areas of Bosnia. Based on existing literature (Allcock 2000, Bose 2002, Bringa 2002, Sells 2003), most fieldwork and research tends to be site, region or event specific, such as the siege of Sarajevo, the rebuilding of the famous *Stari Most* bridge in Mostar or the Srebrenica massacre, and looks past the wealth of data and information available elsewhere in Bosnia. In many cases, these studies tend to mirror the meta-narrative surrounding the breakup of Yugoslavia that one side or ethnic group was particularly responsible and thereby biases the existing research at worst or ignores other interpretations at best.

The dangers of conducting research in a post-war environment (due to physical dangers such as minefields and old battlefields), coupled with a lack of people to study (due to massive population shifts) has inhibited research. Therefore a survey, however limited, was necessary to gain a fuller appreciation and understanding of how the nationalist landscape and notions of ethnic identity relate to Bosnia and its future.

Sample Size and Selection

The sample size required for this survey was difficult to determine. As noted by Fowler (1987) and Bradshaw and Stratford (2000) there is rarely a definitive answer about how large a sample should be for any given study. Sheskin (1985) concedes this but does provide parameters to determine sample sizes. He writes that "in practice, most researchers attempt to obtain about 400 completed responses" which will normally provide an accuracy level of a 95% confidence level at a 5% confidence interval given that the *sample is representative* (Sheskin, 1985, 35). This reflects basically a quantitative approach and an intuitive logic in which "more is better." As much of my research is qualitative I am not attempting to generalize across the entire population, but am garnering data to identify trends based on the regions and population queried. Although researchers can never be certain that the sample is truly representative of an entire population (Strauss, 1990) the broad spatial coverage coupled with an extremely high (>95%) survey response rate, incorporating Bosnia's major ethnic groups, supports a degree of confidence in the sample size. While this selection is not purely representative, I have attempted to mitigate the effects of potential bias.

My participant selection was based primarily on where I traveled. Given the significant population shifts and regional homogenization due to the war I was able to obtain participants by ensuring that my travel route traversed each ethnic group's territory. Sampling was a combination of (1) opportunistic and (2) convenience sampling (Bradshaw and Stratford, 2000). By using an opportunistic sampling method I was able to follow any "flexible leads and take advantage of the unexpected," such as handing out surveys at offices (Table One) in which the office or agency managers were supportive of my research efforts and even served as gatekeepers. Given that the survey was distributed based on my research travels, the majority of respondents were selected on the basis of access, and therefore is considered convenience sampling.

It was impossible to gather a truly unique random sample in Bosnia. No recent census records, phone books, a transitional population, and lack of readily available public demographics information based on ethnicity made trying to develop a random sample list impossible.[3] Separate governmental agencies just do not have the data and non-governmental organizations (NGO) such as the United Nations (UN) and the Office of the High Representative (OHR) offer only aggregate level demographic data from "best guess estimates" from their field offices. Indeed most of their demographic data is based on the irrelevant 1991 Yugoslav census data. After each day in the field, I would review the ethnic group count to see whether or not all groups were be included in the survey. This usually turned out to be the case.

I utilized a "team concept" in administering the surveys to potential respondents during my travels. Questionnaires were distributed most often by my interpreter who would offer a short explanation of who I was and the goals of my research. The interpreter would also elaborate or answer any questions that the respondent may have had, often translating my answers to the respondent. This method was extremely effective in obtaining collected questionnaires; I estimate that well over 95% of distributed questionnaires were returned to me.

Outside of the team concept survey, I handed out questionnaires to (1) my interpreters to have their family and friends complete the questionnaire, (2) my points of contacts at official institutions, US military offices and non-governmental organizations (NGOs) as listed in Table One. Again this accounted for a high response rate. Moreover my German language skills were a significant aid in distributing questionnaires at the hotels I stayed at as German appears to be the *lingua franca* in this industry in Bosnia. Another reason is the number of Bosnians who worked in Germany as *Gastarbeiters* or were refugees there during the war and had a reasonable command of the language.

Figure One (above) displays the regions I traveled, therefore my spatial coverage of Bosnia. In the somewhat less than four weeks spent in Bosnia I drove over 3,000 kilometers. Given the extensive area and ethnically diverse regions covered and the number of respondents, I achieved a sample size that is useful to develop and identify trends. When coupled with my landscape observations and readings a much clearer picture emerges on the nationalism, notion of ethnic identity and possible implications for the future of Bosnia.

Survey Respondents

The three major sources of survey respondents were: (1) Bosnian employees of International Community and Bosnian state institutions; (2) employees of the hotels I stayed at; (3) family members and friends of my interpreters; and (4) respondents at the various locations I stopped at during my travels. These were primarily outdoor cafes, their store employees and customers. Table One below lists the many organizations and their location. Respondents were assured of their anonymity and that the survey was voluntary.

Table 1 Office/Institution	Location	Entity
US Embassy, Attaché Section	Sarajevo	FED
US Embassy, Field Office	Banja Luka	RS
Office of Defense Cooperation (ODC), EUCOM, DoD	Sarajevo	FED
Headquarters, Multinational Bde (N), Eagle Base	Tuzla	FED
UN High Commissioner for Refugees (UNHCR)	Sarajevo	FED
Office of the High Representative (OHR) HQ	Sarajevo	FED
OHR Field Office	Banja Luka	FED
OHR Field Office	Tuzla	FED
OHR Field Office	Doboj	RS
OHR Field Office	Livno	FED
Organization for Security and Cooperation in Europe (OSCE)	Prijedor	RS
International Orthodox Christian Charities (IOCC)	Banja Luka	RS
IOCC Field Office	Drvar	RS
"DON" nongovernmental organization (NGO)	Prijedor	RS
Lighthouse Youth Organization NGO	Prijedor	RS
Faculty of Sciences, University of Banja Luka	Banja Luka	RS
Hotel - Holiday Inn	Sarajevo	FED
Hotel - Hotel Firenca	Banja Luka	RS
Hotel - Senad od Bosna	Lukavac	FED
Hotel - Doboj Inn	Doboj	RS
UNITIC Office Building tenant businesses	Sarajevo	FED

It was crucial that members of each of the three ethnic communities were included in the survey. My travel route went through municipalities of both the Federation and Republika Srpska. Sarajevo and Banja Luka are overwhelmingly Bosniak and Serb respectively. Croat respondents were primarily found in Canton X Herceg-Bosna and Canton II Posavina. Table Two provides a demographic breakdown of respondents (May-June, 2004.)

TABLE 2	Rep. Srpska	Federation	BiH
Male	65	69	134
Female	42	40	82
Total	107	109	216
Bosnian	4	32	36
Bosniak	13	39	52
Croat	5	24	29
Serb	83	9	92
No answer	2	5	7

The questionnaire was standardized in an attempt to minimize any survey-related error. The respondents were exposed to the same question protocol, in this case self-administered questionnaires, so that any differences in the answers can be interpreted as reflecting differences between respondents rather than differences in the process (Fowler, 1990).[4]

Survey Questionnaire

The difference between the answers of members of the various ethnic groups permits the measurement of that data.

Sources of error in surveys can be mitigated when properly constructed and administered. Fowler (1990) notes the four major sources of error:

(1) The sample itself, by leaving potential respondents out, not reflecting the sample population, or respondent's refusal to answer any or all of the questions.

(2) The questions on the questionnaire. Prone to misunderstanding, unwillingness to answer honestly or when the respondents do not know the answer.

(3) Interviewer questioning may be a source of error. This was mitigated by having self-administered questionnaires.

(4) Data reduction or by entering the results incorrectly.

The questionnaire is organized on four pages and begins with a short introduction, thanks to the respondent for participation and a map of Bosnia clearly denoting the IEBL (Appendix B). The questionnaire comprises of ten closed ended questions. The survey was prepared in (1) English, (2) Serbo-Croatian (Latin script), (3) Serbo-Croatian (Cyrillic script), and one was eventually produced in (5) Bosnian or *jekavica* dialect of Serbo-Croatian (Latin script), the vernacular in Bosnia.

The first set of questions beginning on page two addresses the ethnic communities' perception of (1) the IEBL's importance, the (2) effects of dissolving the DPA entity system and establishment of a strong central state, the (3) impact of an independent Kosovo on Bosnia, and the (4) prewar national group identification.

The first set of six questions on page two were closed-end, Likert rating scale type questions, which are typically used to form the basis of aggregated opinions or attitude rating scales (Peterson, 2000). As I required data and measures of the opinions and perceptions of the respondents, the Likert scale is appropriate, allowing for analysis by statistical techniques if desired.

There is no consensus on the number of scales intervals and categories to be used. Peterson (2000) writes that typically five, even up to nine are found in some research work. Based on time available and ease of respondent completion, I chose five intervals of strongly agree, agree, unsure, disagree, strongly disagree. Considering that one of the goals of these questions was to make generalizations of the ethnic communities towards certain subjects and then comparing the outcomes between the groups, five categories sufficed (Peterson 2000).

Realizing that an indifferent attitude could prevail as an outcome, five categories make sense and an odd number of categories were used. The usage of "strongly agree, agree, not sure, disagree, strongly disagree" as the verbal stimuli in the response categories better reflects the level of intensity that the respondent feels (Peterson, 2000).

Given the known myriad of differences between the Bosniaks, Croats and Serbs who all fought against one another at various points during the war, the polar aspect to these rating scales best reflects the opposite meanings to these groups – therefore the results are less problematic to interpret. Additionally questionnaire design and space considerations also suggested using five intervals.

Page three has three questions that are modeled on Dr Francisco Gil-White's (1999) research on the concept of primordialism and his method of obtaining empirical data to support a primordialist approach to national identity. My versions of Gil-White's questions only differed in reflecting European identities as the basis of comparison in the scenarios presented instead of Gil-White's Central Asian ethnic identities.

Otherwise they are identical closed-end questions of three response choices.

The fourth and last page also contains the closing demographic questions. I did not seek extensive demographic data and limited this portion of the survey to gender, age, nationality, home municipality and occupation. By recording the municipality in which the questionnaire was given I was able to tie survey location to the landscape. In order to cloak of respondent anonymity and to set them at ease, I did not seek names, income, marital status, or number of children.

Questionnaire Distribution and Training

A major issue in surveying is the uniformity in canvassing responses from participants. Are the people conducting the survey trained to answer questions correctly and do they understand the languages well enough to elaborate on any details of the questionnaire (Sheskin, 2002, Fowler, 1990). To ensure that the surveying was uniformly conducted I had to train each of my interpreters on the questionnaire. Initially I would have them answer a questionnaire and then we would discuss any potential pitfalls that they believe they could encounter, I would clarify any points of the questions and finally we would discuss the rationale and meaning behind the questions so that when the interpreter conducted the survey there would be no obstacles.

Through this method of training the survey process was exceptionally smooth, although there was one incident in which I experienced hostility.[5] Respondents were made to feel comfortable as the interpreters would introduce me and explain the purpose of the survey. Almost every person approached to participate agreed to do so. When people expressed concern about answering certain questions, such as their *opština* or ethnic identity, they were reassured that the survey was anonymous, but if they persisted they were told that a non-response would be fine. This accounts for the seven respondents who did not give their ethnic identity in the demographics section of the questionnaire.

Survey Data Analysis

The survey questionnaires produced ordinal data and responses to two sets of questions. The data were analyzed using the SPSS software package. The first set of questions primarily engaged nationalist and political issues and measured responses based on the level of agreement with a given statement. The responses, which were the variables, are based on a Likert scale and are: strongly agree, agree, unsure, disagree, and strongly disagree. The Likert scale was used as it provided for an effective translation into Serbo-Croatian, ease of execution in Bosnia and usefulness in tabulating the responses and conducting statistical measures of the data. The responses were further grouped by group ethnicity determined from responses in the demographics section of the questionnaire. By grouping the responses to the statements based on nationality any deviations between the ethnic groups could be used to develop themes present and differences among the groups. Statistical measure, including the Chi-square test, indicates that the data are significant.

The second set of questions dealt with the respondent's notion of ethnic identity transmission. All had three closed end answer choices. As in the first portion of the survey, analysis using a software package presented simple statistical data that was used to group and interpret how people conceived of ethnic identity and how it is transmitted within their culture. Statistical significance was determined in the same manner as before and revealed that the data obtained was statistically significant. Discussion of the results is at Chapter VIII and the data output from the SPSS software package is at Appendix E.

Challenges of the Survey

There were numerous challenges in preparing and administering the questionnaires. Translating was problematic in that the survey had to be translated first from English into Bosnian, Croatian or Serbian and then using either the Latin and/or Cyrillic text. All three languages, although only having subtle differences, are present in Bosnia. In order to complete this step quickly, I had the English version translated by an acquaintance into the pre-war official Serbo-Croatian. This would cause some problems for me when I canvassed respondents in Bosniak and Croatian regions.

Most of Bosnia's inhabitants speak the *jekavian* dialect of Serbo-Croatian not the *ekavian* in which my surveys were written. The version of my survey was seen as Serbian and understandably both Bosniak and Croat regions made note of my surveys. The surveys had to be re-translated into the vernacular while in Bosnia after an incident with a Croat in Glamoć, Canton X.

Initially, language barriers made it difficult for me to answer respondent questions about the survey, or about my own role in Bosnia. The majority of Bosnia's inhabitants suspect conspiracies or fear that some latent power is trying to obtain personal information. Indeed, several people refused to participate, fearing that there was a sinister purpose behind the survey or offering the attitude of "why should I fill this survey out, Westerners have come and conducted surveys for the last ten years but nothing changes." Public apathy and even antipathy was present in Bosnia.

To overcome my language shortfall I found myself "retreating" to German in order to clarify any concerns or additional information requirements. The ideal locations for me to distribute surveys on my own were in the hotels where I stayed, in the offices of official institutions such as the Office of the High Representative (OHR), the US Embassy and its Field Offices, Organization for Security and Cooperation in Europe (OSCE) offices and some other organizations. In these institutions English was readily accepted, German more so in hotels and civilian establishments.

To expand the available pool of respondents I resorted to using my hired interpreters in the survey process. Their role was instrumental in obtaining a larger sample and distribution. At every travel stop location I would have my interpreter pass out surveys and answer any questions a respondent may have. This turned out to be an excellent decision and prevented most awkward moments.

Another challenge was time and money, both of which were limited. I did not have the population lists from which to draw a sample from the whole population. As national identity in Bosnia today is relatively homogenous by region (entity, canton or municipality) by distributing the questionnaires during my travels I believe I obtained a good distribution. By collecting questionnaires in places like Sarajevo, Tuzla, Banja Luka, Doboj, Mostar, Cantons II Posavina and X Herceg-Bosna I touched upon the major population centers of Bosnia.

Some advantages I did possess were the (1) prestige or official backing of both the US Army and Kent State University and (2) my ethnic heritage. These advantages worked differently in different ethnic communities. In the Bosniak and to a lesser degree Croat communities the status of a US Army officer assisted greatly in finding willing respondents and in collecting completed questionnaires. My Serbian heritage was significant in doing the same in Serb regions of Bosnia. However it could have been a significant disadvantage in the other two communities had it been known.

Interviews & Discussions

The majority of opportunity interviews and discussions came about from conducting surveys or from casual conversations with locals. Based on the survey interviews and discussions, I interpreted what the landscape symbols, whatever they may be, represent as opposed to merely observing them and searching for a simple metaphorical meaning (Mitchell, 1996). This approach allowed me to tie the physical "thing" and its representation, allowing for a fuller understanding of how the landscape is actually perceived and comprehended by different national groups.

By interviewing respondents, or simply through discussions with the locals, I was able to capture ideas, feelings and perceptions that the represented national groups may have. This anecdotal data coupled with observation and survey data allowed for comparison and complemented these methods. In some cases the interviews provided information that was not readily apparent from a photograph or survey questionnaire and therefore allowed me to capture more in-depth knowledge and understanding. When observing the landscape and noting new churches, interviews allowed me to discern whether or not they were brand new or recently reconstructed from the war. In several instances I discovered from locals that the church or mosque was simply built as a sign to inhibit refugee returns and claim the territory by another national group.

An example would be deciphering what a newly built mosque "means." Was it built to address the needs of a growing returnee Bosniak community or was it built in a former Croatian region, thus representing new Bosniak territory and meant to inhibit the return of Croatian refugees?

Documents as Resources

Although not a separate method *per se*, using documents in my research has been necessary and complements the aforementioned methods. Books, periodical manuscripts, maps, official documents, cartoons, and Bosnian newspapers are all critical to understand the history of the region and to understand the recent events, Bosnia's history and its people. Any attempt to analyze and understand the landscape, questionnaire responses and interview data is useless without a significant appreciation of the historical background. Moreover the history of Bosnia is very dynamic as numerous political and social issues are wrestled with daily, making the use of current information sources necessary. The political atmosphere in Bosnia changes almost daily and requires that Bosnia be followed closely in the current press, which includes electronic media. By meeting OHR representatives and establishing a good repertoire and professional relationship I was able to ask their assistance in keeping me abreast of current events in Bosnia. The result has been to receive daily news updates from the OHR representatives and speedy responses to any questions that I have asked of them either through the internet or phone calls. Critical documents and sources which I am currently using and will continue to use while in Bosnia are:

- Official government statements from various political actors; culled primarily from official and news websites.
- Region studies and histories (noted in bibliography).
- Dayton Peace Accords (DPA).
- UNHCR – statistics; refugee return, property claims.
- Electronic media – government websites, news organizations, etc.
- Responses to questions from personal contacts (interpreters, OHR reps, military contacts, etc.).

Methodology Conclusion

Tying together the data and information obtained through the three methods of (1) observation of the landscape, (2) survey questionnaires, and (3) the interviews and discussions permitted me to analyze the differences among Bosnia's national groups. The grouping of the responses by nationality, graphically depicted in the survey section, presents strong divergences and processes among Bosnia's constituent national groups that weigh heavily on the future of Bosnian state and "Bosnian" identity.

The nationalist representations present in the landscape, the responses to the survey and the information rich interviews and discussions provide an understanding that contributes to the nationalist discourses present in Bosnia. The following sections present my findings.

---

[1] The IEBL possesses numerous meanings. It is the acknowledgement of a Serb Entity, it is an obstacle to Bosniak/Muslim desire for a strong central state centered in Sarajevo, and to the Croats it represents what the Serbs won and they lost (an entity or statelet) through the Dayton Peace Accords. The vandalism of many of the IEBL markers attests to their being sites of contestation.

[2] I was able to contact (1) the Federal Bureau of Statistics and (2) the Agency for Statistics of Bosnia and Herzegovina, however both agencies replied that their information was based on the 1991 census. A new census may be conducted sometime in 2005 if it is deemed politically acceptable.

---

[3] Prior to my departure for Bosnia in May 2004 I contacted the Federal (entity) Bureau of Statistics and the Agency for Statistics of BiH in the hope of obtaining demographic data. Both responded that they do not have demographic data based on ethnicity and the only data available for ethnic breakdown is the 1992 statistics. Moreover, during my travels I had the opportunity to speak with entity representatives in the RS who told me that perhaps in 2005 there would be a new census but that it would be a political decision.

[4] I must note that while most respondents were given questionnaires by me or a translator, some were provided to gatekeepers, such as a hotel manager, to be further distributed to respondents. In each case I (or the translator) went over the questionnaire to ensure the gatekeeper understood it and could answer respondent questions.

[5] While administering surveys in Glamoć, I was almost accosted by a Croat who did not like the version of the survey, which had the *ekavian* dialect, usually considered Serbian. This incident highlights the level of tension and even hatred still present in some regions of Bosnia. I decided to prepare the *jekavian* dialect version after this incident.

CHAPTER IV

BOSNIA'S HISTORICAL BACKGROUND

"Violence was, indeed, all I knew of the Balkans: all I knew of the South Slavs."

Dame Rebecca West, 1942

No understanding of today's Bosnia and Herzegovina can be achieved without introduction to its pre-war historical development. This chapter briefly overviews the relevant history that has shaped and impacted Bosnia's development into today's state. Indeed many of the charges and counter charges levied by Bosnia's national groups find their sources in historical grievances and to comprehend Bosnia nowadays one has to understand its past.

Formation of Bosnia's Early Religious Communities

Prior to the Ottoman Empire's arrival and after the Eastern Schism of 1054, the Balkan lands were situated between the domains of the Western or Latin Christian Church and the Eastern or Byzantine Christian Church (White, 2000). The Eastern Schism created two dominant churches in early Christianity, Catholicism centered in Rome and Eastern Orthodoxy centered in Constantinople. The ecclesiastic boundary cut across the lands of the former Yugoslavia. Islam did not have a major presence in the Balkans until the arrival of the Ottomans.

In early medieval Bosnia, the Bosnian church was originally part of the Dalmatian Archbishopric of the Catholic Church. It was a fairly independent church and was subjected to Catholic and Western power politics when Hungary attempted to assert control by launching a crusade against the Bosnians (Malcolm, 1994). The Hungarians were successful in depicting the Bosnian church as heretical and thus garnered papal permission to invade in 1235. A subsequent assault by the Tatars against Hungary succeeded in bringing the Hungarian crusade to a premature end in 1241. Unable to take Bosnia by force, Hungary persuaded Rome to place the independent minded Bosnians under the ecclesiastic control of the Hungarian archbishop in Kalocza.

The Bosnians reacted to this decision by breaking from Rome in the 1250s. The Bosnian nobility founded their Bosnian church. Fine (2002) asserts that the Bosnian church was a mainstream church with standard Christian/Catholic views. It was not a dualist church, or Bogomil, as is typically conveyed in most literature on Bosnia (Bringa, 1995, Malcolm, 1994). For close to one hundred years the Bosnian church remained independent. The Bosnian Church enjoyed its heyday in the fourteenth and early fifteenth centuries (Malcolm, 1994).

Recent research on religion in medieval Bosnia thoroughly refutes the notion that Bosnia was Bogomil during the fourteenth and fifteenth centuries (Fine, 2002, Malcolm, 1994). Most evidence contradicts the two major sources used to purvey the Bogomilism theory in the region. Adherents to this theory use the examples of mass conversion to Islam by the Bosnians as an act of revenge against the proselytizing and persecution by the Catholic and Orthodox churches and the medieval gravestones, called *stećci*, of Herzegovina which are thought to be Bogomil (West, 1937).

In 1340 the Bosnian *ban* (equivalent to duke), Stjepan Kotromanić, accepted a Franciscan mission into central Bosnia in order to avoid another threatened crusade. By the end of the decade he accepted Catholicism and all of his successors, except for one, were Catholic until the Ottoman conquest in the 1460s. According to Fine (2002), all Christian religions were tolerated under what can only be understood to be an enlightened ruler. The Orthodox were found in Herzegovina, or Hum, and along the Drina river, in the east, Catholics in the north and west of Bosnia, and the Bosnian church in the center and most regions of Bosnia.

The Bosnian church, as opposed to the Catholic and Orthodox neighbors, was a purely monastic organization. The monasteries, although possessing features of both Catholicism and Orthodoxy, were unique in that the only Bosnian churches present were those structurally attached to the monasteries themselves. Therefore the church never had the territorial structure that the other churches maintained and remained relatively weak. A contributing factor was the harsh and mountainous terrain of Bosnia which made travel and communications extremely difficult, thereby inhibiting effective centralized control by any power.

It was not until five years before the Ottoman conquest that religious persecution began. In return for aid that never materialized to any great extent, the papacy required the elimination of the Bosnian church. The choice for Bosnian church clergy was either conversion to Catholicism or exile. Malcolm (1994) writes that as the church was being dismantled, many of its adherents accepted refuge in Raška with the Orthodox clergy. Others were forcibly converted to Catholicism by King Tomas in 1459. For all intents and purposes, Papal actions broke the back of the Bosnian Church (Malcolm, 1994).

Figure 2 – Map of the Medieval Kingdoms of Bosnia (Malcolm, 1994).

Fine (2002) asserts that, unlike other medieval states, the religion of the Bosnian ruler did not dictate the religion of his subjects. In fact he writes that religion was "worn loosely" and people changed faiths based on economic, political or marital reasons (Fine, 2002, 10). He contradicts the Bogomil narrative on Bosnia that the members of this Bosnian church converted en masse to Islam in protest of the persecution suffered at the hands of the Catholics. As the Ottoman Turks conquered Bosnia in the late 1400s, many Catholics fled west to Dalmatia, or north to Croatia. The approaching Turks forced many Orthodox to flee Serbia into Bosnia in order to avoid their depredations.

According to Fine (2002) the appearance of Muslims in Bosnia came from two sources. The first source was the Muslim migrants that came with the Sultan's armies. The second, and by far the largest component of Islam in Bosnia, came from the converts. He writes that there was no wholesale conversion, but a gradual process in which converts came from all the Christian churches and it was not until the seventeenth century that a majority of the Bosnians became Muslim (Fine, 2002, Malcolm, 1994). It was a multi-directional process in which Catholics became Orthodox and vice versa and each had members contribute converts to Islam (Bringa, 1995). The Bosnian church itself never really proved a challenge to the Ottoman overlords as it was already defunct and powerless upon their arrival.

The reasoning for conversion was simple. In Bosnia, prior to Ottoman arrival, there existed three competing churches that lacked clergy members. The church members were also much less devoted than what was typically found elsewhere in the medieval world. And finally, Islam appeared as a dynamic new faith and God's favor was shown by Ottoman military success. Those that remained Christian tended to be Orthodox or would convert to Orthodoxy from Catholicism (Fine, 2002). The Orthodox Church was part of the Ottoman administrative structure, known as the *millet* system, which oversaw the Sultan's Orthodox subjects. Only the Franciscans were able to receive a charter from the Sultan to operate in central Bosnia after 1340; otherwise the Catholic Church was absent from Ottoman controlled Bosnia.

The Ottomans established an administrative scheme, called the *millet* system, in which membership in a community was based on faith. People were classified by their religion; no ethnic or national divisions were recognized. Six non-Islamic *millets* existed over the course of the Ottoman Empire in its conquered territories: the Greek Orthodox, Gregorian Armenian, and Jewish, the largest, and Roman Armenian, Roman Catholic, and Protestant, smallest of the six (Stavrianos, 2000). Each *millet* had its spiritual leader, the Serbs were organized within the Greek dominated Orthodox *millet*, with the Patriarch of Constantinople [Istanbul] its head.

The Christian *millets*, into which all Christian subjects of the Sultan fell, were second-class citizens while the Islamic *millet* had the most favored status (Fine, 2002, Stavrianos, 2000). The Muslims controlled the land through a feudal system and many Bosnian Muslims were able to rise high in Turkish society and assume posts of importance within the Ottoman Empire (Pavlovich, 1988). An elite of Bosnian and Ottoman Muslims developed in the towns and cities from which the Sublime Porte (the term used to connote the Ottoman government) ruled Bosnia. The peasants, termed *rayah* (Turkish for cattle) by the Ottomans, worked the Muslim feudal estates and were overwhelmingly drawn from the Christian *millet*.

Excluding the elite, the population of Bosnia was primarily composed of peasants or shepherds. Fine (2002, 8) emphasizes that both the Muslim and Christian villages manifested ties across faiths and that "religion stood at a considerable distance from formal religious institutions." Formal religious institutions were centered in religious ritual and constituting peasant understandings of religion. Practices, rather than religious doctrine, were the bulk of a peasant's religious belief system. Interaction at the village level across all the three faiths, supported by local priests, *hodjas* and Franciscans, allowed for the development of a truly Bosnian culture. This unique culture was shared by all Bosnians and was distinct from that of neighboring regions (Fine, 2002). Fine (2002) also believes, based on his observations, that this general Bosnian feeling was still alive into the late 1980s.

Certain critical aspects of the Ottoman Empire in its relations with its Christian populations receive little to no elaboration by many authors, including Allcock, (2000), Fine (2002), Malcolm (1994), Mazower (2002), and Stavrianos (2000). The *devshirme*, or child levy (commonly called "blood tribute" by the Serbs), in which Christian male children were taken from their homes to serve in the Sultan's elite *Janissaries* or the state administrative apparatus, receives scant attention. If it is acknowledged, one is left to believe that this event was beneficial to the abducted and provided many with a way out of a poor future. Through this system, many of these youths reached positions of great power within the Ottoman Empire. However, the preponderance of the blood tribute would serve as soldiers in the campaigns of the Sultans. In no uncertain terms the Christians were second-class citizens in the Ottoman Empire. Christians were oppressed; the record exists in the large scale uprisings of the Serbs in the 1590s, 1640s, 1650s and 1690s (Pavlovich, 1988). As the empire declined, becoming known as the "sick man of Europe," the historical evidence indicates that the corruption, misrule and oppression by the Ottoman masters against the Christian millet was cruel, indifferent and harsh (Gerolymatos, 2002, Jelavich, 1983, Pavlovich, 1988, Stavrianos, 1965). This aspect of the Ottoman period of rule would cause immense suffering for the Bosnian Muslim population during the 1991-95 war as it was used as grounds for avenging past wrongs done to Christian Croats and Serbs.

Bosnia, Ethnicity and Nationalism

The notion of an "ethnicity" arrives in Bosnia during the 19th century when Bosnian Christians began to acquire ethnic and national ideas penetrating Bosnia from Serbia and Croatia. Fine (2002) claims that this is the first time Serbs (as Orthodox Christians) and Croats (as Catholics) come to be known as separate nations within Bosnia. Until then Fine (2002) writes that there was no internal ethnic or religious warfare. Bosnia remained under Ottoman suzerainty from 1463 to 1878, however in 1875 a major revolt by the Serbs of Herzegovina broke out that threatened to cause a major war among the Great Powers of Austria-Hungary, Britain and Russia as they maneuvered to support their perceived interests in the region. The Serbs suffering under a famine and Turkish oppression sought to achieve union with the Serbs in neighboring Serbia and free themselves from the Turk. The *Nevesinje* Revolt, as it is called, ended in failure for the Serbs. The overall situation in the Balkans was eventually resolved and stabilized with the Treaty of Berlin in 1878. Bosnia was transferred to Hapsburg control to prevent Serbian acquisition of Bosnia and at the same time allowing the Ottoman Empire to retain nominal control (Stavrianos, 2000).

The 1878 Treaty of Berlin allowed the Austro-Hungarian Empire to occupy and administer Bosnia, although it ostensibly remained part of the Ottoman Empire. This occurred with much consternation on the part of Bosnia's three religious groups. The Austrians imported a secular school system that found the Muslims worried that they would be compelled to convert to Catholicism – the religion of the Hapsburg Empire. The "loose fit" or more liberally practiced Islam was now seen as a problem by educated Muslims. The lack of a sophisticated Islam coupled with the retained Christian traditions and the power of the Austrian state led many to worry about conversions, which did occur in many localities (Glenny, 2000). The Muslim elite involved themselves in the affairs of the villages in an attempt to stave off any threat to the Muslim religion. This resulted in rising tensions, where none had existed before, between the sophisticated elites of the urban centers and the Muslims in the rural regions. This moderate resurgence also strained the relations with Bosnia's Christian population which had always viewed the Muslims skeptically as they maintained most of the power and privilege due to the Ottoman legacy.

In the late nineteenth century, the Hapsburg Minister Benjamin von Kallay, Bosnia's administrator, attempted to weaken the predatory ideologies of the Croat and Serb nationalism by advocating that all communities embrace the notion of *bošnjastvo*, or Bosniakdom (Malcolm, 1994). This was an endeavor to supplant the growing disparate nationalisms by reviving the common notion of a Bosnianess, or *bošnjak,* which was inclusive of all (Magaš, 2003). It was a complete failure among Bosnia's Christian population but did lay the seeds of a Bosniak identity among the Muslim elites (Glenny, 2000). This idea of Bosnianess was flawed by the very fact that fourteenth century Bosnia was Christian and the term "*bosanac*" for all its merit was a regional, not national, distinction.

The Catholics were also caught in a dilemma. Pope Leo XII, supported by the Austrian emperor, appointed a foreigner and non-Franciscan as the archbishop of Bosnia. This is the first instance since the medieval Bosnian state and Ottoman period that a bishop, who could exercise authority in Bosnia, was appointed by the Vatican. Archbishop Josip Stadler arrived in Sarajevo in 1881, much to the dismay of the Franciscan clergy and their parishes. To this day tension still exists between the Catholic clergy and the Franciscans.[1]

Bosnia would be annexed outright, in what was called the Annexation Crisis, by Austria in 1908, and remain under Habsburg control until the end of the First World War. Sarajevo, Bosnia's largest town, served as the administrative center and capital of Austria's new province. It was a period in which the Catholics received a favored position and the Muslims would in many instances also be in the Emperor's grace. The Orthodox Serbs, the vast majority of whom lived in the rural areas, were still in the position of second-class citizen in Bosnia. The 1914 assassination of Archduke Franz Ferdinand and his wife, Sophie, by the Serb nationalist, Gavrilo Princep, would lead to the First World War and to the widespread executions and massacres of Bosnia's Serb population, a fact rarely mentioned in the history books.

The post-World War I Kingdom of Serbs, Croats and Slovenes was in essence a Greater Serbia. Serbia had been a loyal ally to the British, French and Americans and suffered horrendously during the three years of Central Power occupation. The Serbian Karageorgević royal dynasty became the monarchy of the newly founded Kingdom, to be renamed the Kingdom of Yugoslavia in 1929, which would rule in some form until 1941. The most vociferous opponent to Belgrade during this period was the Croatian nation. Hitler would play upon these animosities once World War II erupted.

Fascism and Religious Persecution in World War II Bosnia

Yugoslavia was quickly overrun by German, Italian, Hungarian and Bulgarian forces in April 1941. Shortly thereafter, Croatia was established as an independent fascist state with new boundaries incorporating most of Bosnia and a portion of Serbia (see Figure 3). As Bosnia only had a 20% Croat population, the new Croatian fascist leadership of the *Ustaše* actively sought Muslim support in its plan to eradicate the Serbs, Jews and Roma. On July 22, 1941 Milan Budak, the Croatian Minister of Education, elucidated the state's plan for the Serbs when he announced that a third would be killed, a third converted, and a third expelled (Trifković, 1998). It is at this time that the ethnic element of World War II Bosnia assumed a religious dimension, creating intractable hatreds that linger to this day and have been used as grounds for national revenge.

The Catholic Church, particularly the Franciscan Order, helped implement *Ustaše* policies. The Franciscans were active in the conversion of the Serbs, and played a major role in the *Ustaše* regime and in running the death camps (Fine, 2002, Trifkovic, 1998). The *Ustaše* campaign of destruction and terror against the Serbs provoked a Serb nationalist response, resulting in both a vicious guerilla campaign against the Axis invaders but also against the *Ustaše* and hapless Croat civilians and villages. By the end of the war it is estimated that between 350,000 to over 700,000 Serbs were exterminated and 200-300,000 were converted to Catholicism (Ivanović, 2002, Jelavich, 1983).

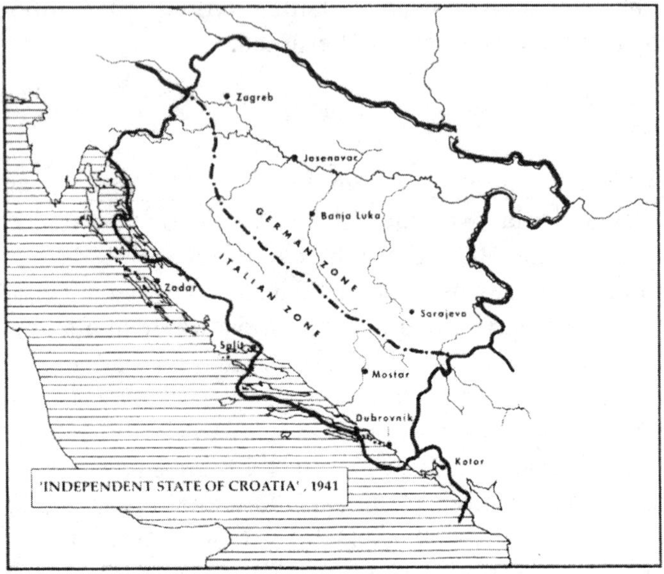

Figure 3 – Map of the Independent State of Croatia 1941-45 (Malcolm, 1994).

Bosnia became a scene of bizarre horrors as massacre and revenge massacres took place between the various national groups. The Serbian dominated Yugoslav government in exile Royalist Movement, or "*Četniks*" under the leadership of General Draža Mihailović, a former Yugoslav officer, fought not only the *Ustaše* and Germans, but also the growing communist *Partisans*. A civil war within a world war was being waged in the former Yugoslavia.

Josip Broz Tito, as the leader of the Communist Partisan and popular front Antifascist Council for National Liberation of Yugoslavia (*AVNOJ*), rose above the ethnic strife (West, 1983, Pavlowitch, 1992). He was able to call the Yugoslav peoples together under the slogan of "*bratsvo i jedinstvo*" (brotherhood and unity). His Partisan cause included all of the ethnic groups of Yugoslavia, but it was the Serbs that were greatest in numbers. In the course of the war, Tito succeeded in leading Yugoslavia to liberation. The *Ustaše* leadership fled in massive numbers, some through the Catholic Church, while others were captured, imprisoned or executed. The *Četniks* were discredited and fell apart as the Soviet troops moved into Yugoslavia in pursuit of the retreating Germans. The living memory of the nightmares experienced in wartime Yugoslavia would be rekindled with the rise of nationalism in the late 1980s.

Secularism, Citizenship and Identity in Tito's Bosnia

In 1945 Yugoslavia was a Communist dominated state, divided into six republics, each based on a dominant ethnic group. The only exception was Bosnia, which included Serb, Muslim and Croat nationalities. Tito recognized that nationalism posed a constant threat to the new state. He also realized that strong adherence to one's religion correlated to a strong tie to one's national community which could lead to separatist nationalism (Bringa, 2002). Religion was anathema to Communism and Tito's credo of "Brotherhood and Unity" and he therefore strove through rhetoric and his dreaded *Uprava Državne Bezbjednosti*, or *UDBa* (Department of State Security - the secret police) to eliminate these nationalist threats.

Yugoslavia did progress as a country, by some accounts phenomenally well, but a policy of decentralization over the years left increasing power in the hands of the separate Yugoslav republics. By 1968, the Muslims, after realizing that they did not fit in as "Muslim Croats" or "Muslim Serbs," became an officially recognized nation in Yugoslavia. Their label, "Muslim" [*Musliman*], possessed a double meaning. Similar to the Jewish community, the new, officially declared Muslim was a member of a religious community and also an ethnic group.

For most of the 45 years following World War II, Bosnia was a secular society. The "loose" religious characterization coupled with an anti-religious stance of the Communist Party leadership meant that religion played little to no role in Bosnia. The *muezzin*'s call to prayer from the local Bosnian mosque was not a common occurrence and rarely, if ever, heeded in large towns and cities. Intermarriage was widespread, roughly 40% of urban marriages were mixed and over 20% of urban Bosnians declared themselves "Yugoslav" or "other" in the years before civil war (Fine, 2002). The 1991 census notes that of Sarajevo's

525,980 inhabitants, 16% of the people identified themselves as "Yugoslav or other."

In urban centers people tended not to declare themselves in ethnic terms, but as Yugoslavs or perhaps Bosnians. A certain harmony existed between all ethnic groups, again primarily within urban settings. Bosnia's five largest towns – Sarajevo, Banja Luka, Tuzla, Zenica and Mostar accounted for barely one quarter of Bosnia's 4.4 million citizens in 1992. Three quarters of the population were in rural or small town settings where attitudes were remarkably different from those in the cities (Bose, 2002). This points to a disconnection in the identities of urban and rural communities – one that would dramatically impact Bosnia and Yugoslavia in the early 1990s.

A Muslim nationalist political agenda, albeit small and powerless, did exist in Yugoslavia beginning in the 1970s. Tito's wide ranging and close cooperation with Yugoslavia's non-aligned alliance partners, including oil-producing Middle East states, enabled many Yugoslavs, including Bosniaks, to work or study in these states. Under the mantra of education, many Bosnian Muslims studied Islamic theology at major Islamic teaching institutions. In earlier days these Islamicized intellectuals and students would have remained in an isolated place within Yugoslav society. After 1990, however, these same men gained prominence and political power in post-Dayton Bosnia.

The Bosnian rural folk and villagers tended to be much more conservative in behavior and in matters of religion and ethnicity. Urban Bosnians saw themselves as European, if not cosmopolitan, while the villagers kept up their religious practices (Bringa, 1995, Fine 2002). Islamic values and practices clashed with the urbanites' secular views on life. Moreover, the urban Muslim had more in common with the urban Serb or Croat as opposed to the Muslim villager. In many, if not most, cases entire villages were made up of single ethnic communities. The true secularism of the urban centers simply did not exist in the smaller towns, villages, and countryside. This situation was endemic within all of the pre-war Yugoslav republics.

Religion's Vicious Revival in Bosnia

As Croatia and Slovenia began their secessionist moves in early 1991, Yugoslavia descended into chaos and the ethnic tensions within Bosnia mounted. Both Serbia and Croatia, through their state controlled media and propaganda, sought to sway their ethnic brethren in Bosnia to their side. In the 1990 Bosnian republic elections, three nationalist parties won. These were the Bosnian Muslim *Stranka Demokratska Akcija* (Muslim Party of Democratic Action or SDA), the Croat *Hrvatska Demokratska Zajednica* (Croatian Democratic Community or HDZ) and the Serb *Srpska Demokratska Stranka* (Serbian Democratic Party or SDS). According to some authors it was only the *SDA*, the Muslim Party of Alija Izetbegović, which called out to other groups to join their political party in the early days of the secession. The reasoning is simple: Izetbegović realized that the Muslims would not survive without the Serbs or the Croats as they were trapped between the stronger Croatia and Yugoslavia (now consisting of Serbia and Montenegro).

Although much of the leadership of the SDA was composed of former Communists and secular ethnic Muslims, its leader Izetbegović was a religious Muslim. He authored the 1969 book Izlamska Deklaracija (The Islamic Declaration) in which he theorized that a modern, technological state could exist while keeping the values of Islam. Indeed, in 1984 Izetbegović had been tried and convicted with fellow co-conspirators of belonging to the Muslim nationalist political activists and being traitors to Tito's Yugoslavia.

Much rhetoric and propaganda was made of Izetbegović's treatise by the nationalist Croat and Serb leaders and by the SDA's internal political opponents. Croat and Serb leaders stoked fears that an Islamic state was the goal of Izetbegović and his SDA. By overtly tying the Bosnian Muslims to the support provided by Islamic states such as Iran, with their links to terrorism, and by coupling the Muslims with an oppressive Ottoman past, the Bosnian Serb minority was easily persuaded to view the Muslims as a reemerged deadly enemy. In 1991 and leading up to the independence referendum of 1992, an atmosphere was created that guaranteed the Bosnian Serbs would not agree to Bosnian Muslim moves towards independence.

In the April 1992 referendum on Bosnian independence, the Muslims and Croats voted to secede from Yugoslavia whereas the Serbs chose to boycott the referendum altogether. It is commonly misunderstood that Yugoslavia's Constitution permitted republics the right to secede – which it did – but only if the majority of each of a republic's constituent people voted for secession. This was not the case in Bosnia, or in Croatia, in which the Serb populations vehemently protested secession. The Bosnian Serbs immediately began their rebellion with the support of the Yugoslav People's Army, or *JNA*, which by now was primarily officered by Serbs. The Bosnian Croats after initially supporting the Muslims turned on them as they were armed and supported logistically by Croatia. It wouldn't be until later in the war that the West would coerce the two back together as common allies against the Serbs.

---

[1] An example of this can be seen in the Mostar region in which the Archbishop of Mostar is attempting to reign in the activities of the Franciscans at the nearby pilgrimage site of Medjugorje. Indeed fighting and acts of intimidation occur commonly between the two Catholic organizations.

CHAPTER V

THE CIVIL WAR IN BOSNIA AND HERZEGOVINA

"Bosnia... was in a sense a microcosm of the country as a whole... It had been fought over repeatedly by Turks, Austrians and Serbs, and most of the national trends and tendencies were represented there, all at their most violent. The population was made up of violently Catholic Croats and no less violently Orthodox Serbs, with a strong admixture of equally fanatical local Moslems. It is hard to imagine the savage intensity of the passions that were aroused or the extremes of bitterness which they engendered. The lesson we were having was an object lesson, illustrated by burned villages, desecrated churches, massacred hostages and mutilated corpses."

Fitzroy Maclean, 1943 (from Bose, 2000)

"The situation in Bosnia was not simply that of one nation invading another. It was a civil war about territory in which the Bosnian Croats and the Bosnian Serbs sought to secede from the State and join with their compatriots in neighboring Croatia and Serbia."

General Sir Michael Rose, 1998

The recent civil wars in Yugoslavia were the defining event for all the successor states. The events and experienced memories haunt Bosnia today – both through psychological trauma and atrocity but also through the ramifications of the Dayton Peace Accords. The war in Bosnia was over national territory and even identity, and should be scrutinized and looked at closely to further understand the recent role of Bosnia's three national groups and the International Community in establishing contemporary Bosnia and Herzegovina.

Civil War Comes to Bosnia

The ethnic fragmentation in Bosnia was well underway before the April 1992 referendum. The wars in Slovenia and Croatia polarized Bosnia's inhabitants, with both Croats and

Serbs aligning their sympathies with their brethren. The Bosnian Croats made no secret of their desire to affiliate with an independent Croatia, and the Serbs defiantly maintained their position of remaining in Yugoslavia. Izetbegović did not desire to see the Bosnian Muslims left in a rump land-locked state between its larger neighbors (Nation, 2003). Given the demographic reality of a higher Bosnian Muslim birth rate, Nation (2003) asserts that the Izetbegović administration aimed to hold together a unitary state in which Muslims would eventually come to dominate.

In the early stages of the war, although clearly possessing an ethnic and religious component, the military and police forces in the capital city of Sarajevo were multi-ethnic. A third of the defenders were Serb, even the commander Jovan Divjak was a Serb (Fine, 2002, Nation, 2003).[1] However, given the atrocities in the rural areas, the siege of Sarajevo and the latent ethno-religious antagonisms, the fear of an Islamic component in Bosnia was a self fulfilling prophecy. By the fall of 1993 Muslim nationalism had moved closer in character to the virulent Serb and Croatian versions.[2] The Muslim leadership, confronted with the efforts of the International Community leaders to promote ethnic partition as part of the solution, began to embrace the notion of a Muslim nation state as a goal. Outside of the International Community, Izetbegović also supported the notion of a state dominated by the Muslims, an essential incentive for Serb and Croat mobilization.

Moreover with the various sanctions and weapons embargoes in place on the former Yugoslav republics, the Bosnian Muslims turned to their co-religionists in southwest Asia and the Middle East for materiel, financial and moral support. The notion of a multi-ethnic Bosnia was quickly lost in the early fighting – it had become an “us versus them” scenario in which religion and ethnicity became the key component. Foreign Muslim fighters, or *mujahadeen*, were invited by Izetbegović to help the battered Bosnian Muslim army, forever changing the character of both the war and the Bosnian Muslims (Shrader, 2003).

The influx of Muslim refugees changed the character and political atmosphere of most Muslim towns and cities, but especially Sarajevo. As the Muslim refugee population grew, it did so with an increasing rural constituency. Given their treatment at the hands of the Serbs and Croats, these Muslim refugees readily adopted an intolerant stance towards Bosnia's non-Muslims. Tensions would develop between the secular Sarajevans and the new refugees. The entire character of Sarajevo was forever altered. The Muslim leadership now produced fanatical magazines and newspapers, the Mustafa Cerić, as the *Reis-ul-Islam* (head of Bosnia's Muslims), spoke out against mixed marriages and a platform was adopted that Islam should be taught in public schools (Fine, 2002).[3] The prewar cultural world that embraced multi-ethnicity and harmony was turned on its head. Public offices, governmental administrations and the army, once multi-ethnic were now permeated with Islamic symbolism and beliefs. This new visible Islam was all pervasive and in contrast to the marauding paramilitaries of the Serbs, such as Arkan, and the resurrected Ustaše of the Croats.

The Muslim-Croat Federation was nominally a coalition between the two against a militarily more powerful Serb force. However, by the summer of 1992 the Croats made clear their intent to create their own state of Herceg-Bosna, centered on Mostar. On July 3, 1992 the Croats seceded, declaring Herceg-Bosna a sovereign state.[4] In fact the Bosnian Croat's military, the *Hrvatsko Vjece Odbrane* (Croatian Defense Council or HVO) was directly controlled by the Croatian Army (Nation, 2003). Friction between these erstwhile allies was present since the war's beginning.

The complete breakdown of the Croat-Muslim alliance occurred in early 1993. Tensions between the two in distribution of weapons and supplies, disposition of forces, command and control between Croat and Muslim commanders as examples, had been endemic. There were incidences of local fighting between the two in late 1992 in central Bosnia (Nation, 2003). By April 1993 the two allies became enemies as open fighting in Gornji Vakuf, Zenica, the Lašva Valley and in Mostar itself, began in earnest (Nation, 2003, Sells, 2003, Shrader, 2003). This infighting led to brutal massacres of Muslims in Ahmići (April 16, 2004) and Stupni Do (October 1993) by the HVO. The Croat siege of the Muslim controlled part of Mostar was in every way as horrendous as the Serb siege of Sarajevo.[5]

Given the numerical superiority of the Muslims, military action would increasingly favor the *Armija Bosne i Hercegovine* (Army of Bosnia and Herzegovina or ABH) as long as they could stave off defeat. By September 1993 the Croats were checked on the battlefield and the Muslims began to turn back HVO gains. Without any direct intervention by forces from Croatia, the HVO found itself in a standoff with the ABH. A truce in February 1994 brought an end to the "war within a war."

A unique "sideshow" of the war in Bosnia was the Bihać pocket in northwest BiH where a local Muslim strongman and successful Yugoslav businessman, Fikret Abdić, defected from Izetbegović's Muslim government (Burg and Shoup, 2000). He was able to organize several Muslim brigades in his home region of Velika Kladuša, declaring an Autonomous Province of Western Bosnia in September 1993 and gaining control of most of the Bihać area (O'Shea, 1998). His battlefield gains would be rolled back the following spring of 1995 by the ABH 5th Corps.

The outbreak of fighting between Croat and Muslim allies and the internal war among the Muslims in northwest BiH reveals a sequence of shifting alliances and association at regional levels (Nation, 2003, Burg and Shoup, 2000). On many occasions the Serbs would support Croat military efforts against the Muslims. There were numerous times during the civil war that it degenerated into a series of confused struggles for local control, alliances of convenience, and with no sense of a larger strategic purpose being present (Nation, 2003). Indeed, Abdić coordinated an unsuccessful coup against Izetbegović in early 1992 while he was detained by JNA forces. His goal was to keep Bosnia within the remaining Yugoslav state. This illustrates that, even within the Bosnian Muslim political leadership, competing positions on Bosnia's future were prevalent (Burg and Shoup, 2000).

As fighting erupted in Bosnia, the Yugoslav military units were still withdrawing from Croatia into Bosnia under UN brokered cease-fires. These forces, in addition to those already stationed in Bosnia and the JNA forces from Serbia proper, all took part in this fight. Having inherited much of the JNA's arsenal before it left Bosnia, the *Vojska Republike Srpske* (Bosnian Serb Army or VRS) gained control of most of Bosnia by mid-1993 (Figure Four below).

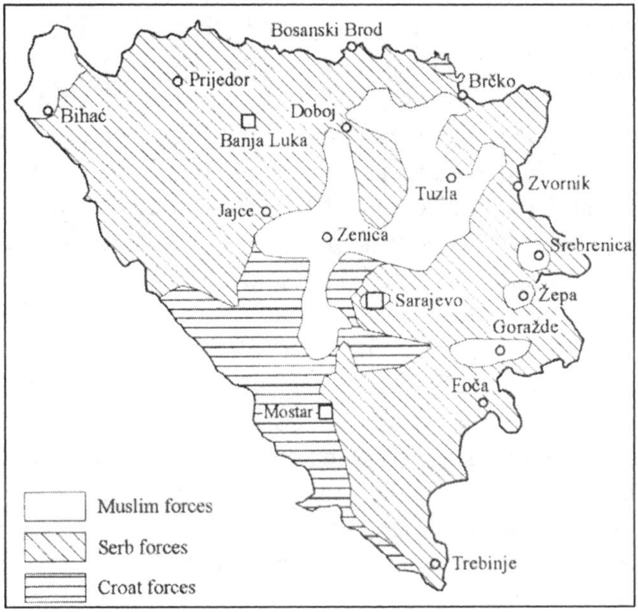

Figure 4 – Map of approximate areas of control, May-June 1993 (Burg and Shoup, 2000).

There were several efforts by the International Community to end the war. The Lisbon *Cutilheiro* Plan, which fell apart in March 1992, the Vance-Owen Plan rejected by the Serbs in May 1993, and the Owen-Stoltenberg Plan rejected by the Muslims in September 1993 are the best known. Over 80 UN resolutions were passed on the former Yugoslavia. Indeed the only major action by the International Community was to deploy UN Protection Forces (UNPROFOR), which grew from 1500 troops in August 1992 to over 23,000 by 1995 (Nations, 2003).

Sanctions were in place on all of the warring parties in the former Yugoslavia, but since the Serbs and Croats had the preponderance of war materiel, only the Muslims and the ABH suffered under them. The International Community and NGOs provided much needed humanitarian aid, but this effort was simply "containment with charity," according to Nation (2003, 172) and Woodward (1995).

Given the public outcry of Serb atrocities and ethnic cleansing, US policy in the region shifted towards assisting the Muslims. It must be noted that the media focus and sensationalism given Serb misdeeds were all but absent when atrocities were perpetrated by Croat and Muslim forces against the Serbs (Burg and Shoup, 2000). The role of the media in the escalation of fighting and violence in Bosnia cannot be understated. In mid-May 1993, the Vance Owen Plan's rejection was due in no small part to the Clinton's Administration proposed policy dubbed "Lift and Strike" – lift the arms embargo against the Muslims and conduct selective NATO air strikes against the Serbs. Neither the Bush or Clinton administrations were convinced of US vital interests in the region and were indecisive in their resolve until 1994.

Nonetheless, by June of 1993, six UN safe havens were established in Bosnia: Sarajevo, Goražde, Srebrenica, Tuzla, Žepa and Bihać. However, "safe haven" was a euphemism as the enclaves were encircled by the VRS and indefensible, and were used on many occasions to launch Muslim attacks against the Serbs (Nation, 2003, Burg and Shoup, 2000). It is estimated that more than 3,000 Serb civilians and soldiers were killed by Bosniak soldiers and paramilitaries operating from Srebrenica (Rohde, 1997, CIA, 2002).

The continuing humanitarian catastrophe and graphic imagery televised around the world led to greater Western initiatives to halt the fighting. The February 1994 *Markale* Market massacre in Sarajevo, in which 65 people were killed and over 200 wounded allegedly by a Serb shell, helped to galvanize the IC to resolve the conflict.[6] NATO set an ultimatum for the Serb forces to withdraw all heavy weaponry from a 20 km "total exclusion zone" around Sarajevo (Nation, 2003). With strong Russian involvement this was accomplished.

Serb encroachments on UN safe havens, such as Goražde, violation of UN imposed "no-fly zones" and incidents with UNPROFOR led to military action by NATO against the Serbs. The US became more involved in Bosnia as the US-NATO relationship, upcoming mid-term elections, reputation in the Muslim world and America's stature as a global leader were questioned (Nation, 2003).

Western Intervention

Throughout 1994, a more assertive Western approach, primarily dominated by the US, slowly started to impact events on the ground. It was hoped that some accommodation and therefore progress towards a negotiated peace could be achieved through the use of diplomacy and military action. From January through March, the yearlong plus fighting between Croats and Muslims was ended by their Washington Agreement settled in Petersberg, near Bonn, Germany. It allowed the SDA and HDZ to put aside their differences in order to concentrate on a common foe – the Bosnian Serb Army (VRS). However, the Washington Agreement did not give rise to common institutions or any meaningful commitment to cohabitation (Nation, 2003).[7]

Building on the limited success achieved under the agreement in forming the Federation of Croats and Muslims, efforts were made to reinvigorate international efforts with the establishment of the Contact Group in April 1994. This international body, composed of the US, the UK, France, Germany and Russia, was used as a forum to pursue peace initiatives and collaboration.[8] In reality, due to increasing US action, the US wound up taking the international lead through the Contact Group (Nation, 2003 and Burg and Shoup, 2000).

By the end of 1994 and into 1995 the Federation armed forces, to the dismay of its Croat members, were penetrated by Islamic religious extremism. As the war dragged on and atrocities mounted, the influx of new fighters from the devastated Muslim regions coupled with foreign fighters led to the introduction of Islamic symbols and use of quotations from the

Koran in army units. One of my Bosnian Serb interpreters related an event he experienced during the war, fighting as an infantryman near Bihać, in northwestern Bosnia. On one early pre-dawn morning the Serb lines were attacked by the nearby Muslim forces. Moments before the infantry attack began, the entire Muslim lines erupted into chants of "*Allah Akbar*" (God is great). He told me that the hairs stood up on his neck and the Serbs were terrified – the intended effect of the Muslim commander no doubt.

The Contact Group formulated a framework for a 51/49 percent territorial division between the Muslim-Croat Federation and the Serbs. Offered to the two sides in July 1994, it was eventually rejected by the Serbs, apparently not willing to surrender territorial gains. The year ended with Goražde nearly falling to the Serbs, minor violations of the Sarajevo exclusion zone by both sides, and the fall of Bihać to Muslim government control. The relationship between UNPROFOR with its peacekeeping troops on the ground in Bosnia, and NATO which favored direct military action via air strikes grew tense.

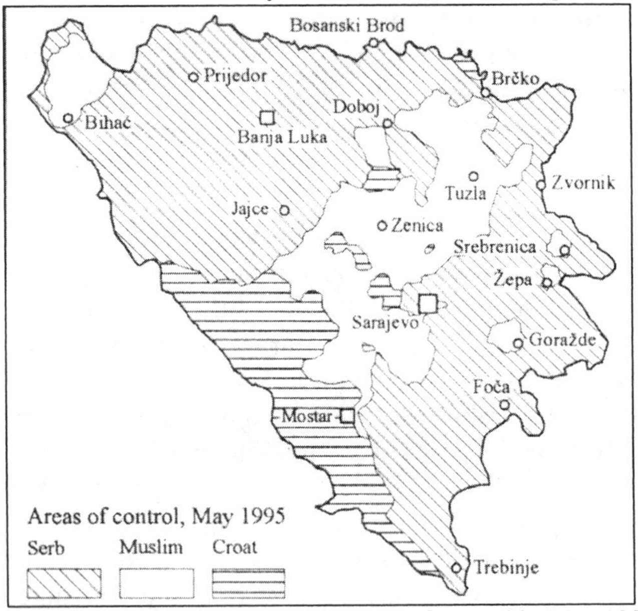

Figure 5 – Map of approximate areas of control in May 1995 (Burg and Shoup, 2000).

The End of Serb Military Hegemony

As 1995 dawned an eerie status quo existed in Bosnia. The Serbs held their gains,and the HVO and ABH were not capable of mounting anything other than local offensives. The only force capable of engaging the Bosnian Serb Army was the Croatian Army, which had been enhanced due to US funding, training through US contractors and weapons shipments from Germany and others (Nation, 2003, Burg and Shoup, 2000).[9] The HV would seize western Slavonia in western Croatia in spite of UNPROFOR's presence, driving tens of thousands of Serbs into Serb held Bosnia and Serbia proper. These same forces would play a role in Bosnia later.

By May NATO was launching air attacks against Serb positions for violating ceasefires in Sarajevo. In retaliation for the air strikes, the Serbs took 400 peacekeepers hostage, and used many as human shields on targets deemed to be bombed by NATO planes (Nation, 2003). The events were a profound humiliation for the entire UN peacekeeping effort in the Balkans.

The antagonism between the Bosnian Serbs, and the UN and NATO was exacerbated even more by the events around the UN safe havens of Srebrenica and Žepa in July of 1995. The Serbs overran the two towns in a matter of hours, pushing aside Dutch peacekeepers in Srebrenica and massacring several thousand male Muslim prisoners from both towns (Nation, 2003, CIA, 2002, Burg and Shoup, 2000).[10] Although not unprovoked, as the safe havens were never demilitarized and were used as bases from which to launch attacks against the Serb villages, the massacre was unique due to the scale of horror perpetrated and the level of planning required to execute the operation. The Bosnian Serbs would forever be judged unfavorably by these events.

Indeed, "ethnic cleansing," which has become commonly associated with the wars in the former Yugoslavia, was characterized by such events in Srebrenica, Ahmiči and elsewhere. The securing of contested areas for one's own ethnic faction resulted in the destruction of the enemy's homes, churches or mosques, cemeteries and national structures – the removing of the historical footprint of the other ethnic group's presence. This phenomenon was practiced by all three sides and by late summer 1993, the former Yugoslavia had over 4 million refugees and displaced persons (Nation, 2003).

Later in July and August 1995 the Croatian Army would prepare and launch an offensive called Operation Storm (*Oluja*) to regain control of the Serb occupied regions, the UNPAs, of Croatian territory. With tacit US approval and indeed air support, the Croats pushed the Serbs out in a matter of days, flooding Bosnia and Serbia with tens of thousands of refugees. It was the largest ethnic cleansing of the Yugoslav wars, perhaps 250,000 people were made refugees (Nation, 2003, Burg and Shoup, 2000, Glenny, 1996). The Bosnian Serb Army was unable to assist the Krajina Serbs as it was heavily engaged with Bosnian Croat and Muslim offensives that were launched in coordination with the Croatian Operation Storm. Milosević's Serbia, under tremendous Western pressure, abandoned its Krajina Serb allies to the Croatian onslaught.

By the end of the Croatian and Federation offensive, the Serbs in both the Krajina region of Croatia and in Bosnia had lost significant territory. In addition to this disaster, another shelling incident in Sarajevo on 30 August gave NATO the pretext to conduct extensive air operations against the Serbs. The air raids were substantial and intended to break the siege of Sarajevo (Nation, 2003). This resulted in accelerated Muslim-Croat advances and, with the increasing loss of Serb held territory, the Contact Group's 51/49 percent territorial division was becoming a reality. Indeed, there was a real fear that the HV and Federation forces would take even more Serb territory and, in order to halt these advances, the UN and NATO feigned military action to get them to heel (Silber and Little, 1997, CIA, 2002).

Figure 6 – November 1995 Areas of control and the Dayton Inter-Entity Boundary Line (Burg and Shoup, 2000).

Although the Bosnian Serb Army was not knocked out of the war, it could not engage Croatian and Bosnian Croat and Muslim forces along its entire front and roll back the significant territorial gains. The military balance of power had dramatically changed to the detriment of the Serbs. Through diplomacy led by the US's Richard Holbrooke, a ceasefire was declared on October 5, 1995. The battlefield gains of the Croat-Muslim alliance would set the stage for peace negotiations and the resultant Dayton Peace Accords' territorial division into two entities, one dominated by the Serbs, the other by a Muslim-Croat arrangement.

---

[1] During the wars early years, the Army of Bosnia-Herzegovina (*Armije Bosne i Hercegovine* – ABH) was fairly multi-ethnic. It was commanded

by Šefer Halilović, a Muslim, the Bosnian Croat Stjepan Šiber as Chief of Staff and the Bosnian Serb Jovan Divjak as the Deputy Chief of Staff.

[2] During the Owen - Stoltenberg July 1993 peace talks Izetbegovic began to see himself as the leader of Muslim interests. Muslim national interest took precedence over Serb and Croat concerns.

[3] To this day Cerić advocates a theocratic state alienating non-Muslims and secular Muslims daily and his actions have contributed to the still festering relations between all communities. His overt actions to control state media and impose "the logic of religious totalitarianism" have not gone unchallenged, even by the Muslims. *Oslobodjenje*, Sarajevo, 23 November 2004.

[4] The flag of the newly declared state was identical to Croatia's state flag. A clear indication of Croatia's sponsorship of Bosnian Croat moves towards secession from BiH and possibly integration into Croatia.

[5] The Croats at one point were threatened with sanctions by the UN; however, the siege never attracted international attention as Sarajevo.

[6] Much evidence exists to indicate that the massacre was staged by Bosnian Muslim forces in an attempt to garner world sympathy and compel military intervention against the Serbs.

[7] The Washington Agreement is hailed by many as the US's first success in its diplomatic efforts in Bosnia.

[8] Italy would subsequently join the Contact Group, which to this day remains active in policy formulation in the Balkans.

[9] Military Professional Resources Inc, or MPRI, was composed of retired US Army generals and officers. It was instrumental in developing the Croatian military into a potent and competent force. Jane's Defense weekly provides fairly detailed and definitive information on where and from which country Croatia received major weapons systems during years of alleged weapon's embargoes on the region; Germany is prominent in providing arms from former East German Army stocks.

[10] The events at Srebrenica have established the narrative of sole responsibility for the war on the Serbs. Estimates of deaths range anywhere from a couple thousand to over ten thousand and have recently been disputed in the press (Copley, 2003). My visit to the memorial park at

Potocari yielded a count of a little over 900 graves in June 2003. Although up to two thousand are still in a mortuary in Tuzla awaiting DNA identification, most of the numbers bandied about by the media are gross exaggerations.

CHAPTER VI

POST DAYTON BOSNIAN TERRITORIALITY AND SPATIAL IDENTITY

"Once people's sense of national identity is secured, the appeal of radical nationalist politicians will evaporate and a reasonable politics and economics can emerge."

General Charles Boyd, 1998

Territorial behavior is understood primarily through two theoretical understandings, one a determinate variety explained under the notion of biological or genetic territoriality and the other as socio-political (Sack, 1986, Storey, 2001). Territoriality in contemporary Bosnia, at its several political scales, is underpinned principally via the socio-political theoretical framework. Although the first theoretical understanding does weigh true regarding human nature to defend one's home (or space) and that humans are territorial by varying degrees, which did play a role in the bitter civil war, it is in the post-Dayton Bosnia that we see territoriality developing and manifesting itself through the socio-political theoretical approach. Certainly it is the Dayton Peace Accords which reorganized Bosnia administratively, nationally and politically. It set the stage for all Bosniaks, Croats, and Serbs to establish pursue their territorial ambitions within a post-war setting.

The Re-Territorialization of Bosnia – the Dayton Peace Accords 1995

The civil war in Bosnia was ended through the use of coercive diplomacy on the part of the United States. By launching an extensive air campaign against the Serbs, their leadership was compelled to negotiate. US policy, which by early 1995 had come to dominate Western diplomacy in Bosnia, sought an end to the fighting, rather than ending the warring faction's political differences and grievances. Therefore from the outset the accords were less than perfect. US led efforts resulted in recognizing the institutionalization of the Bosnian Serb republic and resultant *de facto* partition of Bosnia and Herzegovina into separate territories (Burg and Shoup, 2000).

After American arm-twisting the Dayton Peace Accord was initialed on November 21, 1995 at Wright Patterson Air Force Base in Ohio (Bose, 2002). Slobodan Milosević represented the Bosnian Serbs, Franjo Tudjman the Bosnian Croats and Alija Izetbegović Bosnia's Muslims. Although the fighting was ended, the partition of Bosnia yielded three nationalist statelets whose populations are still deeply divided on fundamental issues of identity and allegiance

The Dayton Peace Accords territorially organized Bosnia into two entities, the Republika Srpska (RS) and the Muslim-Croat Federation. The entities are separated by a 1200 km long Inter-Entity Boundary Line (IEBL) that in most areas reflects the former lines of confrontation. In many places this boundary is indeed physical as numerous minefields still lace the Bosnian countryside. The RS is administratively divided into municipalities which mirror the pre-war municipality structure except in cases where the boundaries are truncated by the IEBL.

The Federation on the other hand is a bit more complex. It is divided into ten cantons which are then divided into municipalities. As in the case of the RS, these municipalities reflect pre-war administrative organization. Until 1992 Bosnia had 110 municipal districts and as of 2002 it has risen to about 145 due in large part to the winding route of the IEBL. In some cases like Mostar, which went from one to six, these new municipalities were created to accommodate the tensions between the Croat and Muslim communities, allowing them to live in their own mono-ethnic municipalities (Bose, 2002).

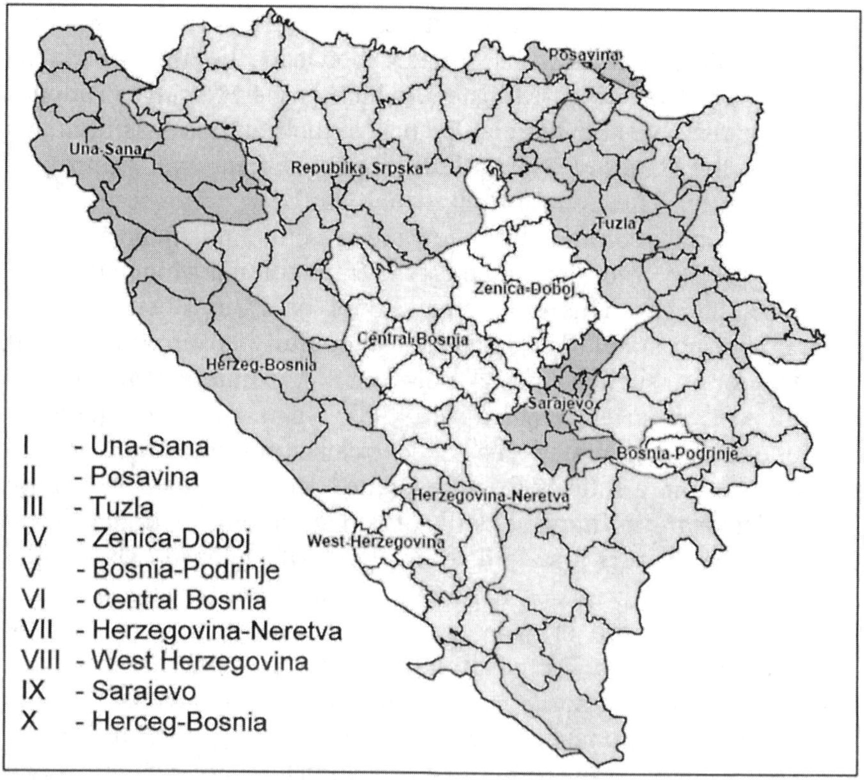

Figure 7 – Map of Bosnia displaying Republika Srpska and the Federation's cantons (source UNHCR GIS map unit Sarajevo 2004).

Each entity possesses its own constitution and entity institutions such as a judiciary, police force, health care, postal and telecommunications systems. These are just some of many such institutions within each entity. However in the Federation the complexity arises with the further devolvement of institutions to the canton level. Of the ten cantons, five are predominantly Bosniak, three Croat and the last two mixed. Each canton possesses the responsibility for its police forces, education policy, social welfare administration, and so on. The canton is clearly the decisive layer in the Federation's multi-tiered framework of government (Bose, 2002).

Partitioning of Bosnia into two entities poses great problems for state building and the exercise of authority.

Although common state structures do exist, such as the Tri-Partite Presidency (which rotates between the three national groups), a Council of Ministers, which is the Executive Branch, and Legislative and Judicial Branches, their authority is limited.[1] In fact the state level institutions are threadbare and wanting of real power. The Central Bank which has been very successful in establishing a common currency and effective monetary policy is run by a Governor appointed by the International Monetary Fund (Bose, 2002). This appointee cannot be from Bosnia or any neighboring state. The intent is to hopefully ensure no partisan behavior in such a critical position. A common Ministry of Defense was established in 2005 and the International Community celebrated this state level institution as a clear sign of success in a bitterly fractured state. But upon closer scrutiny the Bosnian military is still organized along national lines. Although there is a state level Ministry of Defense (MOD), the Army's three brigades are mono-ethnic, there being a Croat, Muslim and Serb brigade and each stationed in its respective national territory. For all intents and purposes, the central government's authority is limited to the conduct of foreign affairs, international commerce and fiscal policy (Nation, 2003).

Outside of the state of Bosnia and Herzegovina and its two entity pseudo-state arrangement, the United Nations and NATO (now the European Union) play an even larger role. The implementation of the DPA clearly envisioned a dual process. The United Nations would oversee the political and civilian administration of Bosnia through the Office of the High Representative (OHR) and the military provisions of the DPA would be enforced by NATO. The integration of these two international bodies is limited and their responsibilities and chain of command are separate. This was done purposefully as the US, primarily, had little faith in the UN being able to fulfill the military clauses of the DPA based on its lackluster performance in the previous three years as UNPROFOR.

The OHR is headquartered in Sarajevo with several field offices located in the major towns of Bosnia. The High Representative's powers are absolute as he possesses full executive authority over BiH. Parenti (2000) and the nonprofit research group European Stability Initiative (2003) liken the position of High Representative to a colonial administrator or European *Raj*. The HR can fire elected officials, fine organizations and even nullify laws as he sees fit and he has therefore come under increasing criticism for what is often being seen as inhibiting democratic growth and process. The OHR and NATO have exerted full territorial control of Bosnia since 1995.

NATO has been charged with enforcing the military provisions of the DPA. At the end of 1995 over 57,000 NATO soldiers, close to 20,000 being US, were deployed into war ravaged Bosnia, they initially separated the warring parties and aggressively maintained a ceasefire. The original and unrealistic one year mandate has been extended ever since 1995 and just recently came to an end. On November 24, 2004 NATO was replaced by the European Union's (EU) Force, or EUFOR, composed of about 7,000 soldiers. The mission remains the same but reflects today's geopolitical realities in which the Balkans has been subsumed by the "Global War on Terror" focus in US foreign and military policy. The US has effectively disengaged from Bosnia after nine years of NATO occupation.

The Dayton Peace Accord brought an end to the most horrific warfare and slaughter seen in Europe since the Second World War. It did not however, provide a viable concept for building a new state. The process of partition has inexorably drawn the ethnic communities further apart. Haris Silajdzić, a prominent member of Izetbegović's wartime administration, noted in 2000 that Bosnia is "now too strong to die, but too weak to function as a self-supporting state" (Bose, 2002). As such, there has been a renewed call by the Bosniaks and even some members of the International Community for a revision of the DPA, or convening a "DPA II," a call that the Serbs vehemently stand against as it would clearly threaten their statelet and perceived security. (Anderson, 1999). Indeed as Burg and Shoup (2000) note "there has been no reduction in the strength of the nationalist parties, and little evidence of either grass roots ethnic reconciliation or the interethnic elite cooperation that would be necessary to make power-sharing work and avert a return to war in the event Western troops are withdrawn." At the state-level, the territorial framework of Bosnia consists of two pseudo-states, the Republika Srpska and the Federation. However, when looking below this scale at cantons and municipalities, three territorial statelets can be said to exist in which each national group maintains power.

The Control of Bosnian Space

The Bosniaks, Croats and Serbs are using/employing territorial strategies to attain and/or maintain political and ethno-national control over space. In most instances these strategies are overt – the construction of signs, monuments, symbols and churches/ mosques or through the re-naming of place. The use of boundary signs between the Federation and Republika Srpska along the Inter Entity Boundary Line is a potent example of this strategy. Not only does this political boundary act as a "fence" to delineate Serb territory, but it is also one of many mechanisms to inhibit non-Serb refugee returns. Refugee returns are achievable only through the presence of NATO's Stabilization Forces (SFOR).

One instrument used to reaffirm control of territory is the removal of other group's presence. The destruction of cemeteries, churches, and mosques was a method commonly used by all three sides during the war (see figures 8 & 9). By removing such markers, political (and military) leaders hoped to discard the claims and physical history of those driven from the region, making it extremely difficult, if not impossible, to re-establish their presence.

Figure 8 – Damaged Muslim tombstones in the vicinity of Modrić (June 2004).

The same phenomenon can be witnessed at the canton level in the Croat controlled regions of the Federation. Power within the Croat cantons is possessed by the Bosnian Croats, although there are no boundary markers comparable to those along the IEBL. The political institutions within these cantons establish a hostile atmosphere making it extremely arduous for non-Croat returnees to return and resume their pre-war lives. Moreover, the cantonal administrative institutions, dominated by Croat nationalists, use economic measures to overtly inhibit non-Croat returns. The inability to repossess homes, obtain former employment or pensions, and procuring permits and licenses to start businesses are insurmountable challenges to returnees. The use of the judiciary, law enforcement and even health services by entity and cantonal authorities to withhold support to and intimidate these disenfranchised returnees is a potent, although covert mechanism that maintains national control within "their" territory. All three national groups use these measures, but my observations suggest that while the Office of the High Representative acts ruthlessly in countering the Serb discriminatory practices, it ignores the plight of Bosniak and Serb returnees in Croat controlled cantons.

Figure 9 – Damaged Orthodox Church in the vicinity of Maglaj (June 2004).

Based on interviews at the Canton X, OHR offices in Drvar and Livno little to no concern is displayed towards the abhorrent condition of returning refugee Serbs. My interpretation of the discussions leads me to believe that the Croat political power and control in their cantons deters outside influence. Indeed, most of the forestry industry in Canton X was Serb-owned prior to the war but through a corrupt cantonal privatization plan only Croats were offered the right to purchase these lands. This forestry industry employed much of the Serb populace, however today few are employed in the Croat firms and those that do work there occupy menial labor positions (based on 11 June 2004 interviews in Glamoć and Livno).

The responses to territoriality in Bosnia were and are conditioned within the wider social and political environment. It is certainly influenced by nationalism. The breakup of Yugoslavia led to the political reorganization of the people based on nationality – the national party represented the interests and rights of its nation. This is also typical of the former East Bloc states in which national parties replaced the communist party (Sugar and Lederer, 1994). Most of the fighting in the former Yugoslavia centered on the control of national spaces. In Bosnia's case it was the 1995 DPA that provided BiH a constitution that legitimated Serb political space within the framework of an administratively and politically weak Bosnian state structure. The Croats gained control of Cantons II, VII, VIII and X, this was, however, far short of their goal of a Herceg-Bosna state. This dissatisfaction manifested itself when elements of the Croat leadership attempted to create self-rule in the region and to disband the Croat portion of the Federation Army in 1999.[2] This uprising was dealt with harshly by the OHR and NATO. The leaders were jailed and political and military measures were taken to safeguard the integrity of the Federation. The US recognizes and legitimates the territoriality of the Croats and Serbs by having placed Embassy Field Offices in the RS capital of Banja Luka and in Mostar, the center of Croat power in BiH.[3]

Sack's (1986) writings on territoriality invoke a much more political reading. To him territoriality is a reflection of power (see also Storey, 2001). The controlling of space thereby affects, influences or controls resources, but it also exerts power over individuals within a specified territory or by excluding people from it. The wars of Yugoslav secession were a series of attempts at either maintaining or asserting control of spaces in a self-destructing Yugoslavia. Place is vital to people and serves in many instances as a component of national identity.

Serbs see Republika Srpska as a guarantee, in accordance with the DPA, of their security and future (Figure 40). Gottman (1973) asserts that territoriality confers security by having defensible space and allowing for the economic organization of that space for self-sufficiency. Others argue that such needs are based on characteristics developed from early childhood in which a space that provides comfort and safety must be maintained – it is innate territorial behavior (Storey, 2001). These aspects serve well in helping to explain why this sense of security is replicated within a nation and territorial state. I am not suggesting that this is the main reasoning to explain national group attempts to maintain power within the political administrative units of Bosnia, but simply are a component within the overall rationale of having one's own state, entity or territory – a visceral component at the individual level played upon by nationalist leaders and political parties during the civil war.

Places within Bosnia mean different things to its three antagonistic inhabitants. As a result of the war and the DPA, the Republika Srpska is increasingly comprehended as purely Serb territory. It possesses all of the trappings of statehood and serves to provide the perception of security from the Muslims.[4] It is at once inclusive of Serbs but exclusive of non-Serb communities. The Republika Srpska poses as the obstacle to the Bosniak or Muslim community imaginings of a unitary, sovereign state centered on Sarajevo. At a much lower scale, the Croat community desires its own entity but must settle for power and control at the cantonal level, as the junior member in the Muslim-Croat Federation.

The bond between place and nation is a phenomenon that strengthens over time. Given that active processes are in place to conflate territory with national identity, it suggests that separate national territorial spaces are developing in Bosnia. The marking and renaming of places in Bosnia is an overt manifestation of one national group's control over place, lending permanency to the Bosniak, Croat, and Serb places in Bosnia and Herzegovina. Coupled with the process of removing the historical trace of another ethnic group's dominance, the supremacy of the three national groups within their respective spaces is assured.

Spatial Identity

Although some states such as Belgium, Canada and Switzerland have been able to fitfully accommodate major national groups within their boundaries, Bosnia still lacks the social and political will by its national groups to submerge Bosnia's internal differences: religious, political, territorial or otherwise. Certainly these antagonisms have been aggravated by the recent civil war, its aftermath and the role played by the International Community in its reconstruction and recovery.

Gottman's (1973) notion of a "sacred soil" that members of a nation will die for is a critical aspect of the notion of spatial identity. The spatial identity of a nation embodies a group's territorial perception of itself which may or may not coincide with the territory it controls. Moreover, if the group doesn't control the territory entirely, it would like to do so. Examples of this are legion in the Balkans, with the ideas of a "greater Albania," "greater Croatia," or "greater Serbia." In each of these examples, hard-line nationalists assert that their national and state boundaries should include all of their national compatriots. As Kaplan (1994, 585) writes, "When spatial identities overlap, as between separate states that claim common territory or between two or more national groups within a state that cannot reconcile separate spatial identities, regional conflict often ensues."

The fears that Bosnia's dominant group, the Muslims, will submerge the Croat and Serb identities through control of the government are real. The friction is based on the unwillingness of the Croats and Serbs to submit to the authority of Muslim-dominated Sarajevo. The inability of the Muslims to have a state congruent with their notion of spatial identity – that is the internationally recognized boundary of Bosnia and Herzegovina – will continue to be a source of tension between ethnic groups that will hinder Bosnian state and national formation. It will be a source of permanent tension between the ethnic groups in Bosnia.

The national identities of Bosnia's three groups are found at three different spatial scales: the state level of the Bosniak, to the entity level of the Serb and to the cantonal and municipal level for the Croat. For inter-ethnic group accommodation to be achieved, the spatial identity of one group should not compromise that of another (Kaplan, 1994).

So how does this affect the notion of a Bosnian spatial identity? The Serbs have been overt in their dismissal of assuming "Bosnian" as part of their spatial identity through the naming and re-naming of place – "Republika Srpska," "Srpski Brod," and so on. My survey results imply that Serbs in Bosnia do not perceive themselves as Bosnian (see chapter IX, appendix

C and figure 45). Neither do the Croats. The Muslim respondents identified themselves as either Bosniak or Bosnian – both terms encompassing the state name.

There does not appear to be any near term accommodation between Bosnia's three national groups in adjusting their spatial identity or spatial ideologies. In fact the current status quo is greatly under threat as the Muslim nationalist Party of Democratic Action (SDA) pushes for the revision of the DPA and abolition of the Republika Srpska, and as the nationalist Serb Democratic Party (SDS) calls for Republika Srpska's independence and union with Serbia.[5]

The label Bosnian (or Bosniak) imparts the idea that the state of Bosnia belongs to this group. On the other hand, "Bosnian" Serb or "Bosnian" Croat only indicates their presence in Bosnia. Dropping the qualifier of "Bosnia" is of no concern as both peoples look to their respective bordering states for support and even identity. No Croats or Serbs ever identified themselves as "Bosnian" Croat or Serb to me. Moreover, their territory was always identified as Croat or Serb.[6] The symbolic locus for the Croats and Serbs is not in Sarajevo, but either in Mostar or Banja Luka at the state level or in Zagreb and Belgrade at the international scale.[7]

Only through the capacity of the Bosniaks, Croats or Serbs to "extend or modify" their spatial ideologies can a successful outcome be achieved. Whether Bosnia succeeds as a sovereign state or one day dissolves depends on whether the national groups can co-exist within the current DPA mandated territorial and political framework. Each group's perception of itself and its territory was hardened, if not reified in the civil war. Although it may be difficult to imagine a state like Canada, the United Kingdom or Belgium plunging into a civil war over spatial ideologies, it is sadly a realistic possibility in Bosnia as it struggles to develop as a state. The notion of forging a common Bosnian national identity and territory was not achieved at the Dayton negotiating table. The Bosniaks alone associate their collective identity and interests with the development of a functional Bosnian state (Bose, 2002). The presence of the OHR and NATO, now EU forces, calms ethnic tensions and compels "good behavior," thereby maintaining the political integrity and territorial integrity of the Bosnian state.

---

[1] Ironically, the Constitutional Court (Judicial Branch) is the most robust central institution and in which non-Bosnians play a critical role. Of nine judges, three are appointed by the president of the European Court of Human Rights! The other six are equally appointed from Bosnia's three ethnic groups.

[2] This incident is the subject of a highly contentious and ongoing court case known as the "Croat self-rule case." In which several local Croat leaders are being tried for treason and actions against the state.

[3] The creation of a permanent airline flight between Mostar and the Croatian capital of Zagreb was announced in October 2004, illustrating the strong Croat presence in Mostar and ties to Croatia itself [*Dnevni List*, Sarajevo, 21 October 2004]. The Serbs have had daily flights from Banja Luka to Belgrade for several years now.

[4] The survey results in Chapter IX provide evidence that the Serbs are adamant on maintaining their entity even at the risk of going to war. My many discussions with Serbs reveal that they honestly believe or perceive that without the DPA entity system their very existence as a national group in Bosnia would be threatened and they would be at the mercy of an OHR backed Bosniak/Muslim regime dominating Bosnia, a fear that drove many to support the war.

[5] The political situation in Bosnia is more tenuous and unstable today than in the last several years. The SDA's political leadership has openly called for the abolishment of RS and revision to the DPA imposed constitution. On 22 September 2004, Bosnia-Hercegovina Presidency Chairman Sulejman Tihić of the SDA used his address to the 59th UN General Assembly in New York to openly advocate constitutional revision. It is a demand for a stronger central government. The response of the Serb community has been predictable; it will not renegotiate the DPA. The acting chairman of the SDS, Dragan Čavić (also the Bosnian Serb president), stated on 25 September 2004 that the RS did not want to change the Dayton Agreement, but if the political pressure of the Federation for a constitutional rearrangement of Bosnia-Hercegovina continues, the SDS would ask the international community to grant the Serbs the same rights as it did to the Albanians in Kosovo and the Montenegrins in Serbia-Montenegro, including the right to self-determination. In fact the probable resolution of

the status of Kosovo and its anticipated independence has led many Serbs to counter SDA inspired political moves to abolish the entities with outright independence of the RS and eventual union with Serbia [sources BBC Monitoring Reports, various dates in September and October 2004].

[6] It must be noted that in Sarajevo, a couple of Bosnian Serbs did advocate a Muslim position towards Bosnia. One young Serb woman working in the US EUCOM's Office of Defense Cooperation (ODC) was "more Bosniak than the Bosniaks." I realized after speaking with her office colleagues that she was married to a Bosnian Muslim. In any case, and outside of this example, the differences between Bosnia's ethnic groups are striking. Another aspect I unexpectedly discovered was Serb support inside the Federation for a more centralized Bosnian state. The reasoning was simple; these Serbs located in the dismal Canton X saw their rights better protected via Sarajevo than from a powerful Croat canton controlled from Livno.

[7] There are some subtle deviations. The Serbs of eastern RS are much more radicalized than the Serbs in the western half of the RS and at times look to Pale, the wartime capital of the Serbs, to pursue their political positions against the more moderate Banja Luka. This aspect is diminishing with time and the extreme nationalists moderate their rhetoric. Of course compelling "good behavior" by the OHR is done through providing financial and political support to the moderates within the RS.

CHAPTER VII

ETHNIC AND NATIONAL IDENTITY IN BOSNIA

"Religion is intimately connected to the expression of ethnic/national identity that distinguishes the Serbs, Croats, and Bosniaks from each other."

Tone Bringa, 1995

A key factor in developing a Bosnian identity is that its citizens must feel they are stakeholders in the success or failure of the state. However the three major ethnic groups, the Bosniaks (Muslim), Croats and Serbs, are developing and strengthening their identities along diverging paths. Only the Muslims, or Bosniaks, primarily are attempting to construct a true Bosnian identity.[1] Certainly the aspect of incongruent identity creation in Bosnia is detrimental to developing a unitary state of Bosnia and Herzegovina. As is commonly the case since the 1992-1995 war, no true shared sense of Bosnian identity, or even citizenship, exists.

Indeed when looking at the research data I compiled from my 2004 trip to Bosnia, it suggests that the Croat and Serb understanding of national identity has a *primordialist* component. Genealogy is important to them. Bringa (1995) and others note that by stressing the idiom of shared blood and a perception of common origins as the basis of their collective identity, the Croats and Serbs manifest aspects of primordialism. The Bosniaks and those who chose to self-identify as Bosnian may be labeled as *instrumentalist* given the creation of these new state-based identities. Indeed here also my data suggests this difference from the Croats and Serbs. The label "Bosnian" has historically been a territorially based title, much as someone being an Ohioan or a New Yorker – but not automatically as a nation state-centered identity. Therefore the regional term of Bosnian (*Bosanac*), one inclusive of all three confessions, has lost its meaning for the most part and has been overwhelmed by the three ethno-national categories of Bosniak, Croat and Serb. Moreover, many outside of Bosnia associate Muslim with being Bosnian – without consideration of the Croats and Serbs.[2]

Bosnia is unlike other regions in the former Yugoslavia where language differentiated peoples, such as Slovenian, or Macedonian (see Velikonja, 1994). In Bosnia, language or race are not factors in identity formation. Religion is a factor and one that is normally neglected as a dimension of nation and nationalism in scholarship today (Hastings, 1997).

The dominant distinguishing cultural feature of the Bosniaks, Croats and Serbs is indeed religion. The Bosniaks are Muslim (a very moderate form of Sunni Islam), the Croats are Roman Catholic, and the Serbs are Eastern Orthodox. It is religion that provides each national group a source of cohesion, rituals and emotionally powerful symbols. In Communist Yugoslavia religion had no official public presence; it was one's private matter and impacted little in society. Moreover, the Communists actively discouraged religious activity and beliefs, stressing the atheist aspect of Tito's Yugoslavia.

Although acknowledged to be the critical component of identity in Bosnia, little attention is paid to religion's role in the development of Bosniak, Croat and Serb identity (Sells, 2003). Most treatises on nationalism in the state of the former Yugoslavia treat religion as an equal among the myriad of cultural attributes, such as language, although it is the critical difference between the ethnic groups and has been so historically.

Ethnic and National Identity in Tito's Yugoslavia

How nationality and ethnic identity was understood in modern Yugoslavia (1945-1990) is essential to understanding it today. Nationality in the former socialist and multi-ethnic Yugoslavia differs from modern, Western notions. Citizenship and nationality are virtually synonymous in Western European usage. However, national identity was different from citizenship in the former Yugoslavia; indeed this is the case in most former socialist states. Everyone held Yugoslav citizenship, but no one held Yugoslav nationality (Bringa, 1995, 2002).

Narod (*narodnost*) is commonly translated as "nation" or "ethnic group" whereas *nacionalnost* is translated as "nationality" or "ethnicity." Yugoslav was never an option as a nationality, only as an ethnic minority or as an "undeclared" category for state administrative purposes (Bringa, 1995). Therefore an individual's relationship to the state differed from the Western sense of it and allowed for manipulation and individual choice. Indeed, everywhere in the Balkans the basis of political division was drawn along historically ethno-religious lines (Allcock, 2002).

Yugoslavia possessed a three tiered system of nationalities policy. The first category consisted of the six "nations of Yugoslavia" (*Jugoslovenski narodi*): Serb, Croat, Slovene, Macedonian, Montenegrin, and Muslim (*Musliman*).[3] Each had a national home based in one of Yugoslavia's republics and a constitutional right to equal political representation. A unique exception is that the Croats and Serbs also had Bosnia and Herzegovina as a national home, in addition to the republics of Croatia and Serbia. Bosnia was a national home to the Croat, Muslim and Serb nations.

The second category was that of nationalities of Yugoslavia (*narodnosti*) which endowed its members with language and cultural rights. Included here are ten groups of which the largest were the Albanians and Hungarians. This category encompassed the non-Slavic members of Yugoslavia (Sells, 2003). The third category was the "other nationalities and ethnic minorities," which included Vlachs, Greeks, Jews, Russians and those who classified themselves as "Yugoslavs" (Bringa, 1995). As noted by Allcock (2002) this system inevitably consigned some to the status of second class citizenship.

The end effect is that the Yugoslav League of Communists, through such processes, privileged certain national identities. This therefore inhibited any effort to institutionalize citizenship as a Yugoslav (Allcock, 2002). The primary catalyst of Yugoslav unity and identity was Tito. After his death in 1980 it was no longer to taboo to discuss nationalism and one's national loyalties.

Bosnia's Muslims

Post 1945 the status of Muslim identity within Communist Yugoslavia's Bosnia was transformed. Initially the League of Communists' strong devotion to secularism attempted to subsume Muslim identity within the cloak of Yugoslavism. The final declaration of a Muslim "nation" was a long and difficult process. In the 1948 census Bosnian Muslims were categorized as "indeterminate Muslims" (*neopredelni Muslimani*); in 1953 "indeterminate Yugoslavs" (*neopredeljeni Jugosloveni*); in 1961 as "Muslims in the ethnic sense" (*Muslimani u etničkom smislu*); in 1971 as "Muslims in the sense of nationality" (*Muslimani u smislu narodnosti*); and eventually listed as a "nation" (*narod*) – *Muslimani* in 1981 (Allcock, 2002).

The elevation of Muslims to *narod* status granted them an equal presence in any governmental body, council or committee. There had to be an proportional number of representatives from all three *narodi* in Bosnian official bodies and institutions. To this day Tito's actions leading to Muslim national recognition helps to explain why his and Partisan statues and monuments are cared for in Muslim areas of Bosnia.

Many scholars have written that Bosnian Muslims had become so secularized in Yugoslavia that their ethnic identity was free of religious labels; all that remained of their faith was the ethnonym "Muslim" (Bringa, 2002). Bosnian Muslims, especially in the rural setting, have to be understood in the historical, geographical, political, and socioeconomic context of a lived Islam. Although becoming much more Islamic since the war, a good deal of a Bosnian Muslim's religion consisted primarily of customs and traditions and not one of strict Islamic ideologies and doctrines. It was openly admitted to me by several Bosniak acquaintances that Muslims drink alcohol and even eat pork, but to a much lesser degree than before the war and rarely outside of the home. This may indicate a change in the salience and interpretation of religion among Bosnia's Muslims.

European Muslims are considered by some as an historical remnant of the Ottoman Empire, thereby invoking a sense of not belonging to Europe. Although possessing a state in the 13th and 14th centuries that had a common identity, Bosnia fell to the Ottoman Empire in 1463 at a time of its state development (Magaš, 2003). It was also during this period that many Bosnian nobles, elites and merchants converted to Islam in order to retain their properties and power within the new empire. During Ottoman control, the ruling Muslim elites never transitioned to being nationally minded as they had become part of the ruling body. This would become problematic with the encroachment of Serbian and Croatian nationalism of the 19th century.

A significant historiographical dilemma exists in understanding Bosnia. There is little written evidence of the Bosnian Church and the interpretation of Christianity and its practice during its medieval existence (Bringa, 1995). Most of what does exist comes from Croatian or Serbian sources, including medieval documents, and in many cases defines the Bosnians as being heretics or occasionally adherents "gone astray" from the Catholic or Orthodox churches. This has served to fuel nationalist arguments as to why Bosnia should be incorporated into a Greater Croatia or Serbia.

Bosnia enjoyed no state-national idea during the Ottoman period (14th-19th centuries), but existed as a territory whose ruling Muslim elites remained loyal vassals to the Ottoman overlords. In contrast the Serbs and Croats enjoyed histories of state individuality and had institutional links to the past: the Serbs enjoyed a national church and emancipation from the Turks in the early 19th century and the Croats possessed a state parliament in Zagreb (Magaš, 2003). Moreover, the continuities that the Croats and Serbs share with their church and national history are absent in the context of Bosniak history.

Magaš (2003) argues that Bosnia began to re-appropriate its state tradition and therefore aspects of Bosnian identity with the 1878 Treaty of Berlin in which Austro-Hungary assumed administrative control of Bosnia. With this project she asserts that "the tools for forging a modern sense of nationhood" were in place and allowed Bosnia to exist as a territorial unit first within the Dual Monarchy and then in royalist and communist Yugoslav state. With the process and assumption of *narod* status in the

1970s and 1980s Magaš asserts that the early Christian and Ottoman cycles came together, forming a linear historical path characteristic of unified nations (Magaš, 2002). The 1992 hoisting of the colors of the Kotromanić dynasty over the entrance to the national parliament in Sarajevo supposedly symbolized the healing of the rupture in state tradition. Given that no Bosnian state structure existed from 1463 to 1992 indicates a very fragile position even though Bosnia possessed Yugoslav republic status post-1945.

The term *Bošnjak* was used as a counter to growing Croat and Serb nationalism in Austro-Hungarian Bosnia. It revived the concept of *Bošnja Ętvo* ("Bosnianess" or "Bosnianhood") and while the term was not originally exclusive to Muslims, it became a way for the Muslim gentry sought to offset the threat of growing nationalisms in Bosnia (Banac, 1984 and Bringa, 1995).

A historical discontinuity as a nation exists in Muslim nationalist discourse. The Muslim assertion of linkage between a people and territory does not exist and has only been manufactured through nationalist discourse. The real debate trying to be addressed is "who is the legitimate owner of Bosnia and its territory?" The establishment of the historical continuity between a people and a specific territory is a crucial element in the nation-building process.

Official sanction was given to the term Bošnjak, or Bosniak, to identify Bosnian Muslims by the Republic of Bosnia and Herzegovina first president Alija Izetbegović. Politically it was clear that the term would establish the Muslims with a continuous historical link to Bosnia as a state and a territory by its very name (Bringa, 1995).

Being a Bosnian Muslim in communist Yugoslavia was difficult if one wished to practice his/her religion. No consideration was made of Muslim dietary practice in factories, schools, or governmental buildings and institutions; no designated collective prayer areas were available to Bosnian Muslims. For Islam, just as for other religious denominations in Yugoslavia, public worship and displays of any nationalist nature were considered anti-Communist and treacherous by the authorities, the Communist Party and legal code. Even the practice of giving traditional Muslim names was discouraged for members of the Muslim Communist Party in the 1950s and 60s.

It was not until Tito's Yugoslavia started to crumble in the 1980s that public worship was seen again. All ethnic groups in Bosnia, as elsewhere in Yugoslavia, saw increased activity and participation at churches and mosques. As Communist control loosened, the revival of the national religions was assured. Even before the civil war, a process of Islamification began to take hold in certain areas of Yugoslavia. Sarajevo's first medressah (*medresa*), an Islamic educational institution, opened in 1978 and its first class graduated in 1982.

There are several reasons for this. Firstly, Yugoslavia's close relationships and cooperation with non-aligned Muslim countries of the Middle East led to Yugoslav Muslims being educated in Middle Eastern states and even the sponsorship of a limited number of mosques in Yugoslavia.[4] Secondly, a radical Islamic movement had existed below the surface in Bosnian society. Alija Izetbegovic's *Islamic Declaration* and the *islamska zajednica* (the official organization of the Islamic community in Bosnia in the 1980s) were clear indicators of the rise of religion within Bosnia's Muslim community.

Lastly, the relaxed treatment and attitude towards religions and national matters contributed to this Islamification process taking hold in Bosnia. The war radically altered this process. The influx of Islamic fighters, several thousand by some estimates, and materiel and financial support of Middle Eastern and other Islamic states intensified this process also. The net effect has led to a revival of Islamic beliefs and practices among the Bosniak community. No longer can they be charged as being an "historical remnant of the Ottoman Empire" or the most secular of communities in the former Yugoslavia. Islam is now an integral part of being a Bosnian Muslim – it is a key component of their identity that separates them from Bosnia's other ethnic communities.

Bosniaks are appropriating the notion of a Bosnian identity. This is both an inadvertent and overt process. The rejection of a purely Bosnian identity by the Croats and Serbs has resulted in the Bosnian Muslims assuming it within the label of "Bosniak." Even the International Community, such as the UN High Commission for Refugees (UNHCR), has labeled the Muslims as Bosnian in public documents.[5] By assuming the title of Bosniak the Bosnian Muslims are stressing their territorial rights (Hamourtziadou, 2002).

Croatians and Serbians

The Croats and Serbs of Bosnia share some strong similarities in their ties to a Croatian and Serbian homeland, respectively. As outlined above, both national groups were recognized by the former Yugoslav system as *narod* in their "homelands" of Croatia and Serbia as well as in Bosnia. Certainly this complicates the notion of a Bosnian identity, when these groups looked either west or east to their brethren. They identified themselves as belonging to national groups whose spatial presence far exceeds that of Bosnia. The identity of the Croats and Serbs in Bosnia surpasses the boundaries imposed and recognized by the Dayton Peace Accords. This is acknowledged by Dayton's acquiescence to Croat and Serb demands of possessing "national" territory within the Bosnian Federation: one at the cantonal level the other at the entity.[6]

As written earlier, religion plays the significant role in Bosnia. During the war enemies or victims were identified based on religion, whether or not they professed a belief or were identified as belonging to a certain religion based on names, dress or official documents such as voter registration lists (Sells, 2003). The history of both these peoples is closely aligned with their religion, its institutions and politics, and pre-dates the arrival of Islam in the region. This poses a dilemma for those asserting a clear historical tie between the Bosniaks (or Muslims) and Bosnian territory.

The background of Serbian and Croatian national identity outside the Bosnian context must be briefly addressed as it directly impacts the Croats and Serbs of Bosnia. Both nations possessed territorial medieval states prior to being submerged within massive empires for a major portion of their history. For the Croatians it was within the Hapsburg and then Austro-

Hungarian Empire. The Serbians on the other hand were left to Ottoman domination for close to five hundred years.

The state territory of King Tomislav's descendants form the basis of Croatian nationhood (White, 2000). A 1925 monument to him in Livno, Bosnia attests to this tie with Bosnia's Croats. Likewise for the Serbs, the legacy of their greatest medieval ruler Stephen Dušan, is a major historical factor in framing Serbian national identity. Both were adherents to Christianity - Roman Catholicism for the Croatians and Eastern Orthodoxy for the Serbians. This historical-religious connection to their medieval past is significantly weaker in the case of the Bosniaks.

By usurping the history and symbology of Tvrtko's Bosnian kingdom, they have attempted to establish an artificial tie to the past, creating an aura of historical legitimacy for the new state. However, it is problematic to envision a clearly traceable and definable lineage between a Christian medieval state and a modern Muslim state construction. This is especially contentious as religion played a crucial role in feeding the internecine violence and atrocity of the civil war and is still the major divisive characteristic in Bosnia.

The Serbians were able to maintain an independent church until 1459, when the last Serbian fortress of Smederevo fell to the Turks. Although now under the Greek domination within the Ottoman *millet* system of administration, the maintenance of a bishopric at Ohrid preserved some semblance of Serbian Orthodox church independence.[7] It was not until 1557 that the Grand Vizier Mehmed Pasha Sokolii-Sokolović established the Patriarchate of Peć as the seat of the autocephalous church of the Serbian Orthodox Church. White (2000) writes that Peć served as the depository of memories and as such was able to maintain the identity of the region's people.

In the absence of any state structure, the revived Serbian Orthodox Patriarchate became an institution of great importance again. Its ecclesiastical territorial jurisdiction spread from the Adriatic littoral to Budapest and from the Serbian enclaves in Croatia to those in Bulgarian areas. In addition, the church owned vast tracts of land and estates, thus making it a feudal overlord to the Serbian peasantry. Paul Pavlovich (1988) writes, "At the top it was a feudal organization, but with its multitude of clergymen, its reconstructed, or newly built churches and monasteries, it was a gathering place for the Serbian people, scattered over a the wide expanses of the Ottoman Empire, welding them into a whole, acting as their representatives, and promoting the notion of their unity" (Pavlovich, 1988, 18). Indeed when the Serbian state did fall, the "soul" of the Serbian people was able to survive the centuries in their faith and traditions of the past due to the role of the church (Petrovich, 1976).

Like the Serbians, the Croatians experienced medieval statehood, albeit short-lived, and established a strong national legacy of their own. Croatia was initially established under King Tomislav in the late tenth century. It achieved its zenith under King Zvonomir in the early eleventh century, only to pass under the control of the Hungarians when Zvonimir died without leaving an heir in 1089 (Stavrianos, 1965). Croatia was able to maintain some level of recognition, albeit under Hapsburg and Austro-Hungarian suzerainty for most of its history, until 1941 and then again in 1991. The native nobility, unlike in Serbia, was able to maintain its power and privilege within the new framework of the Habsburgs.

A strong tie has always existed between the Croatian people and the Catholic Church. In 1094 a bishopric was established in Zagreb, eventually achieving independent archdiocese status in 1852 after Croatian support in the suppression of the 1848 rebellion in Hungary. Indeed the church was a massive feudal structure that controlled vast tracts of land and was closely allied with the nobility. As in Serbia it was a repository of national history and heritage. However unlike Serbia, Croatia except for a brief period of Ottoman control possessed a nobility and varying degrees of territorial recognition and autonomy in its history under the Hapsburgs whereas the Serbs would have to wait until 1804.

Gerolymatos (2000) attributes several factors that allowed the Balkan nations to maintain their language, culture, and history – therefore their identity. First, cultural memories were passed from generation to generation via the prolific use of folk music, stories, epic poetry and the great oral tradition. Secondly, the Ottoman practice prohibiting Christian subjects from certain rights and customs, the special taxes, such as the child levy and other activities perpetuated their distinctiveness from their Ottoman masters and Muslim landowners. The simple application of Ottoman law was a continual reminder that the Balkan Christians were a conquered people. Increasing Ottoman persecution through the centuries ensured that the Balkan Christians were members of a distinct Orthodox community. The use of the Ottoman Empire's administrative *millet* system for non-Moslem Ottoman subjects reinforced and institutionalized the aspect of distinctiveness and unique identity. Grosby (1995) also specifically addresses the *millet* system used by the Ottoman rulers in the Balkans to recognize distinct communities, such as Orthodox Christians, and the end effect it had in retarding the existence of relative homogeneity that would lead to a national territory of the Ottomans. Although it can be argued that the *millet* system differentiated between religions and not ethnicity, it still set the conditions of exclusion. The separate histories, traditions, language and culture differentiated the Christians from one another within the Ottoman *millet* system.

Both Croats and Serbs make the argument and claim a direct link to their past. It has been used to justify their actions in the war and to denigrate the notion of a similar link for Bosnia's Muslims. Indeed as written in so many books on the subject of Bosnia, I witnessed firsthand on numerous occasions Croats and Serbs stating that the Muslims were nothing but converted (or turncoat) Croats or Serbs. The insult of *Turci* or Turk is commonly used in exchanges among the Croats and Serbs.

The Notion of Bosnian Identity

George White (2000) and others assert that Bosnia qualifies for nationhood, and that the multi-ethnic character of Bosnia will fuse into being Bosnian. Moreover White (2000) asserts that the Bosnian nation derives its being more from territory than from any other cultural characteristic. It is territories that frame national identities and given the common history, shared place and past commonalities Bosnia will become "Bosnian" – not Bosnian Croat, Bosnian Serb or Bosniak (White, 2000).

The very mechanisms claimed to be critical to develop a Bosnian identity are missing. The state structure was overtly left weak and unwieldy at the Dayton Peace Accords in 1995 to satisfy the demands of the Bosnian Croats and Serbs notions of national survival. This mortally wounded the development of a true Bosnian identity as conceived in current ethnic and national identity scholarship.[8] The state of Bosnia and the identity of "Bosnian" are perceived as the desire of the Muslims and now as a detriment to Croat and Serb identity.

Recent history and current events indicate that this will not hold true. While it is true that some Croats and Serbs fought alongside Muslims for a Bosnian state, this certainly was an exception and not the rule in the beginning.[9] Those Serbs that remained loyal to Izetbegovič's Bosnia were called "tame Serbs," "loyal Serbs (*Lojalni Srbi*)," or "Alija's Serbs (*Alijini Srbi*)." Moreover, there were Bosnian Muslim forces in the Bihač region that fought with the Serbs against an independent Bosnia.[10] National Bosnian institutions and governmental structures that bring people together do not exist in Bosnia. In fact the very structure of DPA Bosnia inhibits this as the Croats and Serbs maintain their territoriality within DPA Bosnia. The Croats through the canton system maintain their spatial identity and power in cantons II, VII, VIII, and X. The Serbs possess an entire entity unto themselves, with its capital at Banja Luka.

The perceived threat to Bosnia's Christians is not without basis. Ever since 1994 with NATO's arrival and the West's involvement in Bosnian affairs, a discourse has developed that Bosnia is a Muslim state and most international efforts have reflected this.[11]

The majority of Bosnian Croats, although nominally allied with the Muslims against the Serbs initially, eventually fought against them for a Croat Herceg-Bosna and eventual incorporation into Croatia. Under significant international pressure the Croats were forced to rejoin the Muslims in a "common" fight against the Serbs. However the original Croat nationalist goal of an exclusive Croat territory in Cantons II, VII, VIII and X still remains.

The Bosnian Serbs at the outset fought to stay within Yugoslavia (or as part of the oft quoted Greater Serbia) and then as an independent state when support from Milosević, under strong pressures, stopped. Neither the Croat nor Serb desired a Sarajevo centered Bosnian state, although for different stated goals.

Most newspaper and media journalists and international community representatives addressed the Bosnian civil war as being just another stage in the horrific internecine struggles historically associated with the Balkans. An often heard phrase "These people have been killing each other for centuries" and it should be no surprise that it is happening again. According to some accounts, this failure to look at Yugoslavia's demise in a rational pragmatic manner allowed International actors to de-politicize what was occurring and therefore present the notion that there isn't anything we can do to stop it. Not only was the civil war de-politicized, it was even accorded what can be seen as a "natural phenomena" and part of a cycle for the region. The question is how an identity based on Bosnia can be possible given these arguments by many of the international community.

Identity formation is important and crucial to Bosnia's future. It impacts the state's development. Hartshorne (1969) wrote extensively on the aspect of centripetal and centrifugal forces impacting states. The current role of national identity is one of centrifugal impact; the Croats and Serbs do not see themselves as Bosnian first, national group second. They look to their brethren in neighboring Croatia and Serbia, not Sarajevo. The Bosniaks fully endorse the notion of Bosnian identity, which they see as crucial to Bosnia's survival.

Bosniaks see their identity and future linked with a politically and territorially strong state of Bosnia and Herzegovina. The Serbs wish to preserve their current level of pseudo-statehood of Republika Srpska within the framework of the Dayton Peace Accords. The Croats desire their increasing level of autonomy within Bosnia by maintaining the concept of cantons, some expressing aspirations for an entity as the Serbs now have. The fact that through historical events and the post-1945 communist political institutions and arrangements which strengthened Croat and Serb national ties to Croatia and Serbia proper, any aspirations towards a true Bosnian identity is unlikely. The efforts of the Bosniak and Muslim community to demand such allegiance only adds to alienation on the part of the Croats and Serbs, and animosity towards Bosnia's Muslims. As said earlier, much has to do with who is the legitimate heir to Bosnia. The naming, labeling and categorizing that has gone on regarding identities in the lands of the former Yugoslavia are contested acts because they are essential sources of power in the construction of national loyalties – quite apropos to Bosnia today.

---

[1] Based on a survey of 216 respondents during May and June 2004 in BiH, only 16% identified themselves as Bosnian. The vast majority of them were from Sarajevo. It must also be said that many Bosniaks referred to themselves as such and not as Bosnian. Moreover as documented by numerous scholars such as Tone Bringa (2002) the overwhelming majority of those that declare themselves as Bosnian are Muslims.

[2] An excellent example of this is Honig and Both's Srebrenica, Record of a War Crime (1996) where in the "Note to the Reader" it is elaborated that "Muslim" and "Bosnian" are used interchangeable in their book.

[3] Muslim (*Musliman*) was the only category specifically designated by religion.

[4] Islamic institutions abroad include the Al-Azhar University in Cairo and numerous others in Saudi Arabia, Iraq and Turkey.

[5] A September 21, 2004 "Returns to Bosnia and Herzegovina" chart prepared by the UNHCR lists four groups: Bosnian, Croat, Serb, and other. This acknowledgement by an international body overtly acknowledges the Muslims as the inheritors of post-war Bosnia.

[6] This issue is recognized by the international community and Bosniak leadership. There is a strong push by the state and Federation level Bosniak leadership in tandem with the OHR and NATO to revise the DPA Constitution, thereby eliminating the entity and cantons. [*Oslobodjenje*, pg

6 'BiH – a republic without entities' by A. Terzic, *Dnevni List* pg 8 'Organize BiH as de-centralized state', mentione on front, by Danka Polovina-Mandic, *Nezavisne Novine* pg 12 'Decentralised BiH without entities' by FENA, EuroBlic RSpg 2 'No entities in Republic' by SRNA (source OHR News Roundup dtd 15 Sep 04)]

[7] The *millet* administrative system of the Ottoman Empire divided its subjects into groups based on religion. The three largest were the Muslim, the Greek Orthodox and the Jewish *millets* (Glenny, 2000, 71).

[8] In July 2003 while in Banja Luka, I asked a Serb acquaintance about the national capital at Sarajevo and how it impacted the RS. He looked at me incredulously and remarked, "Sarajevo? We have more in common with Zagreb than with Sarajevo!"

[9] I spoke to dozens of Croats, Muslims and Serbs in July 2003 and May/June 2004. Without exception, every Muslim or Bosniak spoke of the Serbs as an enemy, while some would also mention in passing "but they fought on our side too." Indeed they view the Croats little better, viewing their political moves and media remarks as posturing for their own entity or at the very least, working contrary to the benefit of the Muslim/Bosniak goal of a strong state based in Sarajevo – a Muslim state.

[10] The Muslim XXX Corps fought under Fikret Abdić against Izetbegović's forces in the Bihać region until the end of the war. This alone indicates that not all Muslims sought an independent state and were willing to fight to remain within the rump state of Yugoslavia. This facet of the war is rarely addresses by most authors.

[11] Two examples are offered to provide evidence. The first example involves my meeting with the Political Adviser to BG Timothy J. Wright, Mr. Philip Egger in Tuzla. Our discussions revolved around Bosnia's development as a state and the concerns of the Croat and Serb communities. Mr. Egger stated at several times during the discussions that Bosnia was a Muslim country. After the third or fourth time I asked why he kept calling Bosnia a Muslim country? I stated that based on simple demographics, Bosnia was over 50% Christian (Catholic and Orthodox) and therefore based on being a majority Bosnia was a Christian not Bosnian state. He gave me a befuddled look and said that "we always refer to Bosnia as a Muslim state" and he would have to change the narrative at the headquarters that has existed since he was there. He was startled as he came to realize the significance of my observation. The second observation involves the reconstruction of destroyed Muslim homes. The monumental effort of

international organizations in repairing returnee Muslim homes is matched with the overt lack of home reconstruction of Serb communities. The red roofs of brand new homes were almost exclusively those of Bosniak communities, contrast this with the Serb municipalities of Drvar, Glamoć and Grahovo and exhibit the biased nature of the West's role and actions in Bosnia.

CHAPTER VIII

NATIONALIST LANDSCAPES OF BOSNIA

"Spaces are significant spaces, and the significance with which they are endowed are to be understood in terms of the historical narratives which link people to territory or places."

John B. Allcock, 2002

The landscape of Bosnia and Herzegovina today is one still scarred by the 1992-1995 civil war. Although it has been almost been ten years since the end of the war, the ruins of razed villages, skeletons of large buildings in towns and cities coupled with the effects of large population transfers are still evident. Minefield markers, remnants of old Yugoslav and no longer used NATO military bases, military route markers, hulks of destroyed military vehicles are quite commonplace today. The frenzied activity of Bosnia's Bosniaks, Croats and Serbs in reconstructing and building new churches, mosques, mono-ethnic monuments and memorials coupled with nationalist political administrations have significantly remade and reshaped Bosnia's landscape.

Theoretical Perspectives

Most literature and research involving the study of landscape do not consider the context of war and nationalist politics, or the ramifications of national or ethnic identity upon the landscape. Foote's (1997) research and typology of America's landscapes of violence and his several works on Northern Ireland is one of the few that engages this topic. However the majority of recent publications consider gender, sexual orientation, gentrification, poverty and race as related to the study of landscapes. In each topic, however, the point is made that aspects and vestiges of the landscape can illuminate and provide anecdotal evidence for social and political processes that are taking place. These landscapes tell a story.

Landscapes are a text or narrative, to be understood as part of a greater process which is manipulated by Bosnia's three ethnic groups and one that impacts Bosnia's statehood. These groups are overtly modifying their environment through the use of symbols, icons and buildings/markings unique to a national group in the region. It permits the controlling of space (territory) and one group's interaction with another. So landscape communicates, both blatantly and subtlety – by stressing symbols, names and markers in both social and political life

Landscape is a key element in discerning the development of a Bosnian identity and Bosnia's progress of statehood. It is also a crucial factor in distinguishing the trends and processes that may be detrimental to Bosnia's stable development. Does the landscape composed of monuments, religious structures, unique place-names and symbols reflect a Bosnian identity? Or do these omnipresent monuments, churches and mosques, place-names and symbols represent nationalist ideologies and agendas that actually demarcate a national group's exclusive territory within the international boundaries of Bosnia and Herzegovina?

Landscape studies are often intimately associated with the concept of territoriality which in some instances is viewed as a spatial expression of [national] power (Tyner, 2004). Moreover, the role of landscapes is frequently integral to the exercise of power (Winchester, Hilary, Kong, et al., 2003). The states of the former Yugoslavia all use some aspect of the landscape to assert and reaffirm their independence, control of territory, and to even antagonize neighboring former adversaries.[1]

The "landscape perspective" (Lowenthal, 1997, J.B. Jackson, 1984, Meinig, 1979, Lewis, 1979) developed as a way of looking at ordinary or daily landscapes, people and life. A good example of the everyday landscape and the subtlety of prewar national differences is the architectural variation in houses, primarily in the rural and small town areas. Muslim homes possess a four sided roof while Christian homes were two sided (figure 10).[2] Of course this is not an absolute, as many newer homes do not display these differences, but it is quite common in older structures.

Figure 10 – Four-sided roofs of Muslim homes and buildings in Jajce, Bosnia (June 2004).

In Bosnia the former ordinary and pre-war landscape is now dominated by the effects and aftermath of war. In most areas one cannot travel several kilometers without seeing ruins, nationalist war memorials, and reconstruction. Bosnia is replete with these extraordinary landscapes, which are intended to be read and responded to, as opposed to ordinary landscapes (Foote, 2003). It is now a landscape coded to express power, legitimacy and authority of one ethnic group over another.

Billig's (1995) concept of the "banal" in the manifestations of nationalism is ever-present in Bosnia. Each national group is active in altering the landscape incorporating nationalist symbology at the local level thereby using the landscape as a mechanism to create or maintain hegemony in their respective areas. As such, nationhood is present daily, not necessarily in the consciously waved flag, or fervent national parades and celebrations, but also in the unnoticed flags hanging on public buildings, signs and monuments in the landscape – it is an endemic condition (Billig, 1995). The everyday landscape is used as a mechanism to claim and control territory, developing a sense of national identity and permanency. Landscapes have the inherent ability to naturalize ideologies, identity, power constructs because of their dominance in everyday lives. Landscapes are tangible possessing a visible materiality and corporeality, making that which is socially constructed appears to be the natural order of things.

Pierce Lewis (1979) wrote that by understanding oneself one should take a "searching look at [the] landscape." The landscape may serve as a vehicle to shape and transmit a national or society's collective memory and identity. It may also have the opposite effect by having sites become divisive and contentious; Bosnia is replete with instances of the latter effect. Just as ancient and medieval relics and monuments are used by the Bosniaks to legitimate a tie between the Bosnians of the past and today, other members of Bosnia's society are actively using the landscape to counter it.

Public monuments can be used as a vehicle for the nation-building process and may serve as a centripetal force in unifying the nation or state (Johnson, 1997). In the same manner these monuments can serve a divisive purpose, as seen with the Srebrenica monument that commemorates the massacre of thousands of Muslims at the hands of Bosnian Serb forces in 1995. This is crucial in understanding the processes being used today to reshape the ethnic national territoriality and political atmosphere. As Groth (1997, 4) writes, "landscapes are important archives of social experience and cultural meaning" and understanding them is to understand changes in their communities." Landscapes have the power to institutionalize and legitimize ideologies and social relations by reifying them in concrete form (Duncan, 1988). This form takes shape in myriad ways – the construction of ethno-religious buildings, the renaming of place (towns, streets, squares and parks), the reconstruction of one ethnic groups homes over another's, and the construction of monuments imbued with nationalist symbolism.

Power itself resides in numerous institutions, frameworks and schemes; the state (at several scales), organized religions, economic systems and ideologies all possess power in Bosnia. Particularly relevant to Bosnia is the power of the state structures at multiple levels, such as the entity, canton and municipality, on the landscape. It is direct and overt as shown in the case of Inter Entity Boundary Line markings. Through planning and administrative controls, legal and fiscal mechanisms, the state, in this case the entity or canton is able to control the landscape. At all three political scales: entity, canton and municipality, anecdotal evidence from the landscape suggests that fragmentation and not unification is the goal.

By constructing nationally unique monuments, symbols, names and structures, nationalist leaders are both (1) claiming space and (2) creating an unwelcoming, exclusionary space for other national groups.

Figure 11 – Srebrenica Wall Mural along *Maršala Tito* Boulevard in Downtown Sarajevo (May 2004).

The selective reconstruction of history is also being carried out, sometimes overtly, at other times with subtle markers. This resonates with contemporary ethnic nationalist and political needs and goals. The resurrection of historical and especially recent events is extremely useful in developing and fostering group identity. An excellent example is the now famous wall mural in downtown Sarajevo at the eastern end of *Maršala Tita* Boulevard commemorating Srebrenica (figure 11), depicting a skull on a black background with the words "Don't

Forget Srebrenica" along one side. As noted by Hobsbawm (1993), such pictures tap into an elaborate language of symbolic practice and commentary that reinforces an ethnic group's formation. Here it also feeds the notion of victimhood and legitimates the Bosniak role as the inheritor of the state.

My recent travels and research indicate that Bosnia is not developing as a state in which its citizens view themselves as "Bosnian."[3] In fact, Croatian dominated cantons and municipalities are laced with Croat nationalist symbology, monuments and Catholic Churches. The same goes for the regions dominated by the Bosniaks and Serbs Each ethnic group is remaking its territory. Town, street and place names are changed, new churches and mosques are constructed, monuments laced with nationalist motifs are built in each town commemorating "their" war dead and national suffering. Croat and Serb towns and villages fly their national colors and not that of the Bosnian state, unless forced to fly it by Ashdown.[4]

Nationalism and nationalist ideologies are not an exotic concept, located at the peripheries of modern societies and nations, but are actually at the heart of most nations, including Western nations (Billig, 1995). Ideology as used in my research refers to a belief or meaning that is intended to benefit certain interests, institutions and may determine power relations (Winchester, Hilary, Kong, et al., 2003). Coupled with ideology is the notion of hegemony – these two combined lead to a better understanding of how landscapes may become "powerful." Hegemony operates through a set of ideas and values that the majority of a given place, state, or region are convinced to share as their own. This is not difficult to achieve in Bosnia simply because one's ethnic identity places you in one group or another.

Through this mechanism of ideology and hegemony, the landscape is modified or altered to convey a certain story or establish an ethnic group's claim to that place. This is evident in Bosnia, ethnic groups use the landscape as a palate to exert influence, dominance and control within the political administrative units (entity, canton, municipality), in which their group is preeminent. Most often this power is manifested via political control within these units. Political membership within parties is almost exclusively defined by ethnic background.

Monuments in Bosnia

The Yugoslav communist regime of Josip Broz Tito used monuments as a tool to galvanize the various nationalities under the banner of a Yugoslav identity. Partisan monuments that celebrate Yugoslav resistance to the Axis invaders of World War II dot the countryside and towns of the former Yugoslavia. Within Bosnia these partizan monuments are treated and understood differently by the three national groups (based on personal observation May/June 2004). In Serb areas these monuments are cared for with almost the same level of respect given newly constructed Serb memorials commemorating the losses and sacrifice of the recent fighting. The opposite extreme, however, is found in the Croat areas where these monuments are defaced or left to deteriorate with time. In Bosniak areas the monuments are handled in a more ambivalent manner; they are either well cared for or left alone.

The Tito museum complex in the vicinity of Jablanica along the Neretva River within the Federation commemorating a historic battle between the Germans and Partisans is in a state of great disrepair. The museum building is shuttered, just as the Gavrilo Princep museum in Sarajevo. However the grounds are fairly well maintained for park visitors, the several monuments around the park left uncared for, but the museum café is open and ready to serve park visitors.

Relics of Tito's reign can be seen in the hills overlooking major routes or above towns. In Canton X north of Drvar several stands of trees spell "Tito" and can be seen from miles away (figure 12 below). Looking south at the hillside from Mostar above the Orthodox Church and monastery ruins, the remnants of "Tito, we love you" [*Tito ja ti volim*] outlined in painted stones can still be seen. It was partially destroyed during and after the war. Monuments and landmarks have had a special place and powerful effect in Balkan history.[5] Just as monuments have been used to support or reinforce the cult of Tito (or any other tyrant) or used to mark territory or create places of exclusion, they can also be used to promote unity and rapprochement.

Figure 12 – “Tito” spelled out in a forest south of Bosanski Petrovac in Canton I (June 2004).

A novel attempt has been unveiled in Mostar in which a Bosnian Croat writer, Veselin Gatalo, has developed an initiative to build a monument to kung-fu legend Bruce Lee in Mostar’s Spanish Square which is located along the former frontlines. He stated that "Lee is a true international hero and is a hero to all ethnicities in Bosnia and that's why we picked him." The statue should have been erected by November 2004 and it is hoped it will help erase the city's image as a place of ethnic rivalries (http://news.bbc.co.uk/1/hi/entertainment/film/3620752.stm). Indeed this is the only instance of monument creation in which the objective is ethnic reconciliation

Figure 13 – Croat Memorial at the outskirts of Vitez near the village of Ahmiči (June 2004).

A monument that is certainly contentious is the Croat Catholic cross in the Lašva river valley near the village of Ahmiči. This village witnessed one of the most notorious mass-killings during the infighting between the Bosnian Croats and Muslims. On April 16, 1993 at dawn, Bosnian Croat soldiers murdered one hundred and sixteen civilians. Just outside of Vitez, near Ahmiči, a large cross sits along side the road with a plaque that reads (figure 13 above):

ZA 316 DANA
MUSLIMANZKE OPSADE
VITEZA
UBIJENO JE 653 HRVATA
POKOJ VJEČNI
DARUJ IM GOSPODINE

Roughly translated into English:

In 316 days
of Muslim occupation
of Vitez
653 Croatians were killed.
Lord give them eternal peace

Further on, one comes across the remains of a mosque - a dedication to the Bosniak victims of the 1993 massacre is located nearby (Sells, 2003). The interplay of these overt symbols indicates a region whose inhabitants are far apart from reconciliation and harmony. Indeed further interpretation of these sites may indicate an attempt by both sides to appropriate the status of victimhood and therefore strengthening a perceived rightful and legitimate claim to place.

Reinventing Bosnian Places and Histories

Sarajevo, the capital of Bosnia and Herzegovina, no longer truly represents the formerly multi-ethnic republic of Yugoslavia's Bosnia. Although the capital city of the state and also the Federation, it is being remade into an exclusively Bosniak, or Muslim city (Robinson, 2002). It does not represent a space that is all inclusive of the country's other constituent peoples – the Croats and Serbs. The recreation of Sarajevo through the renaming of place, building of ethno-national monuments and memorials is creating an environment that is hostile to non-Muslims, whether real or perceived and is not unique to Sarajevo.

Most Bosnian urban landscapes appear to be conveying a message that counters the International Community's perception of Bosnia's progress towards statehood. Banja Luka, the capital of the Republika Srpska entity is clearly imbued with the Serbian nation – one also of exclusion; and Mostar, the self styled center of the Bosnian Croats reflects tensions between the Croats and Bosniaks, the Serbs all but wiped clean from the region.

Perhaps the most famous event associated with Sarajevo, the assassination of Archduke Franz Ferdinand and his wife Sophie, is a site destroyed and resurrected. The assassination was carried out by Gavrilo Princep – a hero to the Serbs, a Serb nationalist to the Bosniaks and Croats. The prewar museum, plaque and Princep's footprints in the sidewalk were destroyed at the beginning of the war – both by Serb shells and the wrath of

Sarajevo's residents. The Tito era plaque honored Princep for "fighting tyranny" (meaning Austria-Hungary) and praising him

Figure 14 – Memorial Plaque commemorating the assassination of Archduke Franz Ferdinand in 1914 (May 2004).

for trying to free the people from foreign occupation (BBC http://news.bbc.co.uk/1/hi/programmes/from_our_own_correspondent 2736275.stm Saturday, 8 February, 2003). A new plaque has been reinstalled where the old one was, however now it merely acknowledges what transpired that fateful day June 28, 1914. There is no interpretive commentary. The museum is still shuttered today and was to be reopened in April 2003.[6]

Figure 15 – Wall Plaque commemorating the death of 17 Sarajevans on May 27, 1993.

Sarajevo contains many monuments and memorials to the recent war. As mentioned earlier the wall memorial commemorating the Srebrenica massacre is perhaps the most visible, but there are numerous others. As one walks through the town several memorial wall plaques are evident at locations such as the Markale Market, scene of a horrific loss of civilian life during the war. The plaques memorialize the victims of Sarajevo's long siege and are similar to ones found in Tuzla and elsewhere. A plaque on Ferhadija street in Sarajevo's town center (figure 15 above) marks the location where 17 people were killed on May 27, 1992 and reads (translated in English):

AT THIS PLACE
SERBIAN WAR CRIMINALS
27.5.1992 KILLED 17
CITIZENS OF SARAJEVO

Another prevalent symbol along some of Sarajevo's streets is the now famous "Sarajevo rose." These dramatic relicts of the war are mortar scars filled with a solid red epoxy compound. They appear as flower-like imprints along the sidewalks (figure 16).

Figure 16 – "Sarajevo Rose" in a pedestrian zone in Sarajevo (May 2004).

Renaming of Towns in Bosnia and Herzegovina

During the 1992-95 civil war in Bosnia, 13 towns and municipalities were renamed in the areas under Serb control. The adjective "Serbian" was added to their pre-war names, those that had "Bosnian" as part of the name were replaced with "Serbian" – however, this has not gone unchallenged.

This place name change was clearly seen as a nationalist attempt at recreating the ethnic landscape of Bosnia. On 27 March 2004, the Bosnian Constitutional Court, the supreme judicial institution in Bosnia, instructed the Republika Srpska Assembly to change the names of these 13 towns and municipalities.[7] The court ruled that the use of the adjective "Serbian" is unconstitutional and discriminatory against Bosnia's Bosniak and Croat communities. The original lawsuit filed by a prominent Bosniak politician contended that the name changes discouraged ethnic Bosniak and Croat refugees from returning to their prewar homes.[8] According to Ivan Lovrenovic, writing for *Dani* (Sarajevo newspaper) on 20 July 2001:

> So the adjective "Serb" in the names of certain settlements today does not just have the exclusivist national significance that its creators intended,but emits an even more powerful sense of foreboding and sinister shudder at the memory of those events. The prewar, non-Serb inhabitants of those towns are particularly well aware of this, since it is a psychological tool – and one of the most powerful – invisibly preventing their return.

On 29 July 2004 the Republika Srpska Assembly voted to change the names of the 13 towns and municipalities complying with the Constitutional Courts ruling ("Bosnian Serbs Change Town Names" Reuters, AFP – 29/07/04). In what can only be interpreted as an attempt to skirt the court's ruling, the Assembly decided to add "Republika Srpska" to the town and municipality names. This cosmetic name change was done to address what Republika Srpska authorities and politicians see as a well

Pre-War Names	Changed Names	Current Names
Sarajevo	Srpsko Sarajevo	Sarajevo of Republika Srpska
Drvar	Srpski Drvar	Drvar of Republika Srpska
Sanski Most	Srpski Sanski Most	Sanski Most of Republika Srpska
Mostar	Srpski Mostar	Mostar of Republika Srpska
Goražde	Srpsko Goražde	Goražde of Republika Srpska
Kupres	Srpski Kupres	Kupres of Republika Srpska
Bosanski Kostajnica	Srpska Kostajnica	Kostajnica of Republika Srpska
Bosanski Brod	Srpski Brod	Brod of Republika Srpska
Illidza	Srpska Illidza	Illidza of Republika Srpska
Sarajevo	Srpsko Novo Sarajevo	Novo Sarajevo of Republika Srpska
Stari Grad	Srpski Stari Grad	Stari Grad of Republika Srpska
Orašje	Srpsko Orašje	Orašje of Republika Srpska
Foča	Srbinje	Foča of Republika Srpska

Table 3 - Town/Municipality Name Changes in Republika Srpska as of November 2004

coordinated and deliberate effort to change the name of Republika Srpska if not abolish the Serb Entity entirely.

Another example of a town's name change can be seen in Canton X of the Federation. The former town of Duvno, located north of the *Duvanjsko polje* (Duvno Field), had its name changed to Tomislavgrad. Presumably this name change was made by the Croat majority in a referendum to celebrate the medieval Croatian King Tomislav. No attempt has been made to challenge this name change.

Renaming Of Streets In Bosnia and Herzegovina

The renaming of place of place due to war or significant events is commonplace today, in Bosnia as elsewhere in Europe. Public buildings, parks and streets have been renamed with the leaders of the civil rights movement in America. It is legion and widespread, not being unique to the Balkans.

The capital of both the state of Bosnia and Herzegovina and the Muslim-Croat Federation, Sarajevo, has received geographic interest of late as it has dramatically changed from a truly multi-ethnic makeup to one overwhelmingly dominated by the Bosniaks. Many aspects of Sarajevo have changed, but the changing of place names, specifically street names, is noteworthy.

Shortly after the signing and implementation of the Dayton Peace Accords a new administrative Commission was established by the Sarajevo cantonal authorities. The 15 member commission was almost exclusively composed of Bosniaks, including academics, artists, and writers. Its mission was to rename the city's streets and to remove all symbols relating predominantly to the Serbs.

The results are striking. All signs written in Cyrillic were removed as these were clear reminders of Serb domination of both the former Yugoslavia and Bosnia. In Sarajevo itself 40% of the street names were changed and in the nearby suburb of Iliđza close to 66% were changed (Robinson, 2001). Prewar Iliđza had the largest percentage of Serbs of any Sarajevo suburb, today little remains of their presence. As in *Barsčaršija*, the old Turkish market place and center of Sarajevo, the names of streets and places that were believed to have been there prior to the end of the Ottoman Empire were reintroduced. The names established in the late 19th and early 20th centuries were for the most part perceived as being Croat or Serb. They were replaced with names associated with Bosnians from Sarajevo and Bosniaks from other parts of the new Bosnia and Herzegovina. For the most part, communist and partisan names were removed. A notable exception is that Maršala Tita Boulevard has still retained Tito's name, as he is still revered and admired by some in the city.

The use of names of controversial figures in the renaming of the streets in Sarajevo, while reinforcing a Bosniak identity has led to further antagonism with Bosnia's Croats and Serbs. The use of the term *Šehida*, or holy martyr, has found its place on numerous streets and town squares in Bosniak regions of the Federation (see figure 17 below).[9]

Figure 17 – Square of the Holy Martyr (*Trg Šehida*) in Bosanski Petrovac, Federation (June 2004).

The capital of Republika Srpska, Banja Luka, located to the northwest of Sarajevo has also undergone similar changes. In fact street name changes have occurred so frequently that a local software developer produced a relatively simple program that provides the user both the old and new street names. Of the 354 streets listed and portrayed in the software on a map, 152 have been changed. This represents a renaming of over 42% of the streets in the Serb capital (Appendix A).

I have not determined whether some of these changes, as in Sarajevo, have simply been the reintroduction of pre-Communist place names. Some certainly are not, as can be seen in replacing the name of a main artery Boulevard of Solidarity [*Bulevar Solidarnosti*] with the names of two Serbian WWI heroes, Boulevard Duke Peter Bojović [*Bulevar Vojvode Petra Bojovića*] and Boulevard Duke Stepanović [*Bulevar Vojvode Stepanovića*]. Moreover the majority of changes have been to affect the same change as in Sarajevo, here all reference to Muslim, Croatian and many Communist names have been replaced with Serbian place names, religious historical leaders, monasteries, momentous events in Serb history and legend. One of the noteworthy changes was that of Tito Street [*Titova*] to King Peter I Karageorgević [*Kralja Petra Karađorđevća*], the king who led Serbia before and during the First World War.

The landscape tells a story and must be considered a crucial indicator of the trends and problems associated with nationalism and ethnic identity impacting Bosnia. The newly constructed Serb monuments in Republika Srpska, such as in the vicinity of Sekoviči and Paprać, commemorating the World War II Royalist *Četniks* and recent civil war are clearly perceived as a provocation by the other national groups in Bosnia. They are an overt symbol to returning Bosniak refugees of which national group controls the area and establishes a hostile environment for their return. In such situations, any returning refugees only do so in numbers considered sufficient to prevent harassment by former adversaries. Rarely do returns occur at the individual or family level.

Figure 18 – Serb Memorial in Mayevtsa (*Мајевца*), Republika Srpska (June 2004).

Clearly a pattern has emerged across the landscape of Bosnia. As the Dayton Peace Accords established the state of Bosnia and Herzegovina and permitted national hegemony within various administrative political units, each ethnic group has gone to great lengths to inscribe its territory with its national identity. The pattern focuses marking an ethnic group's territory with mono-ethnic markers of identity. This inscription typically takes the form of numerous monuments, statues and memorials imbued with national symbols (figure 18). A well known Belgrade professor and sculptor, Dr. Miodrag Zivković, has designed numerous monuments typically found in the town squares in Republika Srpska (Figure 19). These monuments are quite dramatic, incorporating symbolized crosses, the Serbian national crest of "four Cs" and Serbs as spiritual figures either floating towards heaven or as standing in a defiant position. I saw these monuments in Bijelina, Brčko, Derventa, Prijedor, and Srpski [Bosanski] Brod; more exist elsewhere in Republika Srpska.

Figure 19 – Serb Monuments to the war in the town centers of Derventa (L), Prijedor (C), and Bijelina (R) (May/June 2004).

The renaming and remaking of place in Bosnia is a continual process in which all three ethnic groups are active. It is a phenomenon not unique to Bosnia. The renaming of place occurs at various scales; from the renaming of streets, histories sites, parks, squares and buildings to the renaming of villages, towns and cities. This "remaking" of place has transpired throughout the ages – by ethnically cleansing regions to providing economic incentives or disincentives in order to populate or depopulate places, place is continually remade in the course of nationalist struggle. With time this inscription gains permanency, casting legitimacy to one's territorial claim and thereby demarcating it as a separate space. Coupled with the inability of the various ethnic groups to reconstruct their monuments and religious edifices, one group's claim strengthens at the expense of the other.

Moreover the re-making of place is found in all successor states of the former Yugoslavia. In Croatia alone, state authorities have stood by while Croatian nationalist extremist groups have dismantled or destroyed over 2,900 of the 4,073 monuments dedicated to the *Partizans* and resistance groups of World War II (Hedges, Chris. "Fascists Reborn as Croatia's Founding Fathers," NYT, 12 April 1997, Saturday Late Edition – Final, Section 1, pg 3).

Tracking these changes and their impacts on Bosnia receives spotty recognition and research. One of the best research efforts to date has been provided by Guy Robinson, et al., in *Remaking Sarajevo: Bosnian nationalism after the Dayton Accord*. According to the authors the capital of Bosnia is being remade by recreating the city's identity and changing the worldview of its inhabitants – which are now predominantly Bosniak. Streets, squares and parks are being renamed to reflect Bosniak (read Muslim) history.

<u>Landscape as Manifestation of Power</u>

Canton X is an excellent example of power, legitimacy and authority of one ethnic group over another reign. It is divided into six municipalities: three Croat (Livno, Tomislavgrad, Kupres); and three Serb (Drvar, Glamoć, Grahovo); however cantonal power is wielded from Croat Livno. Canton X is a miserable place to live if one is a Serb refugee. It is composed of six municipalities, three dominated by the Croats and three by returning Serb refugees. Canton X is ruled by the Croat majority from Livno, the cantonal government seat. The Serb municipalities of Drvar, Glamoc, and Grahovo have had practically no reconstruction. These towns were completely destroyed and although having had prewar Serb majorities, they now possess Croat monuments and symbols located in the town centers or at overt locations such as hilltops and residential areas.

It is an eerie drive to the center of Grahovo, a former Serb town, and seeing every single structure substantially damaged or destroyed and then coming upon a recently built Croat Catholic cross monument with an inscription of the Croatian checkerboard crest [*shachhovnitsa*], commemorating the brave Croat homeland defenders (see figure 20). The plaque on the front of the memorial translated into English reads:

AS A SIGN OF GRATEFULNESS
TO THE DEAD CROATIAN
DEFENDERS
B. GRAHOVO 24. JULY 1999

The same can be seen in the Serb majority towns of Drvar and Glamoc. No such Serb monuments exist as the municipalities do not possess the authority to allow their construction. Political power and authority rests solely with the Croat cantonal government in Livno.

Figure 20 – Croat Memorial Cross in downtown Bosanski Grahovo (June 2004).

This Canton has escaped the headlines and Western scrutiny for some odd reason. In the Republika Srpska inordinate funding have been provided to the Bosniak returnee community to rebuild their homes and businesses – not so for the returnee Serb community in Canton X. The three devastated Serb municipalities are a region of desperation and want juxtaposed to the increasing wealth and material betterment of the neighboring three Croat municipalities of Canton X.

Religious Edifices and Place

The use of religious edifices, notably churches and mosques, is the most obvious and dominant physical symbol on the landscape. Religious structures have been used throughout history by many nations to mark their territory. In Bosnia many of these structures were destroyed during the war and there has been a determined effort by the three ethnic groups not only to rebuild those that have been destroyed where possible, but more so to construct new ones. These churches and mosques mark national spaces and correlate well to the territory inadvertently awarded each group after the Dayton Peace Accords of 1995.

Construction of Churches

During and after the fighting in Yugoslavia, the Croatians, Bosniaks, Serbians and Slovenians used churches and monasteries as evidence of their people's presence in contested regions to legitimize their territorial claims. In Bosnia, more so among the Serbs than the Croats, the Serb Orthodox church has instituted a construction program since before the Bosnian civil war, building new churches in Serb majority areas. Reasons for this energy of construction are twofold. First, the death of Tito and the apparent easing of communist suppression of Yugoslavia's various national religions allowed religious institutions to reenter mainstream society and even politics. The construction of Catholic and Orthodox churches and Islamic Mosques were a natural outcome of this.

Secondly and perhaps more sinisterly, the national religions understood how their role as beacons and traditional keepers of national identity would require an active role in marking their national spaces. Croatia, Kosovo and Bosnia all experienced this "church role" in the post Yugoslavia construction spree.

Figure 21 – Unnamed Orthodox Church under construction east of Bosniak Kalesija in Republika Srpska (May 2004).

From my travels in Bosnia, it is apparent that the Serbian Orthodox Church has been very active in building churches in locations where none existed before. Additionally, they are built at prominent locations, such as along primary roads, major route intersections or in urban centers. Many of these locations are in ownership dispute.[10] While traveling any major route in the Republika Srpska one cannot help but notice the new churches (Figures 21 & 22). They are primarily found at prominent locations such as along major roads, hilltops and at road intersections. In many cases these churches (outside of their new appearance) have no evidence of recent activity or routine use. Closer scrutiny suggests that some of these churches are located in Bosniak areas of the Republika Srpska. Therefore there is no interaction of the site with the locals but only transitory meetings, celebrations by Serbs from distant regions at the church.

Two noteworthy examples involve the Orthodox Church building on confiscated Bosniak land in the Srebrenica region of the Republika Srpska. One is located in Potoćari on a parcel of land neighboring the Srebrenica Memorial Park complex and the other at a major road intersection along Route 19 in Konjević Polje (figure 22 below). Municipal authorities granted permission for their construction.[11]

Figure 22 – Contested Serb Orthodox Church on Bosniak land in Konjević Polje (May 2004).

The church in Potoćari was never completed, however a large wooden cross and rectory are still present (Figure 23). Several factors contributed to the halting of the church's construction. One is the dispute over property rights, the other and perhaps more important factor is location and its symbolism. This site was chosen to promote a response from the Bosniak returnee community and meant as a physical symbol to the same that this territory was now Serb. It also represents an act of defiance towards the International Community in its role in having the memorial park constructed. The High Representative, Paddy Ashdown, halted construction to prevent rising tensions from becoming open hostility between the two ethnic groups and to thwart the intimidation of the returning Bosniaks.

Figure 23 – Orthodox Church and cross located next to Srebrenica Memorial Park in Potočari (June 2004).

Certainly this site is one of contestation. Not only is the property owner at odds both with the Orthodox Church but also with the RS officials and administration that approved the church's construction in the first place, but there exist overwhelming symbolism in this place. The construction of the church on land adjacent to the memorial park is significant on its own. The massacre of thousands of Muslim males in July 1995 by Bosnian Serb forces in the nearby areas of Potoćari, such as the battery factory, has made this place hallowed to the Bosniak community and indeed the world. The park itself represents a sacred space to those that perished and their families.

According to Dušan Antilj, the Minister of the Religious Issues Bureau of Republika Srpska that overseas and tracks the construction and reconstruction of destroyed religious structures, the main priority of this ministry is the reconstruction of monuments that are historical and cultural value. Table Four captures Mr. Antilj's summary of church construction within the RS.

Orthodox Administrative Territorial Units	Total Churches	New Churches	Old Churches
Bosanski Petrovac / Bihac	13	1	12
Banja Luka	68	23	45
Tuzla / Zvornik	82	36	46
Sarajevo (Kupres, Kljuc)	18	6	12
Herzegovina / Trebinje	29	8	21

Table 4 – Orthodox Church construction in the RS 1992-2004 (Antilj, 2004).

Most churches are built from funds that derive from 75% donations from the public and 25% from entity funds (Antilj, personal communication). In this same period no new Catholic churches have been built in the RS due primarily to the reduced presence of Croats and the relatively few that lived there pre-war. There are 22 churches divided among the two bishoprics [*biskupija*] of Banja Luka and Herzegovina and the sub-bishopric [*nadbiskupija*] Posavina (see table below).

Catholic Bishoprics and sub-Bishoprics in RS	**Total Churches**	**New Churches**	**Old Churches**
Banja Luka	6	0	6
Bosnia - Posavina	12	0	12
Herzegovina / Mostar	4	0	4

Table 5 – Catholic Churches in Republika Srpska, June 2004 (Antilj, 2004).

Construction of Mosques

The vast majority of mosques in Republika Srpska have been seriously damaged or destroyed. Those in predominantly Croat regions of the Federation were subject to the same fate. The most infamous destruction occurred in Banja Luka where the sixteenth century *Ferhadija* Mosque was dynamited in May 1993. Today nothing remains of the mosque, even the foundation was removed heavy equipment. The only remaining structure is the mufti's office which is the only Islamic community building in Banja Luka (Riedelmayer, 2002). There are similar locations throughout Bosnia, such as in Prijedor, where all traces of the town's Ottoman era mosque was also destroyed.

Figure 24 – New Mosque in the vicinity of Prijedor, RS (June 2004).

Federation entity authorities have attempted to initiate reconstruction of many of the mosques. However, tremendous resistance by local Serbs has left the destroyed mosques as vacant lots. The only region in which new mosques have been built is in the Kozarac region near Prijedor in northwest RS where there have been major Bosniak refugee returns. In both the Federation and Republika Srpska reconstruction of mosques has occurred only in places of considerable Bosniak refugee returns or due to the mandates of the High Representative Ashdown.

Islamic Territorial Organization in RS	Total Mosques	New Mosques	Old Mosques
Banja Luka	34	3	31
Semberija	14	0	14
Travnik	4	0	4
Mostar	9	0	9

Table 6 – Mosques in the Republika Srpska as of June 2004 (Antilj, 2004).

According to Riedelmayer (2002) during the 1992-95 war, 348 of Bosnia's 1706 mosques were destroyed; 270 by Serb extremists, 78 by Croat extremists. Approximately 838 mosques were also damaged; therefore almost 70% of Bosnia's mosques were either destroyed or damaged.[12] Figures do not include Islamic centers and other institutional buildings.

No entity level institution of religious issues exists in the Federation as in the RS. Official offices that handle religious matters are found at the canton level. The readily obtainable information in Banja Luka was not available (if available at all) to me for the Federation given my time constraints and lack of a central repository for the information. Moreover, the spiritual leaders for the Catholic and Muslim communities in the Federation were suggested as the source, not the cantonal institutions.[13]

Figure 25 – Destroyed Croat Catholic Chapel and cemetery near Derventa (L) and a defaced Serb Orthodox headstone in Potočari (R) (June 2004).

Cemeteries, just as churches and mosques, were not spared from nationalist violence (see figures 8 & 9). As cemeteries are primarily mono-ethnic (being Catholic, Orthodox or Muslim), they imprint the landscape with a nation's presence and have been used as historical evidence to bolster nationalist claims to territory. They therefore became subject to desecration, destruction and even removal by all three of Bosnia's national groups. Removing a cemetery removes a nation's historical presence and even prevents refugee returns to an area. I witnessed dozens of burial grounds lying in ruins during my summer 2004 travels.

Landscapes of Sanctification

Srebrenica

From the position of the Serbs, the Srebrenica Memorial Park is a site of misplaced symbolism. From disputed facts about the Srebrenica massacre, to the International Community's overlooking Serb deaths due to Muslim forces operating out of the Srebrenica safe haven, the meaning and understanding of Srebrenica differs based on the ethnic group engaged in discussions on the subject.[14] The attempted construction of the Orthodox Church next to the memorial park antagonizes the Bosniak returnee community, memorial park visitors, and the

International Community. It also bodes poorly for the notion of a multi-ethnic and harmonious Bosnian state.

Figure 26 – Srebrenica Memorial Park, Potočari, Republika Srpska (May 2004).

For the Serbs it is simple to see a symbol of resistance, both to the West which imposed the memorial park, and the Bosniak returnee community. The RS government was forced to pay one million Euros towards the construction of the park by Paddy Ashdown.[15] A question was asked of me during my several visits to the region, "where is the monument to the hundreds of Serb villagers that were killed by Muslim forces operating out of Srebrenica in the Christmas of 1994?" Most of the slaughtered came from the Kravica region and that name bears the same horrors to the Serb that Srebrenica does to the Bosniaks. To the Serbs who were adamantly opposed to the park's construction in the first place, it is perceived as a reminder of the IC's interference in their "state," the RS, and the West's continued biased support of Bosnia's Muslims as during the civil war. This site does not solicit a unitary collective public memory nor does it evoke a collective reconciliation.

Indeed, following Foote's (2003) research of landscapes, Srebrenica clearly falls into the category of sanctification. The site was officially opened on September, 20 2003; President Bill Clinton was the guest speaker and the ceremony was attended by thousands of Bosniaks and representatives of the International

Community. Plans are to eventually have 10,000 graves marked with white marble gravestones. The memorial is interpreted by many Serbs as a symbol of Bosniak moral victory in the middle of their entity, a territory hostile to its existence. Terrorism experts (Bodansky, 2003, Copley, 2003) warn that this site may become a shrine to radical Islam followers.

The dilemma with the Srebrenica Memorial Park is that it is not a site that inspires all of Bosnia's ethnic groups. It is not a site of Bosnian solidarity, but a symbol of divisiveness. Demanded by one side and contested by the other, it serves as a focal point of national separation not unity. The park itself, a Muslim cemetery, is laced with Islamic features – orientation of the graves East, headstones painted green, Islamic characters on several of the park's monuments (for example). Indeed the very fence that surrounds the park is capped with a minaret-style inspired design (see figure 27). A blue and yellow state flag display of flowers on the hillside at the back of the park can be seen from afar.

Figure 27 – Fence around Srebrenica Memorial Park designed with minaret-style inspired tops (May 2004).

Foote (2003) writes that as time passes monuments and memorials can change in meaning and importance. I submit that as the International Community slowly disengages from Bosnia, the Srebrenica Memorial Park will slowly fall into disuse as the international political climate places less significance on Bosnia and as donor funds disappear. It will remain a contested site in Republika Srpska, overlooked by the Serbs, and occasionally commemorated by the Bosniak community.

Many Serbs that I spoke to do not agree with the highly publicized numbers of Muslim deaths associated with the massacre. For that matter, even the Bosniaks themselves cannot agree to the exact number – estimates range from 7000 to 12,000.[16] Srebrenica Memorial Park is ignored by the Serb community which is now the majority in the region. It is not a site of ethnic reconciliation as many outside of Bosnia hoped for. It possesses a duality of meaning: sorrow and commemoration for the Bosniaks, conflict and resistance for the Serbs. Jonathon Rooper, a former BBC journalist, asserted that the Srebrenica region was a graveyard for Serbs as well as for Muslims and that this memorial park serves neither truth nor the goal of reconciliation (Copley, 2003).

Tuzla – A Symbol of Hope

The use of memorials and monuments within Bosniak regions of the Federation plays a significant role in portraying the Muslim as the perennial victim and the Serb as the aggressor. Both Sarajevo and Tuzla possess many monuments that are very condemning of the Serbs. While these monuments do commemorate the loss of life, they take a strong step in condemning the "other," the "enemy." This helps to define Bosniak identity in contrast to what others, in this case Serbs, are reinforcing their identity and all three groups are guilty of it.

On the evening of 25 May 1995, near the end of the war, an artillery shell fired from Bosnian Serb Army positions around Tuzla exploded in the crowded downtown pedestrian zone. Seventy one people, predominantly young adults and teenagers enjoying a pleasant evening, died. A memorial now marks the site of this atrocity. It is built into a wall bordering this small square (see figure 28). A poem by Mak Dizdar (1917-1971), a World War II hero and renowned Bosnian poet, adorns the plaque.[17] The poem's script:

NA OVOM MJESTU,
25 MAJA 1995 GODINE
SRPSKI FASISTICKI AGRESOR JE
GRANATOM PREKINUO
71 MLADI ZIVOT

PROUCITE FATIHNU
POMOLITE SE,
PAMTITE I
OPOMINJITE

Roughly translated into English:

AT THIS LOCATION
25 MAY 1995
SERBIAN FASCIST AGGRESSORS
USED A GRANATE [artillery shell] TO END
71 YOUNG LIVES

STUDY THE FATIHA
SAY A PRAYER,
REMEMBER AND
RECALL [or warn]

In the hillside city park overlooking Tuzla there is a cemetery where the remains of the victims are interred. Immediately adjacent to the cemetery is a large memorial and monument complex commemorating the tragic event of May 95, the recent civil war and the partisans. Further up the hill behind the partisan wall monument is the recently completed "Peaceflame Park and House" (figure 30). It was constructed with funding provided by the Netherlands.[18] The entire site is well maintained having just been renovated over the past year.

Figure 28 – Memorial to 71 youths who perished in an artillery strike by Serb forces on 25 May 1995.

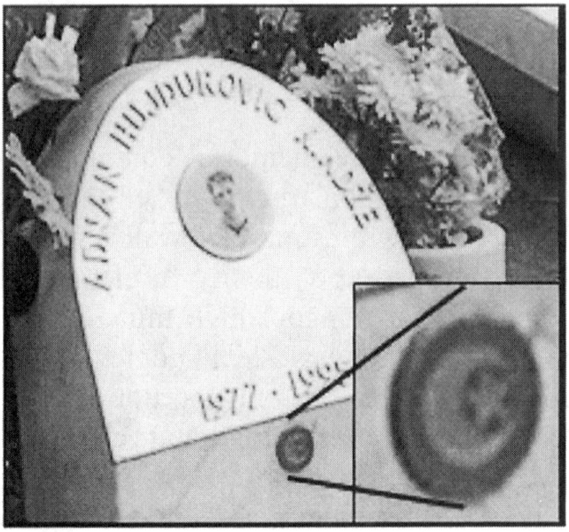

Figure 29 – Grave marker in the Peaceflame Memorial Park with religious affiliation marker highlighted.

This memorial site is one of contradiction but not as acerbic as the memorial in the old town center. The small cemetery at one end of this complex commemorates the innocent victims of the shelling. Religious denomination is understated, although most victims were Muslim, both Croats and Serbs also died there. There are small medallions on the front of the grave markers to indicate Muslim or Christian (see figure 29).

Figure 30 – Partisan Memorial and the Peaceflame Park and House in Tuzla (May 2004).

Further on, the memorial commemorating the victims of the war is simply constructed of an enclosed rectangular space surrounded by white marble walls with the names of the deceased engraved upon them. In one corner stands a structure consisting of four ten foot high minaret like structures covered by an arced stainless steel dome, with a small pedestal underneath. This is the only portion of the memorial complex that conveys a specific national characteristic, in this case Muslim, therefore Bosniak.

The partisan memorial (figure above) was recently painted red representing fires of war. Along its frontage are small plaques commemorating the military units from the Tuzla region that fought against Axis forces. Given what can only be described as a widely varying memorial complex, from graves of those killed on the 25th of May, 1995 to the well maintained Partizan monument, it is very characteristic of the social and political climate of Tuzla. During the war the Tuzla region was characterized as one of moderation, with the level of warfare limited. Moreover, Tuzla never fell completely in line with the extremist SDA nationalist positions emanating from Sarajevo. The Tuzla region, then as now, is dominated by the multi-national socialist party and has often been seen as a political "gadfly" to Izetbegović's SDA. Perhaps if ethnic reconciliation can occur, Tuzla would be where it would begin.

<u>Demarcation and Control of Bosnian Space</u>

Landscapes along boundaries can erect asymmetrical goals - an example can be witnessed in Bosnia along the Inter Entity Boundary Line, or IEBL, which separates the Muslim-Croat Federation from Serb dominated Republika Srpska along this political administrative boundary at every major road crossing, signs welcome travelers from the Federation into the RS. However, in the opposite direction no signs exist delineating the Federation entity. These signs (figures 31 & 32) tell the traveler that they are crossing

Figure 31 – Inter Entity Boundary Line (IEBL) crossing sign near Sarajevo (May 2004).

into a place that is Serb and it is done through the use of Serbian heraldic symbols and colors and the use of not only Latin script but Cyrillic as well. These signs are greatly contested by the central government authorities in Sarajevo and the Bosniak community, frequently being defaced presumably by non-Serbs (see figure 32). These signs serve the purpose of legitimating the RS as a distinct political and ethnic territory, if not that of a pseudo-state. It possesses many characteristics and aspects of a sovereign state.

Figure 32 – Defaced IEBL crossing signs in the vicinity of Mahala (L) and Modrica (R) (May and June 2004).

The landscape of Canton X Herceg-Bosna manifests and legitimates Croatian hegemony. The 1995 Croatian offensive "Operation Storm" drove through this region, leaving destruction and devastation in Serb majority areas. The canton is composed of six municipalities, three Croat and three Serb, however the political power and control resides in Livno the Croat municipality, also the seat of the canton's government. The three Croat municipalities – Kupres, Livno and Tomislavgrad, are in reasonably good economic condition. The major towns are thriving, the population relatively well employed and remnants of devastation all but erased. Turning to the Serb municipalities of Drvar, Glamoć and Grahovo the exact opposite is encountered. Little to no reconstruction of official and government buildings has taken place, the municipalities are scenes of vast devastation and the majority of the population is unemployed. The major employers in these municipalities are Croatian owned and employ little to no Serbs.[19] The Croat cantonal authorities and leaders have constructed several Croatian national monuments in town centers and nearby areas that possess Serb returnee majorities (see Figure 33). The cross in the center of the figure has written across it "To the [dead] Croatian defenders."

Figure 33 – Croatian Catholic crosses: Drvar (L), hilltop in center of Drvar (center), and along main route between Drvar and Glamoc (R) (June 2004).

Reconstruction of the Landscape

It has been noted by international organizations and scholars that by pursuing a vigorous program of reconstructing destroyed sites, the majority of which are religious sites, the mechanism of ethnic rapprochement and "healing" may be introduced. Indeed Sells (2003) concedes that the start of the reconstruction of the Čareva Mosque in Stolac has led to more interaction between the local Bosniaks and Croats and has even assisted in eroding the power of local Croat extremists. Increased international community presence at these places has tended to "quiet" ethnic hostility, although not entirely and not with the same level of success. Attempts to lay the cornerstone for the reconstruction of the *Ferhadija* Mosque in Banja Luka was met with riots in which people were seriously injured and killed.

Nationalist politicians, warlords and religious leaders are aware that the reconstruction of ethnic monuments and the trek towards a pre-war status quo threatens the establishment of their mono-ethnic or homogeneous national spaces. As can be seen in Croatian areas, such as in Mostar, Stolac and Canton X or in Serb Banja Luka and Trebinje, nationalist leaders are critical in delaying reconstruction. Mostar's Catholic diocese is active in hindering and even preventing the reconstruction of mosques and Orthodox churches. Mostar's Serbian Orthodox cathedral [*Saborna crkva*], the *Žitomišličii* Orthodox monastery, the four mosques (one of which is being rebuilt) in Stolac, the Ferhadija Mosque in Banja Luka and hundreds of other religious edifices have yet to be rebuilt. Given the outbreaks of nationalist violence when reconstruction is attempted, many fear that postponement will lead to permanent eradication.

These sites are part of an ongoing process intended to send nationalist messages. A good illustration of this process can be seen in Croat-Muslim Jajce, central Bosnia, which outside of the common fight against the Serbs was also an area of Croat-Muslim infighting in 1992-1994. Here the Ottoman era mosque is being rebuilt by the Bosniak community, having been destroyed by Bosnian Serb forces in 1992. Not to be outdone and to ensure their national presence, local Croat leaders built an elaborate monument to their war dead less than ten meters from the mosque across the street along a café lined pedestrian zone (see figure 34).

Figure 34 – Jajce's Ottoman era mosque under reconstruction (left) and the nearby Croat nationalist monument (June 2004).

The importance of symbolism in the monuments, churches and mosques cannot be understated. The vast majority of them are in lived places; they are part of everyday life. All of the war memorials and monuments I visited had remnants of candles and wreaths – these places are not relegated to the past but are part of an active memory and are critical components of the production and maintenance of nationalist landscapes of Bosnia.

Distinctive national spaces are being established by the reinforcement of national identity on the landscape. Nationhood is reproduced constantly, or as in Bosnia being challenged daily between its antagonistic ethnic groups. In Bosnia, as elsewhere, nationhood can call on mobilization of the nation to react to a threat, whether real or perceived, calling for the ultimate sacrifice. The creation of distinct national landscapes in Bosnia serves the purposes of nationalist leaders in maintaining national territory and national power and may even be viewed as a continuation of ethnic cleansing.

---

[1] An excellent example of this is the former highway of *Bratsvo i Jedinstvo* that connected Belgrade and Zagreb. Traveling east from Zagreb to Belgrade today there is no reference to Belgrade, or that one is traveling towards Serbia. Not until one is within 30 or so kilometers of the border does "Belgrade" show up on Croatia's highway signs – Serbia does not exist! However, the same cannot be said traveling from Belgrade towards Zagreb; Zagreb is posted on all the major highway signs. This in itself is certainly indicative of the chauvinist regime in Zagreb.

[2] During my visit to Jajce, while walking up to the fortress in the town center I made a comment to my interpreter about the damaged or destroyed houses we walked past. I said I wish I knew which ethnic group the homes belonged to. The interpreter told me that it was easy; the four sided roofs were Muslim homes. Unknown to me until then, and in some subsequent readings, this was a unique and traditional architectural difference and marker in Bosnia. However, this is not a rule in construction today and many Bosniaks live in traditional two-sided roofed homes. Reasons for this could be ease of construction, building material costs, and utility of a two-sided versus four-sided roof.

[3] A survey I conducted in Bosnia indicates that few see themselves as being Bosnian. Those that do primarily live in Sarajevo; survey results are in the Survey Section of the dissertation and in Appendices C & E.

[4] The design of the blue and yellow state flag of Bosnia was created and and enacted by foreign civil servants of the OHR. Trofimov, Yaroslav. "In Postwar Bosnia, Overruling Voters To Save Democracy," WSJ, 1 October 2004.

[5] The use of monuments as symbols has gained notoriety in recent times. The use of them by nationalists has brought strong international condemnation. A monument in the northwestern Estonian town of Lihula, financed by Estonian war veterans, had been denounced by critics who said it glorified Nazi Germany and its notorious SS units, which had many Estonian volunteers. Neighboring Russia and Jewish groups vehemently denounced the monument, which was erected August 2004. It was removed on September 2, after the government said it damaged the Baltic state's image. Looking closer to the Balkans, Croatia was also the object of international ire with the placement of a memorial plaque by Croat émigrés to Mile Budak, a writer and minister in the Ustaše in Lovinac and a statue to Jure Francetic, an Ustaše military commander in Slunj. They were removed under heavy security by Croatian police on 27 August 2004.

[6] It is interesting to note that just as in Bosnia where the authorities appear to be foot-dragging in opening the Princep Museum, over the Sava River in Croatia the same situation exists with the Jasenovac Memorial Park. Jasenovac is an infamous WWII death camp in which hundreds of thousands of Serbs, Gypsies and Jews perished at the hands of Croatian fascists – the Ustaše. The museum was closed years ago, and there is a small message on the entrance door that the museum is closed due to renovation. Oddly enough there is no sign of any work at the museum and

during two visits in May and June of 2004 there was no evidence of any renovation being done.

[7] It must be noted that Bosnia's constitutional court is composed of nine judges, two from each ethnic group – Bosniak, Croat and Serb – and three foreigners. Decisions made by this court are final and binding. Source is UNHCR
[http://www.usaforunhcr.org/archives.cfm?ID=1385&cat=Archives]

[8] The lawsuit was filed in 2000 by Sejfudin Tokić and only included name changes instituted by the Serbs. No mention was made in his proposal of the place name changes in the Federation. This is recognized by the Serbs as an initiative for the abolition of Republika Srpska itself.

[9] The town square in Bosnaski Petrovac, in Canton IX Una-Sana has been renamed *Trg Šehida* [Holy Martyr Square] and all street signs have green background – the typical color reflective of Islam.

[10] An excellent example of this is the Orthodox Church constructed in 1996-97 at Konjjević Polje near Bratunac. The church was illegally constructed on the land of Fata Orlovic, a Bosniak returnee. As of September 2004 the municipal and entity authorities and officials of Serb Orthodox Church are trying to solve this problem. Approximately 3000 Bosniaks and 5 Serbs live in Konjjević Polje, and they all agree that Fata Orlovic has a right to demand relocation of the church. Local Serbs claim that they don't even go to that church. Mensur Sehagic, the RS Minister for Urban Planning, Civil Engineering and Ecology claims that this problem should have been solved long time ago, and stressed that the church was constructed illegally. Municipal authorities believe that this case is too big for them and have involved entity authorities and Serb Orthodox Church officials in Bijeljina. Zvornik-Tuzla Orthodox Bishop Vasilije Kacavenda and municipal authorities see the solution as purchasing the land from Orlovic, an option she refuses (source OHR news summaries from BHT 1 and Dnevi Avaz 15 and 16 Sep 04).

[11] Speaking with gas station attendants across the street from the Konjjević church, I was told that the church is only open during major holidays and rarely used on Sundays.

[12] It must be noted that no such similar figures are readily had for the number of Croat and Serb churches destroyed during the war in Bosnia.

[13] The religious head and spiritual leader of the Bosniak community is Mustafa Efendi Cerić in Sarajevo. Cardinal Vinko Pulić of Mostar represents the Catholics in Bosnia.

[14] Greg Copley's (2003) challenges the figures and facts surrounding the massacre at Srebrenica as being vastly inflated and overstated. Forensic evidence allegedly points to the casualty figures being in the hundreds, not thousands. Indeed Mr. Copley is extremely critical of US involvement that serves (-ed) to perpetuate ethnic hatreds and divisions.

[15] The RS was ordered to pay the Foundation of the Srebrenica-Potocari Memorial and Cemetery 1,000,000 Euros by the OHR in 2003. Source [http://www.web.amnesty.org/mavp/av.nsf/pages/Eur_dod].

[16] As a side note, I estimated the number of graves present at the park at slightly over 900. I was told by Bosniak officials in Sarajevo that the remainder of the bodies are in a mortuary in Tuzla, to be buried periodically as the remains are identified by DNA. There are approximately 4000 remains at the morgue. As of June 2004 about 600 have been identified and will be interred in July 2004.

[17] Mak (Mehmedalija) Diždar was born in Stolac, a predominantly Croat region of Herzegovina. He is claimed by both the Bosniaks and Croats as a national hero even though he was of Muslim origin. A similarity can be seen in the appropriation of Nikola Tesla, the world famous inventor, as a Croatian national hero. It is never mentioned in Croatian media that Tesla was a Serb whose father was a Serbian Orthodox priest.

[18] My interpreter Azur, a Bosniak, told me sarcastically that it was built by the Dutch because of the guilt associated with their failure to protect the Srebrenica safe haven. According to an onsite billboard, "The Peaceflame Park and House is a meeting place for the people of the Tuzla region to find and bring peace within each other. This will be initiated by organizing activities, which contribute to personal development and the relief of trauma in a way that is stimulated on an individual and social level. The organized activities are of great variety to meet the local needs. They will consist of various workshops, training courses, individual consultation and seminars containing themes and activities like healing arts, creative and music, dance and drama therapies, capacity building, education, inspiration, meditation, promotion of human rights, strengthening of civil society and democracy, minority awareness, and more.

---

[19] FINVEST, the largest employer in the region is wholly owned by Croats from Croatia. It is alleged to have illegally appropriated vast tracts of woodlands from Serbian owners during the privatization process in Bosnia. From discussions with local Serbs in Drvar, it was asserted that the public tenders were only advertised in Croat regional papers – such as in Mostar, Livno and Tomislavgrad. Therefore no protest could be made or offer by Serbs as they had no idea of the offering in the first place.

CHAPTER IX

BOSNIAN ATTITUDES TOWARD ETHNIC IDENTITY, THE STATE AND BOSNIA'S FUTURE

"The overwhelming concern for Bosnian people is security, the two entities and the state itself have been established on very weak foundations and there is little guarantee that current arrangements, as they stand, will last past international withdrawal. The lack of political security has, in effect, guaranteed continuing support for the three main nationalist parties…"

David Chandler, 2000

<u>Survey Findings</u>

Figure 35 highlights the municipalities in which survey questionnaires were distributed and collected. Detailed data are located in Appendices B, C, D and E.

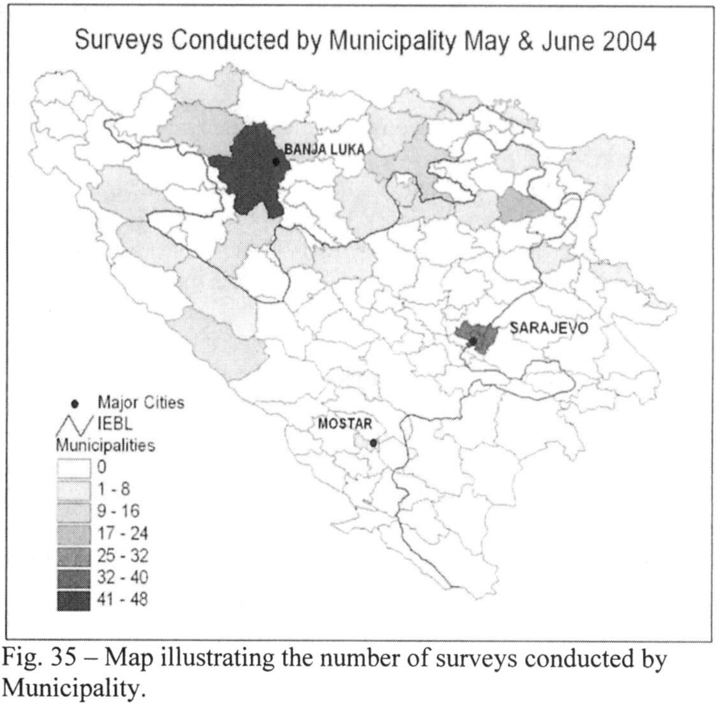

Fig. 35 – Map illustrating the number of surveys conducted by Municipality.

The four page survey administered to 216 people captured the attitudes and perceptions of Bosnia's three major national groups regarding:

- Ethnic identity self identification and understandings of identity transmission.
- How the Inter-Entity Boundary Line, as a major component of the national and political landscape affected views on national territory and Bosnia's future.

The survey also obtained limited demographic data on the population sampled.

Basis of Ethnic Identity

The second set of four questions on pages three and four of the survey engages the notion of primordialism and how Bosnia's national groups comprehend the transmission of ethnic identity. Gil-White's (1999) research and use of an ethnic transmission and acquisition model (ETAM) addresses the evidentiary basis of the primordialist approach to ethnic identity. Many scholars that adhere to the notion of instrumentalist or circumstantialist approaches to ethnic identity and nationalism criticize the primordialist approach as being a concept based on an ineffable or a perceived sense of belonging. Gil-White's field work in central Asia, in which he conducted a question based survey (which I have abridged to better fit my research area) was an attempt to empirically investigate and measure primordialism among nations in a systematic and scientific manner.

By measuring the responses to the sequential questions, Gil-White's questionnaire assists in defining the mechanism or model by which people define their identity. Whether it is a social construction as asserted by scholars such as Anderson (1983), Gellner (1983) and Hobsbawm (1992) or if it is plausible that Geertz (1994), Gil-White (1999) and Grosby's (1995) concept of primordialism is correct, Gil-White's model makes it possible to investigate the two approaches in the field, yielding empirical data to support one's conclusions.

The responses to question number one indicates a preference for the patrilineal notion of identity. Greater than half of the Bosniak, Croat and Serb respondents answered that the identity of a child reflected that of its father, again clearly a patrilineal concept of identity. Respondent # 211 wrote in the comments section that "The children are automatically of the Father's nationality", several others indicated that at the age of maturity the child should choose but until then the child's nationality is that of the father. The data supports Gil-White's (1999) assertion that a primordialist model is active and prevents true changes in ethnic identity in the first generation. If those respondents answering "unsure" are removed from consideration, the results overwhelmingly support the patrilinealism as the mechanism of ethnic identity transmission.

Those that declared themselves to be Bosnian answered the same way only 35% of the time. An explanation can be found here in the same manner in which people in Yugoslavia declared themselves in censuses to be Yugoslav when they were children of mixed ethnic marriages. This would seem to indicate a preference for the approach when looking at self-declared Bosnians.

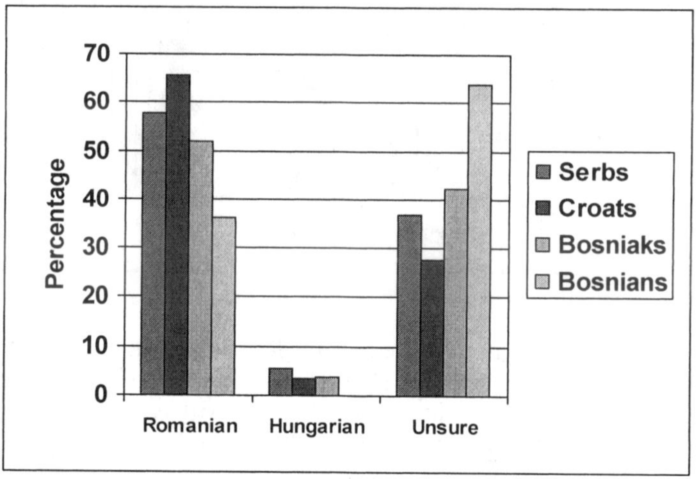

Fig. 36 – Question No. 1 "If the father is Romanian and the mother Hungarian, what is the ethnicity of the child?"

In question number two, a difference appears in how the respondents chose to answer the question. Although a majority of the Serbs answered that ethnic identity still follows the patrilineal line, the other ethnic groups were fairly evenly divided between Romanian and Hungarian. In both questions one and two there is a significant component of respondents that answered "unsure". There are a few reasons for this. Many respondents answered all three ethnic identity questions "unsure" because it appeared that (1) the questions were too long, (2) the respondent did not see the sense in the line of questioning after having taken the first six questions, and (3) some respondents simply had difficulty in comprehending and answering them.[1] There was also a component, based on my numerous discussions with respondents, that the use of Hungarian/Catholic and Romanian/Orthodox was used to replicate Serb/Orthodox and Croat/Catholics, which led some to choose "unsure" and not engage this portion of the survey. In retrospect, perhaps using non-European ethnicities would have averted this perception.

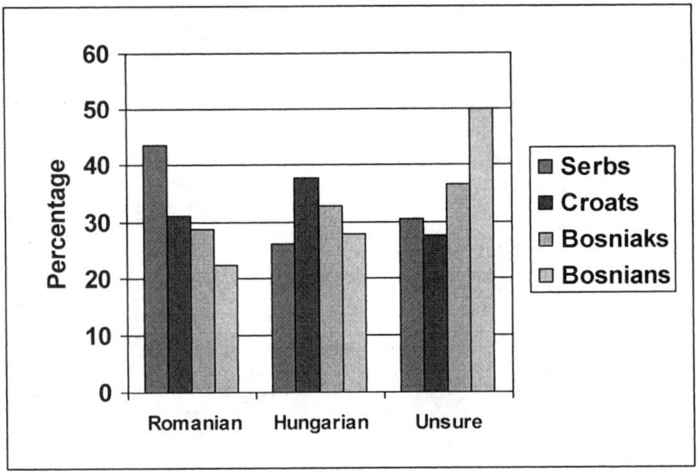

Fig. 37 – Question No. 2 "The father is Romanian, the mother is Hungarian, but everybody around the family is Hungarian and the child has never seen a Romanian, outside of the father. The child will learn Hungarian customs and language. What is the ethnicity of this child?"

In question number three it becomes increasingly clear that the instrumentalist approach to ethnic identity comes to the forefront. In this question all groups come close to or exceed 50% in choosing what they believe the ethnic identity of the child is. In spite of this both the Croats and Serbs had greater than 30% reply that the child was Romanian, regardless of environment, supporting the patrilineal concept and notion of primordialism.

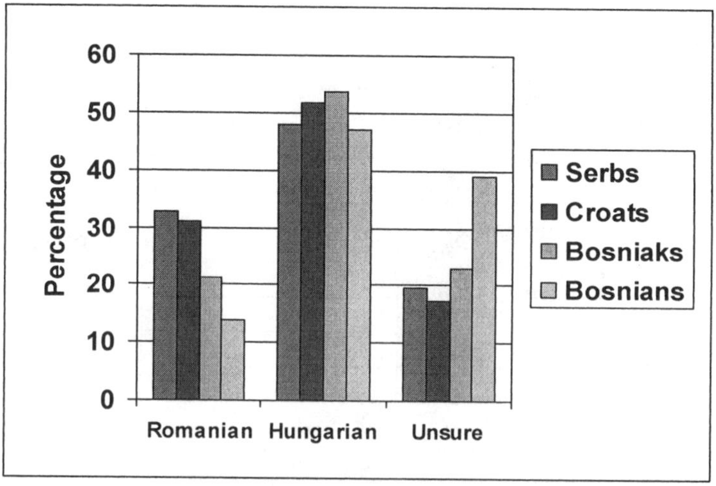

Fig. 38 – Question No. 3 "A Romanian couple has a child that they do not want. They give it in adoption to a Hungarian couple when the child is only six months old. Around the Hungarian family there are only Hungarians and the child grows up never meeting any Romanians. Since he was a baby when adopted, he knows nothing and thinks that his biological father and mother are the Hungarian adopters. He grows up learning Hungarian customs and language. What is the ethnicity of this child?"

Upon closer scrutiny of the response of "Romanian" in the first two questions, there appears to be no difference based on gender, 61.2% male and 38.8% female for the first question and 64.9% and 35.1% for the second. Removing the respondents who answered "unsure," 93.5% chose Romanian in the first question and 54% in the second. Detailed breakdown of the answers based on gender and other factors can be found in Appendix C.

In order to ascertain whether or not survey participants would have answered differently if Bosniak, Croat, or Serb were used instead of Hungarian and Romanian I placed a fourth question on page four, the last page, asking them if they would have responded differently. The response was overwhelmingly no, greater than 80% among all four groups. This indicates that the respondents answered in an open manner, inferring that the same concept of ethnic identity possessed by the respondent could be applied to the people of Bosnia. Indeed less than 10% of the survey respondents replied that they would have answered differently had Bosniak, Croat or Serb had been used.

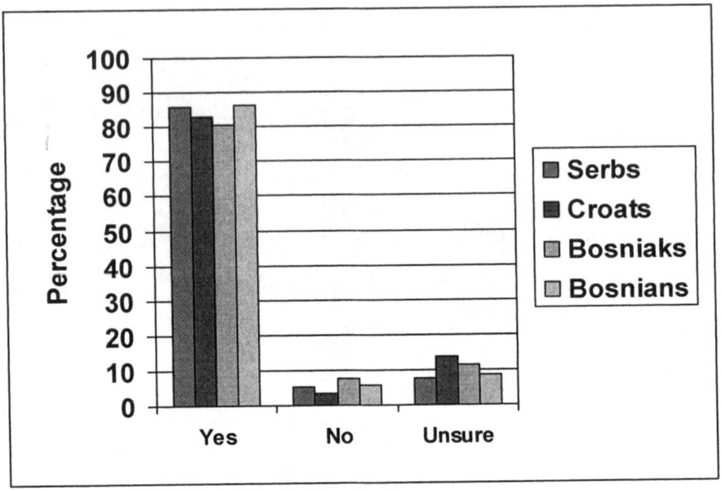

Fig. 39 – Question No. 4 "Would your answers remain the same if Bosniak, Croatian or Serbian were used instead of the Hungarian and Romanian ethnic groups?

This series of questions indicates that there is a primordial and ethno-biological component to how people in my sample population understand ethnic identity and its transfer to following generations. Gil-White's (1999) research allows for the data to tell the story, not ineffable descriptions, intuitions or "feelings" being used to make an argument on behalf of one position or the other. Indeed the primordialist approach to ethnic identity has received scathing commentary from scholars (Eller and Coughlin, 1993). My data suggest that the belief in biological descent is an aspect and requirement of ethnic group membership and is not solely a modern phenomenon as many instrumentalists would argue.

Interpretation of the data does not argue that primordialism trumps instrumental-ism, or vice versa, but it does point to the need in considering the instrumentalist position within the context of primordialism. Ethnic actors do make choices for self-interest, but it is doubtful that people can lose and acquire ethnic statuses the way they may other kinds of statuses or identities (Gil-White, 1999). Moreover, as Gil-White (1999) writes, this data suggest that instrumentalism and primordialism can be merged into a more sophisticated approach to ethnic identity. Smith (1998) acknowledges the importance of hereditary and lineage, aspects within primordialism, but goes further in coupling this with history, national myths, and symbolism of nation within the concept of ethno-symbolism.

When reviewing the comments made in the questionnaires several issues arise (English translations of respondent comments are at Appendix D). Several respondents wrote in the questionnaire that the child should choose its national identity upon reaching the age of maturity, use personal choice, or that the parents should mutually decide (respondents # 16, 63, 113, 130, 158, 159, and 161). These positions certainly support an instrumentalist approach.

Some of the respondents wrote that there was not enough information or the questions should have been better written or prepared, and some chose not to answer for personal reasons and convictions (respondents # 8, 12, 60, and 155). There were others that saw a conspiracy or attempt to blame one ethnic group over the other for the war (respondents # 21, 22, 23, and 24).

I used the software package "Statistical Package for Social Sciences (SPSS)" to analyze the data for significance. The results are at Appendix E and the chi-square test results indicate that the data is statistically significant. Therefore I am able to generalize to the groups of respondents surveyed. Responses did indicate that people see a linkage between ethnicity of the father and that of the child, thus portraying a patrilineal understanding of identity.

One of the most illuminating comments was written by a woman in Sarajevo (respondent #185). She writes that "It is paradoxical that B&H is the only country in which Bosnians and Herzegovinians do not live, but Serbs, Croats Bosniacs. There is no America without Americans; France without the French; similarly there will be no B&H without Bosnians *and Herzegovinians*." She adds further that a new identity should be noted, that of "Bosherk(a)," a combination of both Bosnia and Herzegovina.

Attitudes Towards the Inter-Entity Boundary Line and Bosnian Statehood

The survey's first set of six questions indicate that the Serbs, Croats, Bosniaks and those who identify themselves as Bosnian, differ significantly and measurably in their answers. The answers of those who identified themselves as Bosnian and Bosniak were quite similar. Given that 12 of the 18 Bosnians were surveyed in Bosniak majority areas of the Federation, there is a strong correlation that they too are Muslim. Of the other six Bosnians, five came from Muslim majority towns in Republika Srpska. Given the extent of population transfers and development of mono-ethnic regions since the war it is fairly certain that those who define themselves as Bosnian are Muslim. Moreover as noted in many books written (ie., Honig & Both, 1997, Burg & Shoup, 2000) on the wars in the former Yugoslavia, the overwhelming number of those who declared themselves as Bosnian were Muslims (Bringa, 2002). The responses of the Bosnians and Bosniaks in the survey questionnaires support this position.

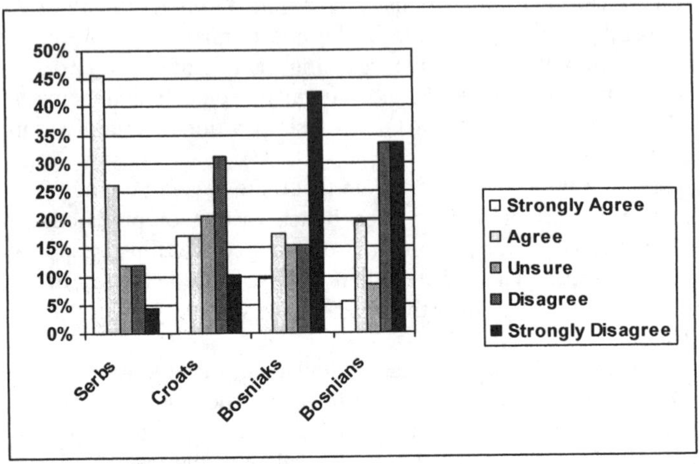

Fig. 40 – Response to Statement No. 1 "The IEBL is important to Republika Srpska" based on ethnic group.

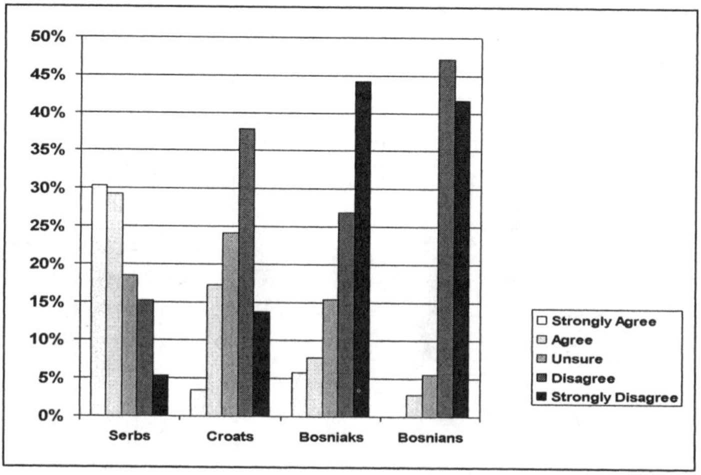

Fig. 41 – Response to Statement No. 2 "The IEBL is important to the Federation" based on ethnic group.

These two figures perhaps more than any other illustrates the chasm between the Serb and Bosnian/Bosniak position in how they perceive the Inter Entity Boundary Line (IEBL). For the Serbs this boundary is their perceived security from Muslim domination and rule from Sarajevo. The Bosnians/Bosniaks view the boundary entirely from a different aspect. It is an obstacle to a strong Bosnian state, inhibiting a strong central authority and thwarting their control of the country.

The Croats response exhibited no clear position. The reason for this is based on their location within Bosnia. Those in Canton X Herceg-Bosna advocate the creation of a third entity on par with Republika Srpska and therefore acknowledge the importance of this boundary. Others in Sarajevo and Canton II Posavina tend to see the boundary as their Bosnian/Bosniak neighbors an obstacle to Bosnia's development.

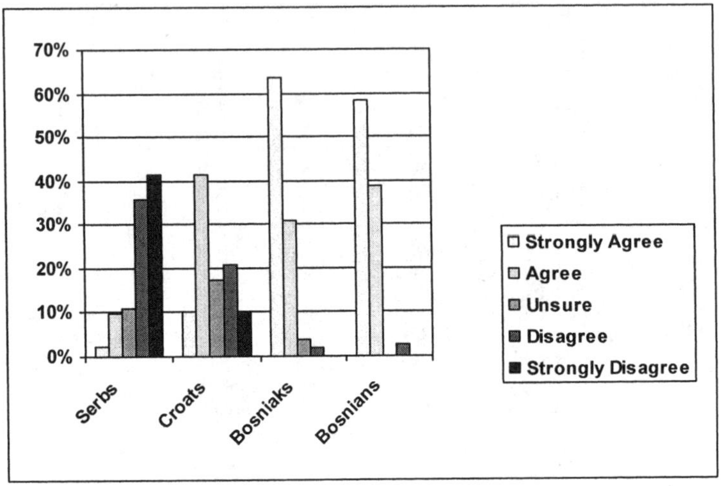

Fig. 42 – Response to Statement No. 3 "Both the IEBL and entities should be dissolved and a strong government and state based in Sarajevo be created in Bosnia" based on ethnic group.

Statement number three was intended to evoke a greater response building upon the differences that arose in responses to statements two and three. The great majority (>77%) of Serbs were in disagreement with such an idea. Opposite them the Bosnian/Bosniaks were absolutely in favor of such an action, with >97% Bosnians and >93% Bosniaks overwhelmingly in agreement. Of note in 1997, 91 per cent of Serbs opposed a united Bosnian state, whereas 98 percent of Muslims supported it (Bose, 2002). It appears that current positions have changed little in the intervening seven years.

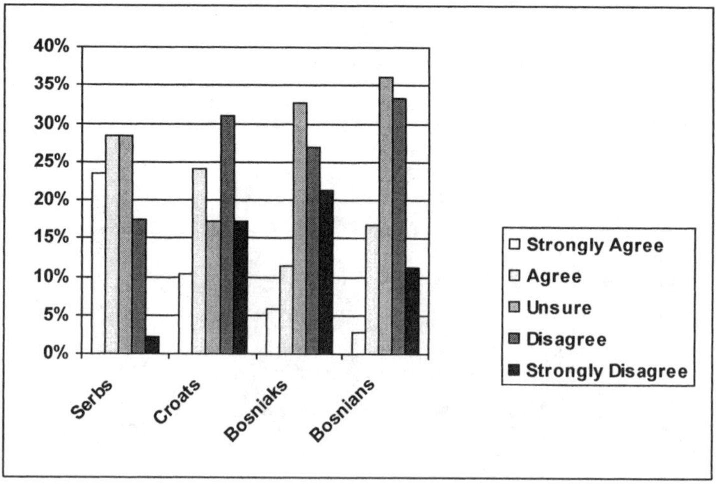

Fig. 43 – Response to Statement No. 4 "There could be renewed hostilities if HR Paddy Ashdown succeeded in removing the IEBL and disbanding the entity governments and creating a strong central government in Sarajevo" based on ethnic group.

Building upon the three leading statements and gauging the level of commitment to their views, I added the potential for renewed conflict as a measure to the strong reactions of the previous statements. As can be seen in Figure 43, the Serbs who feel directly threatened by any changes to the IEBL and therefore the Dayton Peace Accords responded that renewed hostilities were likely. Greater than 57% answered in agreement with this statement. The Bosnians and Bosniaks were both unsure (36% and 32% respectively) or in disagreement (44% and 48% respectively) with the statement.[2]

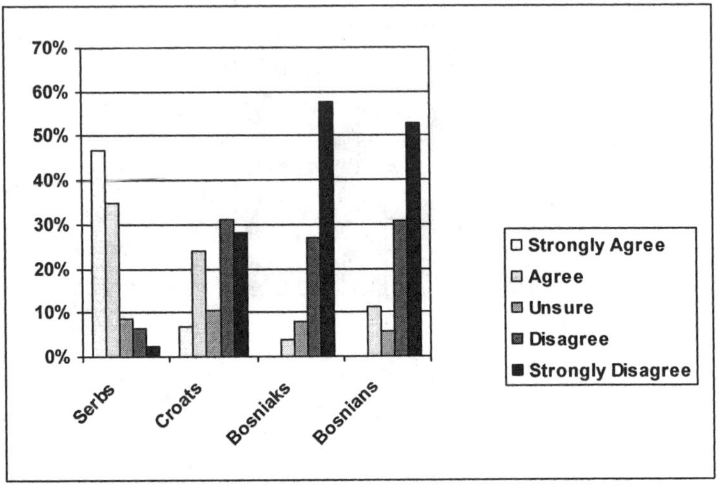

Fig. 44 – Response to Statement No. 5 " If Kosovo is permitted to become an independent state then Republika Srpska has the same right to sovereignty" based on ethnic group.

Statement number five continues to build upon the earlier statements and the notion of Bosnia's future status as a state. Realizing that the Serbs of Bosnia sought to remain within Yugoslavia and not be a part of an independent Bosnia this statement's results infer that the Serbs (almost ten years after the war) do not feel an allegiance to an independent Bosnia. Greater than 81% of the Serb respondents believed that the RS had the right to secede if Kosovo becomes independent. As in the other statement responses the Bosnians and Bosniaks responded in an opposite manner. Greater than 83% of the Bosnians and >84% Bosniaks disagreed with this statement. Once again, the differences in the Croat response were determined by location and their desire for a third entity.

Another result of the survey indicated that the Croats still desire a third entity, to be on equal footing with the Serb entity and their Muslim dominated entity. One couple in Drvar added questions to the survey. In the comments section for respondent # 164 the following was added, "Question 5. Are you for the introduction of a third entity: Yes." Moreover a total of five of the questionnaires had comments indicating that there should be a third entity.

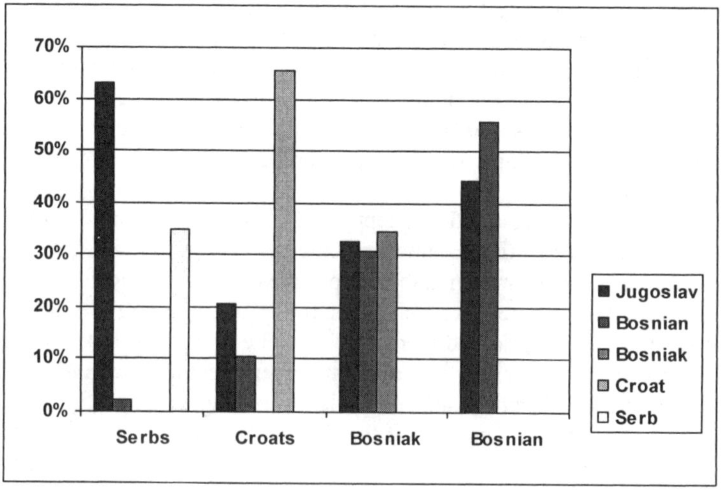

Fig. 45 – Response to Statement No. 6 "Before the war came to Bosnia, you felt yourself to be …" based on ethnic group.

Statement number six is revealing in the sense that the ideal of having been Yugoslav is not equally shared by all ethnic groups in Bosnia. Of course being only nine years after the war, effects of the war have impacted how the people reinterpret their past today. But it does illustrate that there is a residual fondness for the past. Every single person that I spoke to stated that their lives were much better in the "old Yugoslavia." Given the effects of the war and their current economic plight indeed the former Yugoslavia is remembered as the "good old days." Moreover most wished that the war had never occurred and that they should go back to Yugoslavia. However those most brutalized by the war also acknowledged that the "good old days" were long gone and could never be recreated.

Another interesting observation can be seen in the responses of the Serbs and Croats. Over 60% of the Serb respondents felt themselves to be Yugoslav before the war. The Croats on the other hand felt themselves to be over 65% Croat; only 20% chose Yugoslav. The Bosnian and Bosniak groups, similar to the Serbs, chose Yugoslav at a higher proportion than the Croats. An explanation to these differences can be seen as an aspect of hostility towards Serb demographic domination of the former Yugoslavia and their close association with Yugoslavia's founding after World War One as a victorious nation.

In analyzing this series of responses to the IEBL and state, I again used the software package "Statistical Package for Social Sciences (SPSS)."

The results can be found in Appendix E. The statistical measures, including chi-square test, indicate that the data is statistically significant and therefore supports generalizations based on my sample population.

Survey data indicates a lack of unity on the part of Bosnia's national groups towards a common understanding of Bosnian identity. Personal positions toward the status of the entities and strength of central government in Sarajevo are diametrically opposed and based on ethnic group membership.

The survey coupled concepts of (1) identity formation and (2) the role of the Inter-Entity Boundary Line as a significant feature of the symbolic landscape and in national psyches. They indicate that Smith's (1998) ethno-symbolic approach is useful in understanding ethnic identity in the context of Bosnia and Herzegovina. The historical past, reinvigorated by the recent civil war, has refreshed and even created new myths, symbols, national tragedy, heritage and possibly even language(s). Spoken Serbo-Croatian, the official language of the former Yugoslavia, has been replaced by Bosnian, Croatian and Serbian. National ties have been strengthened to the detriment of a Bosnian state centered identity.

This survey highlighted the significant differences between Bosnia's national groups and suggests that a Bosnian identity is overridden by Croat, Muslim or Serb ethnic identity. Moreover, it is the Bosnian Muslims that have assumed the label of Bosnian, inferring further separation of this community from its Croat and Serb neighbors. In looking at the future of Bosnia as a state the survey indicates that here too a significant difference exists based on nationality and that Bosnia's future is questionable at best.

---

[1] In situations where the respondents answered unsure the major reason given was that they felt the questions to be pointless and time consuming to think about it. Whereas the first section was composed of direct, short statements evoking an immediate response, the second section placed more demands on the respondent who often chose the easy "unsure" instead of deliberating whether or not to choose Romanian or Hungarian. As I and the interpreters had to be sensitive to any aggravations expressed by respondents due to the nature of the questionnaire, we avoided pressing the respondent to answer these questions as well as some of the demographic questions.

[2] I must note that it is quite possible that the statement written in several parts could have contributed to the high "unsure" response rate. Some respondents could have agreed with "the IEBL and entities should be dissolved" but may have been in disagreement with the "strong government and state based in Sarajevo" portion of the statement.

CHAPTER X

CONCLUSION

> "In Bosnia nationality is defined by religion, and a religious revival will be at the core of any development of an aggressive nationalism among any of the three Bosnian nationalities."
>
> Tone Bringa, 2002

Bosnia's ethnic nationalities are in continued conflict with one another. Although the Dayton Peace Accords were completely successful in halting and preventing renewed military conflict, any other success has been limited in scope. The Croats and Serbs are not abrogating their national identities in favor of a common Bosnian one. The notion of a Bosnian identity however, is embraced by the Bosnian Muslim community. The interchangeable use of Bosnian and Bosniak, coupled with survey and interview data and analysis buttress this observation.

The Croats and Serbs are actively thwarting the attempts of Sarajevo and the High Representative Lord Paddy Ashdown to inculcate the notion of a Bosnian identity that includes all of Bosnia's constituent peoples. The label is a regional distinction, not ethnic group identification for Bosnia's Croats and Serbs. Survey and interview data strongly suggests that the Serbs, above all, are focused on maintaining their identity and national territory.

Bosnia's Muslims are apparently assuming the identity of "Bosnian." The identification by many Bosnian Muslims as Bosnians on the survey, coupled with the resurrected label "Bosniak," a term which clearly identifies with territorial Bosnia sustains this position. As such their destiny is inseparable from that of Bosnia and Herzegovina. Just as the Serbs, and the Croats to a lesser degree, see their national territory as being critical to their perceived security, the Bosnian Muslims envision a territorially and politically strong Bosnia as vital to their existence. There is no convenient solution to this national linkage between political space and identity. It is somewhat apparent that no national rapprochement or political accommodation is on the horizon.

Smith's (1998) ethno-symbolic approach to understanding identity is especially relevant and useful in appreciating the notion of identity among Bosnia's Croats, Muslims and Serbs. Each group, along slightly different paths, uses religion, shared history, symbols, sacred places, etc., in their understanding of their national identities. The ethno-symbolic approach places great emphasis upon the historical aspects of these characteristics in understanding identity development and in maintaining that a common understanding of a nation's heritage pre-dates nationalism's rise in the 18th century.

This is not to say that certain aspects of primordialism and instrumentalism are not present in Bosnian identities. My data suggests that both the Croats and Serbs incorporate, to some degree, the notion of primordialism, based on their understanding of patrilineal heritage in transferring ethnic identity to their progeny. Survey data suggests that those who identify themselves as Bosnian or Bosniak do not embrace the mechanism of patrilineal identity transference as do the Croats and Serbs. The Bosnian Muslims moreover, are appropriating the historical and symbolic legacy of the former Christian medieval Bosnian kingdom to legitimate a Bosniak and Bosnian (referring to identity and not territorial label) identity. Whereas the Croats and Serbs trace a clear historical and religious legacy back hundreds of years to their medieval states, the legacy of Bosnia's Muslims is discontinuous. By having changed their religion and pledged allegiance to Ottoman suzerainty, Croats and Serbs would argue that Bosnian Muslim claims to a medieval past are illegitimate and they should look to Istanbul for their heritage.

All of these ethnic groups place a heavy premium upon religion, shared histories, and perceived origins in comprehending their identity. The ethno-symbolic approach encompasses this quite well and allows for the differences between the Croats and Serbs on one hand and the Bosnian Muslims on the other. Modernist interpretations of the nation (see Anderson,1983, Breuilly, 1996, Gellner, 1983 and Hobsbawm, 1992), disregard the importance of the historical, even continuous, existence of nations. Many nations existed long before the arrival of nationalism in the 18th century. Pre-modern persistent group identities have existed long before nationalism – but not all nations have followed the same path. Differing contexts and histories led to each nation's uniqueness in developing a national identity. The shared "collective cultural sentiments" (Smith, 1998, 187) are components of the uniqueness of each nation, and are now glaringly absent in Bosnia.

Although the symbolic landscapes of Bosnia escape scrutiny and serious academic inquiry, it is neither irrelevant nor inconsequential why and how the nationalist landscape of Bosnia continues to develop. The ethno-nationalist symbolism and imagery illustrates that there is a definitive ongoing process detrimental to the notion of Bosnia's status as a nation-state and as an identity. Moreover, this process has continued with the signing of the Dayton Peace Accords and cannot simply change overnight without the possibility of renewed conflict. The role of religion as the flag bearer of national identity is reflected in the construction of powerful memorials and monuments with religious overtones. The construction of new churches and mosques also indicate the crucial role of religion but also the influence of external forces on Bosnia.

A landscape of mono-ethnic symbolism composed of statues to national heroes, national churches or mosques, and the re-naming of place reflecting the national spatial identity are all indicative of an active process that is undermining the development of the Bosnian state and are contrary to the notion of a Bosnian identity. Ethnic cleansing has continued however it has done so through a different mechanism. The landscapes of Bosniak dominated areas boldly identify the Serbs as the aggressor, fascists or enemy. The prevalence of this tone and its overt message(s) inhibits the development of rapprochement and reconciliation between Bosnia's Muslim community and Serbs. In all three communities, meanings and understandings of nationalist symbology are apparent and overt, having been used extensively in the civil war and indeed in their national histories. They are meant to mark territory for one nation and provoke a response from another, even to the point of constraining mobility and preventing return.

The meanings and messages inherent in nationalist symbols are powerful mobilizers of the nation. The Inter Entity Boundary Line is perhaps the most powerful of these symbols on the landscape and it is uniquely understood by Bosnia's main antagonists - the Bosniaks and the Serbs. Its representation to the Serb community is one of *de facto* statehood and national security. For the Bosnian Muslims it represents a rewarding of aggression, a flawed political arrangement in which Bosnia is left as a weak state, frustrating Muslim attempts to assume a self understood legitimate control of the entire territory of Bosnia and Herzegovina. To do away with the IEBL is to do away with the Dayton Peace Accord and the state's Constitution.

Through the entity and cantonal political administrative systems the Serbs and Croats continue to create their national spaces within the boundaries of Bosnia and Herzegovina. They do not acknowledge Sarajevo as holding their interests at heart and look to Belgrade and Zagreb instead. The Dayton Peace Accord guarantees the current administrative organization of Bosnia and the Serbs and many Croats see it in their national interest and security to strongly support its continued enforcement.[1] Indeed, based on the surveys the implication is that the Croats are striving for the same political legitimacy as the Serbs, desiring their own entity.

The Bosniaks are at odds with the Croat and Serb communities in relation to Bosnia's statehood. They overwhelmingly support and are advocating the strengthening of the government in Sarajevo, a clearly Muslim city today, and the abolition of the entity and possibly cantonal arrangement in Bosnia. Pending this outcome, the Bosniaks are pursuing the same nationalist activities as the Serbs and Croats by marking their national spaces in which they are the majority. Moreover, Paddy Ashdown has openly advocated for and supported the Bosnian Muslim desires for a stronger central government. A political platform is forming in which the Dayton Peace Accord is being challenged and may lead to renewed nationalist rhetoric and possibly war.

The political and territorial ambitions of the current leaders and parties, nationalist across the board, in Bosnia are diametrically opposed. The presence of NATO, now the EU, and the Office of the High Representative nine years since the end of the war has witnessed an entrenchment of each party's position. Political or even social accommodation is not close at hand. Daily political discourse within Bosnia is dominated by nothing more than charge and counter-charge between the nationalist parties. Political brinkmanship is the order of the day and from this it is not hard to see that renewed warfare in Bosnia is certainly not out of the question.

The political structures inherited by Bosnia via the 1995 Dayton Peace Accords virtually guarantees that no true Bosnian identity will emerge from the civil war. The Croats and Serbs possess demarcated territories at the canton and entity level that guarantee their spatial identity within a weak state. Separate judiciaries, police forces, mono-ethnic military formations, independent health care systems, separate pension systems, national ties to Croatia and Serbia, and more indicate that Bosnia's Croats, Muslims and Serbs are developing along different trajectories.

Celebrating the re-opening of Mostar's *Stari Most* Bridge as a display of success and hope for ethnic rapprochement and reconciliation is misleading. It pales in comparison to the brutal reality of Bosnia's entire nationalist landscape and antagonistic national groups. In the case of Bosnia and Herzegovina, hope is not a method. In the same breath that a Bosniak will argue for a multi-ethnic, harmonious Bosnia, he will blame the Serbs for all of Bosnia's problems and only accept them in a subordinate role or in second-class status. Even during the war, Muslims had a phrase for the Serbs – those that were supportive of a Bosnian state were "tame Serbs," those fighting for remaining in Yugoslavia or as an independent state were called many other things. This is an arrangement that is clearly a non-starter, as it has become in the discourse of a sovereign Bosnia.

I suggest that "reading" the landscape's nationalist markers and assessing anecdotal evidence, provides a better understanding of the presence and power of nationalism in a particular place. By analyzing the process of nationalist landscape creation and the formation of identity, foreign policy and defense elites will be better prepared to deal with ethnic conflict prevention and decision making. Studying nationalist landscapes in tandem with surveys and interviews provides a useful mechanism in identifying nationalist and even separatist trends.

In late November 1996, I sat around a conference table with the all field grade[2] officers of the US 1st Armored Division engineer forces supporting Operation Joint Endeavor. It was to be our last "get together" prior to our redeployment to Germany and the Brigade Commander Colonel Stephen Hawkins (now a Major General) went around the table and asked each officer to speak a few words on what the Army had accomplished and what the officer thought about Bosnia's future. Having arrived in theater shortly before military operations were almost over, I could only speak to Bosnia's future. I simply stated that although the fighting had stopped, I believed that each side would continue the war by other means until their eventual goals would be achieved. Indeed the "other means" have been active since and Bosnia and Herzegovina still does not possess a unitary and sovereign state structure. November 2004 marked a full nine years since the signing of the Dayton Peace Accords and the International Community's saying and behaving as if Bosnia is a state does not make it so.

Bosnia is a land overwhelmed by fragmentary powers. Differing national histories, the role of religion's spiritual leadership, and the living memory of the recent civil war all serve to splinter Bosnia. The notion of a harmonious and multi-ethnic Bosnia exists only in the imagination and hopes of Western leaders and in the discourse created by media and news releases that selectively highlight "successful" events. Only the power and presence of the Office of the High Representative and EUFOR will hold Bosnia together. Another unifying element simply does not exist in Bosnia... yet.

[1] Over 100,000 Serbs still exist as refugees, having fled from Croatia. They have little incentive to return given the lack of security guarantees and no protection from nationalist inspired policies against the Serbs that do return (Amnesty International Report, "A shadow on Croatia's future: Continuing impunity for war crimes and crimes against humanity" (AI Index: EUR 64/005/2004). Many of these Serb refugees currently live in Bosnia and their presence fosters Serb fears of persecution in the absence of the IEBL and DPA political framework.

[2] Field grade officers are typically those in the rank of Major, Lieutenant Colonel and Colonel and considered senior in rank.

Chapter XI

EPILOGUE

> The Embassy of Bosnia and Herzegovina, Washington
> will be holding a commemoration of
> the 11th Anniversary of the Srebrenica Massacre
> on 11 July 2006.
>
> At 7:00 p.m. on the steps of the Embassy you will be able to
> light a candle and hold a silent prayer in remembrance of the thousands of
> innocent lives massacred under the orders of Radovan Karadzic and Ratko Mladic
> on 11 July 1995.
>
> At 7:30 p.m. a film entitled "The March of Death" will be shown in our main
> reception hall.
>
> **Please join us in ensuring that those lives so viciously taken are not forgotten.**
>
> A Book of Condolence will be available in the vestibule area for those
> who wish to express their sympathy in writing.

Invitation from the Embassy of Bosnia and Herzegovina,
Washington DC, July 7, 2006

As I finished preparing this manuscript for publication I received the invitation above from the Bosnian Embassy. In many respects this invitation symbolizes the ongoing tension, irreconcilable differences and latent conflict in Bosnia, a tension I argue is imminently palpable on the landscape and detrimental to rapprochement.

The symbolic landscapes of Bosnia have changed little since 2004. The Bosniaks have had limited success in reclaiming their historical and symbolic presence in the Croat and Serb regions of Bosnia by rebuilding some of their most historic mosques and by successfully returning Bosniak refugees to their prewar municipalities. Of the more than 2,200,000

Bosnians who became refugees during the war, 1,013,000 have returned to their prewar homes.

The Bosniak community has been slowly reclaiming their sacred spaces since the end of the war. Indeed from 1995 to the end of September 2004 roughly 565 mosques were either rebuilt or newly constructed.[1] A unique facet of this new construction is the appearance of "petro-dollar" mosques springing up in Bosnia and indeed elsewhere such as the Sandzak region of Serbia, Montenegro and Kosovo. These mosques are funded by wealthy Middle Eastern states and their architectural style is alien to the Bosnian tradition, reflecting a clearly Middle Eastern appearance and located on hilltops dominating the countryside. These ominous "Saudi modern" mosques will not contribute to the rebuilding of Bosnian Muslim cultural heritage and identity.

Perhaps one of the most salient victories for the Bosniak community has been the launching of the reconstruction of the Ferhadija Mosque, in Banja Luka in October 2005. Mosques in Bijelina, Foča, Jajce, Stolac among many other towns have also been reconstructed or are in the process thereof. The reclaiming of the destroyed mosque property in Devic, along the banks of the Drina, has been especially contentious as a Serb Orthodox church was built on the site where the mosque had once stood. These efforts have been seen by the Serb community as a reassertion of Muslim control and presence in Serb territory and is one example of many that are being pursued in Bosnia today. It is a source of significant inter-ethnic tension that keeps nationalist passions alive and hinders any sign of rapprochement between the ethnic groups. The nationalist landscapes of 2004 are still ever-present in Bosnia today.

Since the completion of the research in 2004, there has been minimal progress in bringing Bosnia's three ethnic groups towards reconciliation and a common desire for a stronger unitary and functional state model. There is no collective Bosnian identity, but one based on ethnic group membership. The replacement of Lord Paddy Ashdown by High Representative Christian Schwarz-Schilling has been interpreted as a sign that Bosnia is becoming easier to deal with and that a hard-fisted administrator such as Ashdown was no longer required, that it is time for the Bosnians to take more responsibility for their own future. Moreover, at first glance the departure of the NATO's SFOR and replacement by European Union Forces, or EUFOR, in December 2004 and the announcement that the Office of the High Representative will close in 2007 may indicate that normalcy has once again returned to the war torn regions of Bosnia and Herzegovina - realities on the ground contradict this. The Bosniaks oppose the abolition of the OHR and the Bonn Powers as they have been the only effective mechanisms to effect change - normally against Serb interests. Nonetheless, international presence will remain with an EU Administrator, the EU Police Monitoring Mission (EUPM) and EUFOR.

Bosnia has made some progress in developing as a state in the interim - an integrated Ministry of Defense, an effective National Border Service, and the introduction of a highly successful national sales tax, or value added tax (VAT). The VAT has been resoundingly successful in helping Bosnia gain sound fiscal footing. These are indeed steps forward and are indicative of actual progress. However this progress has not translated into improved relations between the Bosniaks, Croats and Serbs.

Ethnic reconciliation, rapprochement and social harmony remains distant. Since 2004 Bosnia's three ethnic groups still remain far apart in their future outlook. The Bosniaks are adamant on creating a unified central state centered on Sarajevo, dissolving the entities, and de-legitimizing any Bosnian Serb counter proposals on state structure and Bosnia's future by incessantly lampooning the Serb nation as the perpetrators of aggression and genocide against Bosnia's Muslims. Room for reconciliation and political accommodation is severely lacking. The recent defeat of the 2006 Constitutional referendum, surprisingly by Bosniak assembly member votes, is an indication of this antagonistic relationship. This failure of a compromise draft Constitution acceptable to the Croat and Serb political parties (which viewed the document as a compromise for which they voted) was unacceptable to Bosniak assembly members who entertain an “all or nothing” attitude in pursuit of their political goal of a stronger state and Bosniak hegemony. The voting actually contradicted popular sentiment. A recent United Nations Development Program survey indicated that over 50% of Bosniaks and only 27% of Serbs supported the constitutional changes, reflecting the similar trend discovered in the 2004 survey.

The Bosnian Serbs for their part and in light of the draft constitution’s defeat have derailed the Police Reform process to create a single national level police force. The successful establishment of a national police force, dissolving the entity-level police is viewed by the International Community and European Union as a key step to eventually joining the EU and establishing stronger ties between Bosnia and Euro-Atlantic institutions. The successful secession of Montenegro in May and looming independence of Kosovo has led to calls by some Bosnian Serb nationalists and politicians for the independence of Republika Srpska. However this is widely viewed as rhetoric in the follow-up to the upcoming elections in Bosnia. Nevertheless, as the situation in Kosovo further develops, the IC should be wary of Serb unrest and the potential for instability in Bosnia.

The Bosnian Croats have been advocating the establishment of their own entity to protect and advocate Bosnian Croat national interests. Cardinal Vinko Puljić of Sarajevo has been extremely vocal over what he sees as the discrimination of the Croats in the Muslim dominated Federation. The political platform of the HDZ, the Croat nationalist party, overtly calls for the establishment of a third entity, further decentralizing Bosnia into three entities as the best way to protect the Croat minority. This mirrors Bosnian Croat sentiments expressed in the 2004 survey.

The sense of a shared Bosnian history continues to be elusive. The Bosniaks perpetuate a vision of singular victim hood, accusing the Serbs of aggression and genocide. The Serbs counter that the 1992-1995 war was a civil war in which Serbs, just as Bosniaks and Croats, were victims of the war’s same horrors. These positions have only hardened since 2004, with Bosnia aggressively pursuing a lawsuit against neighboring Serbia in the World Court and the Bosnian Serb political leadership demanding a commission to investigate atrocities committed against the Serbs in wartime Sarajevo. Reconciliation and political accommodation is simply unattainable given the rhetoric and whipped-up hysteria of Bosnia's nationalists and political opportunists.

A May 18, 2006 television report on Sarajevo's state BHTV1 presented survey data that suggested a state of apartheid exists in Bosnia. As noted in the program "60 % of Bosnian citizens are against [ethnically] mixed marriages; one-third do not wish to have neighbors of other ethnicities; and every fourth [citizen] does not want his/her child to go to school with peers who are not members of the same group. Why not be open about it: apartheid has become the lifestyle in this country. In many parts of Bosnia, children are growing up in purely mono-ethnic communities, and teachers and parents are teaching them that the other and the different is actually bad."

The Bosniak desire to abolish the entities and, although to a lesser degree, the cantons only hardens the political positions of all three groups. The ever present IEBL is still a source of enormous contention as it epitomizes the entity structure. Should the International Community support Bosniak goals, war would likely be inevitable.

The notion of an all-encompassing and shared collective Bosnian civic identity is still absent in Bosnia. In the intervening years since this study was conducted, there has been no tangible change in the sense of identity among Bosnia's Bosniaks, Croats and Serbs. Although a united Ministry of Defense has been achieved, the individual soldiers will wear their regimental emblem on their sleeve, which maintains the tradition of their ethnic group therefore manifesting a Bosniak, Croat or Serb not Bosnian identity. Without a shared sense of Bosnian national and civic identity Bosnia and Herzegovina's future remains bleak.

One disturbing facet of this study is what it says toward other other geopolitical situations. To this end, Bosnia and Herzegovina's alleged success must be closely reviewed. The Dayton Peace Accords and international oversight have been extremely successful in stopping the war and maintaining the peace but may have only "delayed a day of reckoning." There are implications and lessons to be learned from Bosnia relevant to the world's situation today. As Iraq reels under sectarian violence and an insurgency, Bosnia (Kosovo too) has been oft identified as the template to successfully end internecine warfare and control ethnic hatreds. As Iraq wrestles under American occupation for its survival and political future, the U.S., its allies and the U.N. had better find a another template to help the Iraqis, as Bosnia is still an unfinished story. Using the "Balkans Solution" elsewhere will only ensure another one.

In closing, political and social accommodation is nowhere near at hand. The Croats and Serbs still preserve their spatial identity within Bosnia via Croat cantons and the Republika Srpska entity. They will not give this up easily to what the Serbs certainly see as the attempt by the Bosniaks to assert hegemony over the state. Should the Bosniaks ardently pursue their goals of a de-facto Muslim state and the Serbs stubbornly resist surrendering their entity, instability will remain an ever-present malaise. Indeed, the parties could be setting Bosnia and Herzegovina on a trajectory towards renewed conflict. Centripetal forces that will strengthen the state or affect reconciliation simply do not exist - it is a dark forecast.

---

[1] Zubcevic, Asim. "Islamic Sites in Bosnia - Ten years on." Islamica Magazine , No. 15, Winter 2005/6.

Appendices

Appendix A

List of street name changes in Banja Luka, Republika Srpska

Appendix A – Banja Luka Street Name Changes as of June 2004

	New Name	Remarks
no change	ŽARKA ZGONJANINA	
no change	ŽELJEZNIĆKA KOLONIJA	
no change	ŽIVOJINA PRERADOVIĆA	
no change	ĐORĐA JOVETIĆA	
no change	ĐURE ĐAKOVIĆA	
VUKE KARADJIJA	ĐURE DANIĆIĆA	
no change	ĐURE JAKŠIĆA	
no change	ĆAIRE	
VILKE VINTERHALTERA	1. KRAJIŠKOG KORPUSA	
no change	1. PRIGRADSKI PUT	
no change	1.KRAJIŠKE BRIGADE NO	
DR. ASIMA KULENOVIJA	12 BEBA	
no change	13. KRAJI[KE BRIGADE	
ELMASSA SARAJLIJA	1300 KAPLARA	
no change	14.SREDNJOBOSANSKE BRIGADE	
no change	22. APRILA	
no change	3. PRIGRADSKI PUT	
no change	4. PRIGRADSKI PUT	
no change	5. KOZARSKE BRIGADE	
no change	6. PRIGRADSKI PUT	
no change	7. PRIGRADSKI PUT	
no change	8. PRIGRADSKI PUT	
ALEJA JNA	ALEJA SV.SAVE	Saint Sava Allee
no change	ALEKSE ŠANTIĆA	Serb Poet [Mostar]
no change	ALEKSE DUNDIĆA	
no change	ANĐE KNEŽEVIĆ	
VAHIDE MAGJLAJLIĆ	ANKE DRAKULIĆ	
BEŠIRPAĆIŠEVA	BAJE PIVLJANINA	
MIRKA VIŠNJIĆA	BANA DR. TODORA LAZAREVIĆA	
SIME ĆOLAJE	BANA MILOSAVLJEVIĆA	
no change	BANIJSKA	
MUHAREMA KARABEGOVIĆA	BANOVIĆ STRAHINJE	
no change	BEOGRADSKA	
no change	BITOLJSKA	
no change	BOŽE NIKOLIĆA	
ANTE MARINIĆA	BOŽE VARIĆAKA	
no change	BOŽIDARA MIŠE BABIĆA	
no change	BOGDANA ŽERAJIĆA	
AVGUSTA CESARCA	BOLANOG DOJĆINA	
GROBLJANSKA	BORE STANKOVIĆA	
no change	BOSE ŽIVKOVIĆ	
no change	BRAĆE I SESTARA GLUMAC	
no change	BRAĆE I SESTARA KAPOR	

	New Name	Remarks
BRAĆE BUKIĆ	BRAĆE JUGOVIĆA	Kosovo Heroes
ŠOŠE MAŽARA	BRAĆE MAŽAR I MAJKE MARIJE	
AVGUSTA ŠENOE	BRAĆE PANTIĆA	
DŽEMALA BIJEDIĆA	BRAĆE PIŠTELJIĆ	
no change	BRAĆE PODGORNIKA	
no change	BRAĆE SOLA	
NASIMA BARUHA	BRAĆE ČUBRILOVIĆA	
no change	BRAĆE POTKONJAKA	
no change	BRANISLAVA NUŠIĆ	
no change	BRANKA GRPČIĆA	
no change	BRANKA MORAČE	
no change	BRANKA RADIČEVIĆA	
no change	BRANKA ZAGORCA	
BULEVAR REVOLUCIJE	BULEVAR CARA DUŠANA	Medieval Serb Emperor
BULEVAR NARODNOG FRONTA	BULEVAR DESANKE MAKSIMOVIĆ	
PARTIZANSKIH AVIATIČARA	BULEVAR SRPSKE VOJSKE	Blvd of the Serb Soldier
RADE VRANJEŠEVIĆ	BULEVAR VOJVODE Ž. MIŠIČA	Serb Fld Marshall Misic
BULEVAR SOLIDARNOSTI	BULEVAR VOJVODE PETRA BOJOVIĆA	Serb Fld Marshall Bojovic
BULEVAR SOLIDARNOSTI	BULEVAR VOJVODE STEPANOVIĆA	Serb Fld Marshall Stepanovic
KASIMA HAŽIJA	CARA LAZARA	Serb Emperor Lazar
ISMETA DEMIROVIŠA	CAREVA ROMANOVIH	
BRAĆA I SESTARA KAPOR	CARICE MILICE	
M.M. KRESIŠA	CERSKA	
3. KRAJIŠKE BRIGADE	CETINJSKA	
no change	DŽINIŠA	
no change	DANILA PEROVIĆA (81)	
no change	DAVIDA ŠTRPCA	
no change	DESPOTA KONSTANTINA DRAGAŠA	
no change	DOBOJSKA	
no change	DOSITEJA OBRADOVIĆA	
no change	DR VELIMIRA ČOLIĆA	
no change	DR. ŽIVKA NJEŽIĆA	
no change	DR. BOŽIDARA ADŽIJE	
DR. BOŽIDARA ADŽIJE	**DR. JOVANA RAŠKOVIĆA**	
no change	DR. KOSTE KRSMANOVIĆA	
no change	DR. MLADENA STOJANOVIĆA	
no change	DR. V. ĆEDE KECMANOVIĆA	
PETRA MEŠAVE I OTOKARA KERŠOVANIJA	**DR.JOVANA RAŠKOVIĆA**	
no change	DRAGANA BUBIĆA	
no change	DRAGOMIRA DRAGE MALIĆA	

	New Name	Remarks
no change	DRVARSKA	
no change	DUŠANA DILJEVIĆA	
no change	DUŠANA JOKIĆA	
no change	DUŠANA SUBOTIĆA (90)	
no change	DUŠKA KOŠČICE	
no change	DUNAVSKA	
no change	EUGENA KUMIČIĆA	
no change	F.G. LORKE	
no change	FILIPA KLJAJIĆA FIĆE	
no change	FILIPA MACURE	
no change	FRANCA PREŠERNA	
no change	FRANE SUPILA	
no change	FRANJE SARAFINA	
no change	FRUŠKOGORSKA	
no change	GAJEVA	
SKOJ-a	GAVRE VUČKOVIĆA	
no change	GAVRILA PRINCIPA	WW I Serb Hero
LABINSKIH RUDARA	GOLUBA BABIĆA	
ŠTROSMAJEROVA	GRČKA	Greek
no change	GUNDULIŠEVA	
MIRKA MANDŠA	HAJDUK VELJKA	
no change	HERCEGNOVSKA	
no change	HVARSKA	
no change	IGMANSKA	
VLADE VITJUKA	ILIJE GARAŠANINA	
no change	BRANKA RADIČEVIĆA	
no change	BRANKA ZAGORCA	
BULEVAR REVOLUCIJE	BULEVAR CARA DUŠANA	Medieval Serb Emperor
BULEVAR NARODNOG FRONTA	BULEVAR DESANKE MAKSIMOVIĆ	
PARTIZANSKIH AVIATIČARA	BULEVAR SRPSKE VOJSKE	Blvd of the Serb Soldier
RADE VRANJEŠEVIĆ	BULEVAR VOJVODE Ž. MIŠIČA	Serb Fld Marshall Misic
BULEVAR SOLIDARNOSTI	BULEVAR VOJVODE PETRA BOJOVIĆA	Serb Fld Marshall Bojovic
BULEVAR SOLIDARNOSTI	BULEVAR VOJVODE STEPANOVIĆA	Serb Fld Marshall Stepanovic
KASIMA HAŽIJA	CARA LAZARA	Serb Emperor Lazar
ISMETA DEMIROVIŠA	CAREVA ROMANOVIH	
BRAĆA I SESTARA KAPOR	CARICE MILICE	
M.M. KRESIŠA	CERSKA	
3. KRAJIŠKE BRIGADE	CETINJSKA	
no change	DŽINIŠA	
no change	DANILA PEROVIĆA (81)	
no change	DAVIDA ŠTRPCA	
no change	DESPOTA KONSTANTINA DRAGAŠA	

	New Name	Remarks
no change	DOBOJSKA	
no change	DOSITEJA OBRADOVIĆA	
no change	DR VELIMIRA ČOLIĆA	
no change	DR. ŽIVKA NJEŽIĆA	
no change	DR. BOŽIDARA ADŽIJE	
DR. BOŽIDARA ADŽIJE	**DR. JOVANA RAŠKOVIĆA**	
no change	DR. KOSTE KRSMANOVIĆA	
no change	DR. MLADENA STOJANOVIĆA	
no change	DR. V. ĆEDE KECMANOVIĆA	
PETRA MEŠAVE I OTOKARA KERŠOVANIJA	**DR.JOVANA RAŠKOVIĆA**	
no change	DRAGANA BUBIĆA	
no change	DRAGOMIRA DRAGE MALIĆA	
no change	DRVARSKA	
no change	DUŠANA DILJEVIĆA	
no change	DUŠANA JOKIĆA	
no change	DUŠANA SUBOTIĆA (90)	
no change	DUŠKA KOŠČICE	
no change	DUNAVSKA	
no change	EUGENA KUMIČIĆA	
no change	F.G. LORKE	
no change	FILIPA KLJAJIĆA FIĆE	
no change	FILIPA MACURE	
no change	FRANCA PREŠERNA	
no change	FRANE SUPILA	
no change	FRANJE SARAFINA	
no change	FRUŠKOGORSKA	
no change	GAJEVA	
SKOJ-a	GAVRE VUČKOVIĆA	
no change	GAVRILA PRINCIPA	WW I Serb Hero
LABINSKIH RUDARA	GOLUBA BABIĆA	
ŠTROSMAJEROVA	GRČKA	Greek
no change	GUNDULIŠEVA	
MIRKA MANDŠA	HAJDUK VELJKA	
no change	HERCEGNOVSKA	
no change	HVARSKA	
no change	IGMANSKA	
VLADE VITJUKA	ILIJE GARAŠANINA	
no change	LJEVČANSKA	
no change	LJUBICE GEROVAC	
no change	LJUBICE MRKONJIĆ	
no change	LJUBIJSKIH RUDARA	
no change	LJUBLJANSKA	
no change	LJUPKA RAČIĆA	
no change	LOŽIONIČKA	
OREŠKOVIĆA	LUKE VUKALOVIĆA	
no change	MAŽURANIĆA	
M. SABITOVIĆA	MAČVANSKA	

	New Name	Remarks
no change	MAJEVIČKA	
MILANČIĆA MILEVIĆA	MAJKE JEVROSIME(464)	
BULEVAR MARKSA I ENGELSA	MAJKE JUGOVIĆA	Kosovo Heroine
SKENDERA KULENOVIĆA	MAJKE KNEŽOPOLJKE	
VRHPOLJSKA	MAJORA DRAGE BAJALOVIĆA	
no change	MAKSIMA GORKOG	
PORODICE MLEČNIK	MANASTIRA GRAČANICA	Serb Monastery
BIHAĆKA	MANASTIRA MOŠTANICE	Serb Monastery
no change	MARIJE BURSAĆ	
PETRIČEVAČKI PUT	MARIJE DIMIĆ	
no change	MARINA DRŽIĆA	
5. KONGRESA KPJ	MARKA KRALJEVIĆA	Kosovo
no change	MARKA LIPOVCA	
no change	MARKA MILJANOVA	
no change	MASARIKOVA	
ZAGREBAĆKA	MEŠE SELIMOVIĆ	
no change	MIŠE STUPARA	
ŠANDORA PETEFIJA	MIŠE LJUBIBRATIĆA	
no change	MIŠE RADAKOVIĆA	
no change	MIHAJLA PUPINA	Serb Inventor
no change	MILANA BRANKOVIĆA	
no change	MILANA BUDIMIRA (235)	
no change	MILANA CVIJETIĆA	
FRANCA STANETA ROZMANA	MILANA KNEŽINE	
JURIJA KRIŽANIĆA	MILANA KRANOVI]A	
no change	MILANA RADMANA	
ŽELJE BARIŠA	MILANA RAKIĆA	
VLADIMIRA NAZORA	MILANA TEPIĆA	
ALI KELEMENDIJA	MILANA TOPLICE	
no change	MILE BEKUTA	
RUŠIDA DŽEHVEROVIĆA	MILEŠEVSKA	
DRAGE JURINČIĆA	MILICE STOJADINOVIĆ - SRPKINJE	
no change	MILOŠA DUJIĆA	
no change	MILOŠA MATIĆA	
NURIJE POZDERCA	MILOŠA OBILIĆA	Kosovo
no change	MILORADA UMJENOVIĆA	
AVDE ČARDEŽIĆA	MILOVANA GLIŠIĆA	
no change	MILOVANA HRVAĆANINA	
no change	MIRE CIKOTE (248)	
no change	MIRJANE JOTANOVIĆ	
no change	MIRKA KOVAČEVIĆA	
no change	MLAĐE ĆUSIĆA	
no change	MLADENA OLJAČE	
no change	MOČILA	
no change	MOMČILA POPOVIĆA	
no change	MOSLOVAČKA	

	New Name	Remarks
ALIJE ALIJAGIĆA	MUHAMEDA MEHMEDBAŠIĆA	
no change	NADE VALENČIĆ	
REDŽEPOVIĆA	NADEŽDE PETROVIĆ	
no change	NATALIJE JOVIĆ	
MIRKA MRMONJE	NEDELJKA ČABRINOVIĆA	
no change	NIKOLE BOKANA	
RADE LIČINE	NIKOLE PAŠIĆA	WWI Prime Minister
no change	NIKOLE TESLE	Serb Inventor
no change	NJEGOŠEVA	Njegosh - Hero
no change	NOVA ULICA	
no change	NOVI SOKAK	
no change	NOVICE CEROVIJA	
no change	NOVO NASELJE	
no change	NOVOSADSKA	
no change	OGNJENA PRICE	
no change	OMLADINSKA	
TRAVNIĆKA	OPLENAČKA	Serb Royal Tomb
no change	PATRE	
FAHRETA DEDIĆA	PATRIJARHA ARSENIJA ČARNOJEVIĆA	Serb Religious Leader
FERHATPAĆINA	PATRIJARHA MAKARIJA SOKOLOVIĆA	Serb Religious Leader
no change	PAVE RADANA	
TEKIJI	PERE DRLJAČE	
no change	PETRA KOČIĆA	
VJEKOSLAVA BAKULIĆA	PETRA MEĆAVE	
ISTARSKA	PETRA PECIJE	
no change	PETRA PRERADOVIĆA	
ZIJE DIZDAREVIĆA	PETRA RAĐENOVIĆA	
no change	PETROVAČKA	
no change	PILANSKA	
no change	PIONIRSKA	
BLEDSKA	PLITVIČKA	
no change	PODGRMEČKA	
RIZE GOLALIĆA	POPA JOVICE	
FRANJE NANUTA	PROTE NIKOLE KOSTIĆA	
ABDUSELIMA BLEKIĆA	PROTE TODORA SRDIĆA	
LUTVIJE SMAILAGIĆ	RAŠKA	
no change	RADE KONDIĆA	
no change	RADE MARJANCA	
SLAVIŠE VAJNERA ČIČE	RADE VRANEŠEVIĆ	
EJUBA KOBAŠLIĆA	RADOJE DOMANOVIĆA	
no change	RADOVANA VULINA	
no change	RAJKA BOSNIĆA	
no change	RAKOVAČKIH RUDARA	
no change	RANKA ŠIPKE	
HRVOJA VUKČIĆA	RAVNIH KOTARA	
MATOŠEVA	RAVNOGORSKA	

	New Name	Remarks
HASANA KIKIŠA	RELJE KRILATICE	
no change	ROMANIJSKA	
OMERA AHMETAŠIĆA	SANIČKIH ŽETELACA	
no change	SANSKA	
no change	SAVE KOVAČEVIĆA	
no change	SAVE LJUBOJE	
BENEŠEVA	SAVE MRKALJA	
ŽARKA VRANJEŠEVIĆA	SAVE TEKELIJE	
HALILOVCA	SENT - ANDREJSKA	
VELJKA VLAHOVIĆA	SIME ŠOLAJE	
ANTE JAKIĆA	SIME MATAVULJA	
no change	SIME MILIĆ JORGIĆ	
no change	SIME MILJUŠA	
AHMETA HADŽIHALILOVIĆA	SIME PANDUROVIĆA	
AVDE KARABEGOVIŠA	SIMEUNA ĐAKA	
AVNOJ-a	SKENDERA KULENOVIĆA	
no change	SLAVKA RODIĆA	
FRANJE KLUZA	SLOBODANA JOVANOVIĆA	
no change	SLOBODANA KOKANOVIĆA	
FADILA MAGLAJLIŠA	SOLUNSKA	WW I Salonika Front
BRAĆE ODIĆA	SR\E ZLOPOGLEĐE	
no change	SREDNJOŠKOLSKA	
FRA GRGE MARTIŠA	SRPSKA	
FRANJE HAZARINA	SRPSKIH DOBROVOLJACA	Serb Volunteers
TRIGLAVSKA	SRPSKIH RUDARA	
RUDARSKA (od broja 46 do broja 86)	SRPSKIH SOKOLOVA	
27. Jula	SRPSKIH USTANIKA	"Serb Rebellion" [1804]
no change	SRPSKIH VITEZOVA	
MEHMEDA DELIŠA	STARINE NOVAKA	
STOJANA VUJASINOVIŠA	STAROG VUJADINA	
no change	STEVANA BULAJIĆA	
no change	STEVANA MOKRANJCA	
AVDE HERCEGOVCA	STEVANA MOLJEVIŠA	
MIŠE JAZBECA	STEVANA PRVOVJENČANOG	
DALMATINSKA	STOJANA JANKOVIĆA	
HAZIMA OMERBAŠIĆA	STUDENIČKA	Serb Monastery
MILANA LIČINE	SV. KRALJICE JELENE	
ZAGORSKA	SVETOG NIKOLE	
MOSTARSKA	SVETOZARA ĆOROVIĆA	
no change	SVETOZARA MARKOVIĆA	
no change	TALIJANSKOG BATALJONA MATEOTI	
no change	TARASA ŠEVČENKA	
no change	TEODORA KOLOKOTRONISA	
no change	TIHOMIRA T. DAMJANOVIĆA	
no change	TINA UJEVIĆA	

	New Name	Remarks
MEJDAN	TODORA OD STALAĆA	
no change	TOME RADULOVIĆA	
no change	TRŽNIČKA	
ZAVNOBIH-a	TRIVE AMELICE	
no change	TRLA	
SAFETA KRUPIŠA	TROMEĆE	
no change	TUZLANSKA	
no change	UŽIČKA	
BOSANSKA	UROŠA NEJAKOG	
BRAĆE RADIĆA	UROŠA PREDIĆA	
no change	VACLAVA HAVLEKA VENE	
JOSIPA BRACE NEMECA	VASE GLUŠCA	
EVLIJE ČELEBIJE	VASE KONDIĆA	
no change	VASE PELAGIĆA	
VORANCA PREŽIHOVA	VASE VIDOVIĆA	
MAJSTORIŠA PUT	VASILIJA OSTROŠKOG	
no change	VELEBITSKA	
no change	VESELI BRIJEG	
no change	VESELINA MASLEŠE	
no change	VIDA SIMURDŽIĆA	
AKIFA ŠERAMETA	VIDOVDANSKA	
no change	VILSONOVA	President Wilson
NEVENKE DADASOVIĆ	VISOKIH DEČANA	Serb Monastery
no change	VLAŠIĆKA	
PAVLOVIŠA PUT	VLADANA DESNICE	
NIKE JURINČIŠA	VLADIKE PLATONA	
9. PRIGRADSKI PUT I V. ROLOVIŠA	VLADIMIRA ROLOVIĆA	
IVANA CANCARA	VOŽDOVAČKA	
DUJE IVEZIŠA	VOJVOĐANSKA	
IVICE MAŽARA	VOJVODE MOMČILA	Četnik
ŠEFKETA MAGLAJLIĆA	VOJVODE PERE KRECE	
HUSINSKIH RUDARA	VOJVODE PRIJEZDE	
RUDIJA ČAJAVECA	VOJVODE RADOMIRA PUTNIKA	WWI Serb Hero
JUSUFA JOJE TULIŠA	VOJVODE SINĐELIĆA	Serb Hero
no change	VRBASKI PUT	
VLADIMIR LENIN	VUKA KARADŽIĆA	Serb Academic
no change	ZDRAVE KORDE	
no change	ZDRAVKA ČELARA	
no change	ZELENGORSKA	
no change	ZEMUNSKA	
no change	ZMAJ JOVINA	
no change	ZORE KOVAČEVIĆ	
no change	ŠARPLANINSKA	
no change	ŠIBALOVIĆA	
no change	ŠPIRE BOCARIĆA (391)	
no change	ŠUMADIJSKA	

Appendix B

Survey Questionnaires

Questionnaire – English Version

Dear Sir or Madam –

I am conducting this survey on ethnic identity as part of my doctoral research work in the USA. A large portion of my research attempts to identify how ethnic identity is understood and created. I would sincerely appreciate a few minutes of your time in completing the following questions. You may elaborate on your answers if you feel it is necessary.

Thank You

The Inter-Entity Boundary Line (IEBL) that separates Republika Srpska (RS) from the Federation (FED) was created by the Dayton Peace Accords (DPA) in 1995.

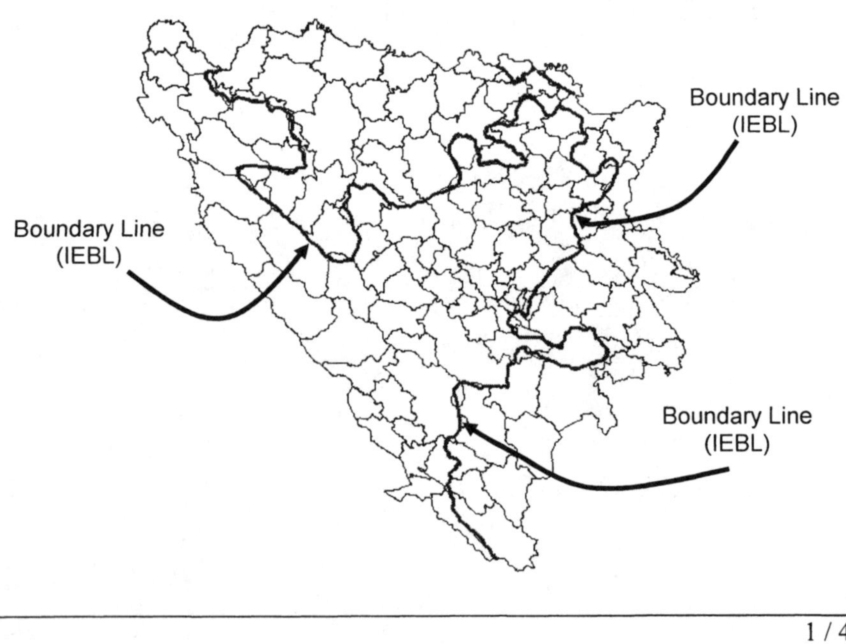

1 / 4

1 "The IEBL is important to Republika Srpska."

Strongly Agree Agree Not sure Disagree Strongly disagree

2 "The IEBL is important to the Federation."

Strongly Agree Agree Not sure Disagree Strongly disagree

3 "Both the IEBL and entities should be dissolved and a strong government and state based in Sarajevo be created in Bosnia."

Strongly Agree Agree Not sure Disagree Strongly disagree

4 "There could be renewed hostilities if UNHR Paddy Ashdown succeeded in removing the IEBL and disbanding the entity governments and creating a strong central government in Sarajevo."

Strongly Agree Agree Not sure Disagree Strongly disagree

5 "If Kosovo is permitted to become an independent state then Republika Srpska has the same right to sovereignty."

Strongly Agree Agree Not sure Disagree Strongly disagree

6 Before the war came to Bosnia, you felt yourself to be (please circle one):

Yugoslav Bosnian Bosniak Croatian Serbian

2 / 4

Question 1. If the father is Romanian and the mother Hungarian, what is the ethnicity of the child?

Romanian Hungarian Unsure

Question 2. The father is Romanian, the mother is Hungarian, but everybody around the family is Hungarian and the child has never seen a Romanian, outside of the father. The child will learn Hungarian customs and language. What is the ethnicity of this child?

Romanian Hungarian Unsure

Question 3. A Romanian couple have a child that they do not want. They give it in adoption to a Hungarian couple when the child is only six months old. Around the Hungarian family there are only Hungarians and the child grows up never meeting any Hungarians. Since he was a baby when adopted, he knows nothing and thinks that his biological father and mother are the Hungarian adopters. He grows up learning Hungarian customs and language. What is the ethnicity of this child?

Romanian Hungarian Unsure

Question 4. Would your answers remain the same if Bosniak, Croatian or Serbian were used instead of the Hungarian and Romanian ethnic groups?

Yes No Unsure

Demographic Data:

Sex (circle one): Male Female Age: ____ Municipality (residence): ________

National affiliation (circle one): Bosnian Bosniak Croatian Serb

Occupation (circle one): Student Professional Worker/Tradesman

Businessman Farmer Other (specify):

Comments:

4 / 4

Appendix B

Survey Questionnaires

Questionnaire - Serbo-Croatian Latin version

?oštovani Gospodine/Gospodjo

Jpitnik koji vam šaljem, dio je obaveznih aktivnosti vezanih za moj doktorski istraživački rad u SAD. Veliki dio mojih istraživačkih napora jeste da ustanovim kako se podrazumjeva i ustanovljuje etnička pripadnost i uticaj Dejtonskog Sporazuma na BiH. Prilikom odgovora, možete ići u detalje ako smatrate neophodnim.

Hvala

Granična linija (Inter-Entity Boundary Line – IEBL) koja razdvaja Republiku Srpsku (RS) od Federacije (FED) je uspostavljena Dejtonskim Sporazumom 1995.

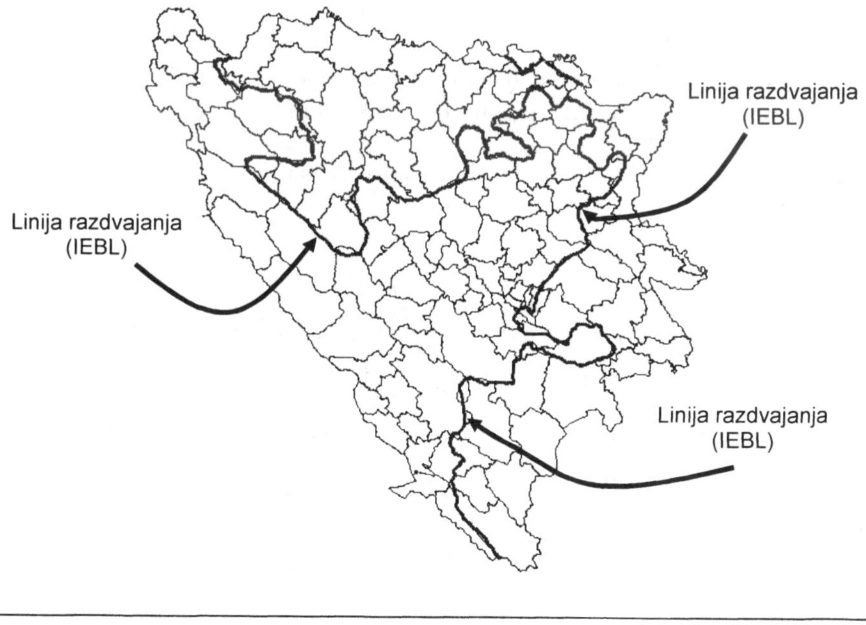

1 / 4

1 "Linija razdvajanja je bitna za Republiku Srpsku."

Slažem se u potpunosti	Slažem se	Nisam siguran/ sigurna	Ne slažem se	Apsolutno se ne slažem

2 "Linija razdvajanja je bitna za Federaciju."

Slažem se u potpunosti	Slažem se	Nisam siguran/ sigurna	Ne slažem se	Apsolutno se ne slažem

3 "Linija razdvajanja i entiteti bi trebali biti ukinuti, i Bosni formirati jaku vladu i državu sa sjedištem u Sarajevu."

Slažem se u potpunosti	Slažem se	Nisam siguran/ sigurna	Ne slažem se	Apsolutno se ne slažem

4 "Moguće su obnove neprijateljstava u slučaju da OHR i Pedi Ešdaun uspiju da uklone liniju razdvajanja i raspuste vlade entiteta."

Slažem se u potpunosti	Slažem se	Nisam siguran/ sigurna	Ne slažem se	Apsolutno se ne slažem

5 "Ako je Kosovu dozvoljeno da postane nezavisna država, onda i Republika Srpska ima isto pravo na suverenitet."

Slažem se u potpunosti	Slažem se	Nisam siguran/ sigurna	Ne slažem se	Apsolutno se ne slažem

6 "Prije rata u Bosni, osjećali ste se kao" (zaokružite jedno)

Jugosloven	Bosanac	Bošnjak Musliman	Hrvat	Srbin

2 / 4

Molimo Vas da na pitanja odgovorite po redoslijedu.

Pitanje 1. Ako je otac Rumun a majka Madjarica, koja je nacionalnost djeteta?

Rumun(ka) **Madjar(ica)** **Nisam siguran(na)**

Pitanje 2. Otac je Rumun, majka je Madjarica, a svi ostali u porodici su Madjari i dijete nikad nije vidjelo Rumuna, osim oca. Dijete će naučiti madjarske običaje i jezik. Koja je nacionalnost ovog djeteta?

Rumun(ka) **Madjar(ica)** **Nisam siguran(na)**

Pitanje 3. Rumunski par ima dijete koje ne žele. Oni su ga dali na usvajanje madjarskom paru kada je dijete bilo samo šest mjeseci staro. U okolini madjarske porodice samo se nalaze Madjari i dijete raste bez kontakta sa Rumuni. Još dok je bio beba, prilikom usvajanja, on ništa ne zna i misli da su njegovi biološki otac i majka zapravo madjarski par koji ga je usvojio. On raste učeći madjarske običaje i jezik. Koja je nacionalnost ovog djeteta?

Rumun(ka) **Madjar(ica)** **Nisam siguran(na)**

Pitanje 4. Da li bi vaši [tvoji] odgovori bili isti da su umjesto madjarske i rumunjske u pitanju bošnjačka, hrvatska, ili srpska etnička grupa? (Opcija)

Da Ne Nisam siguran/sigurana

Demografski podaci

Pol (zaokružite jedno): Muško Žensko Godine: Opština (boravište)

Nacionalna pripadnost (zaokružite jedno):

Bosanac Bošnjak Hrvat Srbin

Zanimanje (zaokružite jedno):

Student Stručnjak Radnik/Zanatlija

Preduzetnik Poljoprivrednik Ostalo (precizirajte)

Komentar:

4 / 4

Appendix B

Survey Questionnaires

Questionnaire - Serbo-Croatian Cyrillic version

Поштовани господине/госпођо

Упитник који вам шаљем, део је обавезних активности везаних за мој докторски истраживачки раду у САД. Велики део мојих истраживачких напора састоји се у томе да установим како се подразумева и установљава етничка припадност. Приликом одговора, можете ићи у детаље ако сматрате за неопходно.

Хвала

Гранична линија (Inter-Entity Boundary Line – IEBL) која раздваја Републику Српску (РС) од Федерације (ФЕД) је успостављена Дејтонским Споразумом 1995.

1 / 4

1 “Линија раздвајања је битна за Републику Српску.”

Слажем се у потпуности	Слажем се	Нисам сигуран/ сигурна	Не слажем се	Апсолутно се не слажем

2 “Линија раздвајања је битна за Федерацију.”

Слажем се у потпуности	Слажем се	Нисам сигуран/ сигурна	Не слажем се	Апсолутно се не слажем

3 “Линију раздвајања и ентитете би требало укинути и у Босни формирати јаку владу и државу са седиштем у Сарајеву.”

Слажем се у потпуности	Слажем се	Нисам сигуран/ сигурна	Не слажем се	Апсолутно се не слажем

4 “Могуће су обнове непријатељстава у случају да УНХЦР и Педи Ешдаун успеју да уклоне линију раздвајања и распусте владе ентитета.”

Слажем се у потпуности	Слажем се	Нисам сигуран/ сигурна	Не слажем се	Апсолутно се не слажем

5 “Ако је Косову дозвољено да постане независна држава, онда и Република Српска има исто право на суверенитет.”

Слажем се у потпуности	Слажем се	Нисам сигуран/ сигурна	Не слажем се	Апсолутно се не слажем

6 “Прије рата у Босни, осјећали сте се као” (заокружите једно)

Југосгловен	Босанац	Бошњак	Хрват	Србин

Питање 1. Ако је отац Румун а мајка Мађарица, која је националност детета?

Румун(ка) Мађар(ица) Нисам сигуран(на)

Питање 2. Отац је Румун, мајка је Мађарица, а сви остали у породици су Мађари и дете никад није видело Румуна, осим оца. Дете ће научити мађарске обичаје и језик. Која је националност овог детета?

Румун(ка) Мађар(ица) Нисам сигуран(на)

Питање 3. Румунски пар има дете које не желе. Они су га дали на усвајање мађарском пару када је дете било само шест месеци старо. У околини мађарске породице само се налазе Мађари и дете расте без контакта са Мађарима. Још док је био беба, приликом усвајања, он ништа не зна и мисли да су његови биолошки отац и мајка заправо мађарски пар који га је усвојио. Он расте учећи мађарске обичаје и језик. Која је националност овог детета?

Румун(ка) Мађар(ица) Нисам сигуран(на)

3 / 4

Іитање 4. Да ли би ваши одговори били исти да су уместо мађарске и румунске у питању бошњачка, хрватска или српска етничка група? Опција)

Да Не Нисам сигуран(на)

Демографски подаци

Пол (заокружите једно): Мушко / Женско Године: Општина (боравиште)

Национална припадност (заокружите једно):

Босанац Бошњак Хрват Србин

Занимање (заокружите једно):

Студент Стручњак Радник/Занатлија

Предузетник Пољопривредник Остало (прецизирајте)

Коментар:

4 / 4

Appendix B

Survey Questionnaires

Questionnaire – Bosnian Dialect version

Poštovani Gospodine/Gospodjo

Upitnik koji vam šaljem, dio je obaveznih aktivnosti vezanih za moj doktorski istraživački rad u SAD. Veliki dio mojih istraživačkih napora jeste da ustanovim kako se podrazumjeva i ustanovljuje etnička pripadnost i uticaj Dejtonskog Sporazuma na BiH. Prilikom odgovora, možete ići u detalje ako smatrate neophodnim.

Hvala

Granična linija (Inter-Entity Boundary Line – IEBL) koja razdvaja Republiku Srpsku (RS) od Federacije (FED) je uspostavljena Dejtonskim Sporazumom 1995.

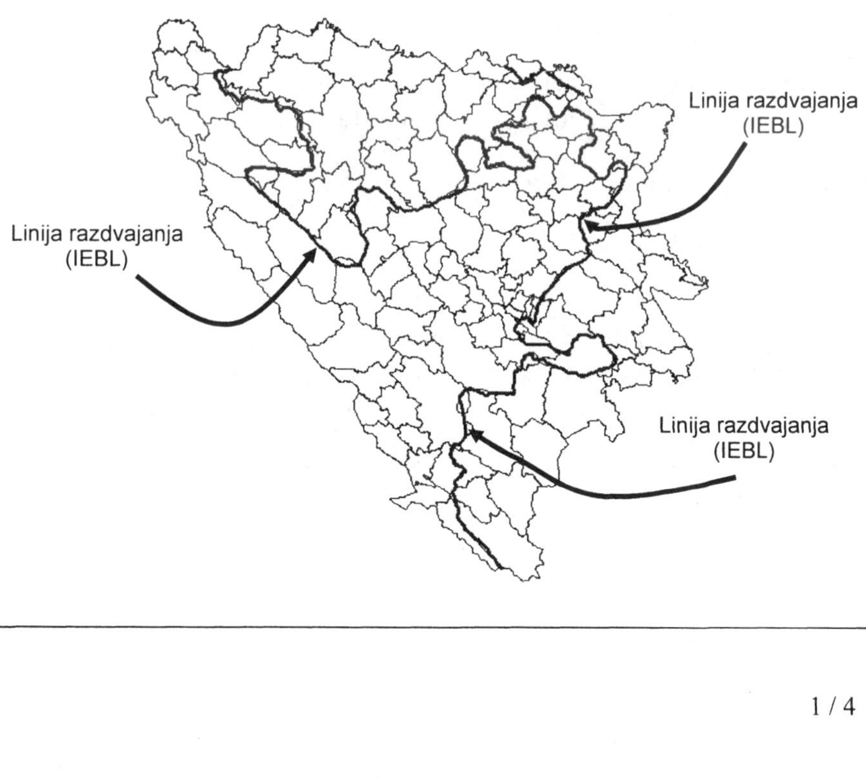

1 / 4

1 “Linija razdvajanja je bitna za Republiku Srpsku.”

Slažem se u potpunosti	Slažem se	Nisam siguran/ sigurna	Ne slažem se	Apsolutno se ne slažem

2 “Linija razdvajanja je bitna za Federaciju.”

Slažem se u potpunosti	Slažem se	Nisam siguran/ sigurna	Ne slažem se	Apsolutno se ne slažem

3 “Linija razdvajanja i entiteti bi trebali biti ukinuti, i Bosni formirati jaku vladu i državu sa sjedištem u Sarajevu.”

Slažem se u potpunosti	Slažem se	Nisam siguran/ sigurna	Ne slažem se	Apsolutno se ne slažem

4 “Moguće su obnove neprijateljstava u slučaju da OHR i Pedi Ešdaun uspiju da uklone liniju razdvajanja i raspuste vlade entiteta.”

Slažem se u potpunosti	Slažem se	Nisam siguran/ sigurna	Ne slažem se	Apsolutno se ne slažem

5 ”Ako je Kosovu dozvoljeno da postane nezavisna država, onda i Republika Srpska ima isto pravo na suverenitet.”

Slažem se u potpunosti	Slažem se	Nisam siguran/ sigurna	Ne slažem se	Apsolutno se ne slažem

6 “Prije rata u Bosni, osjećali ste se kao” (zaokružite jedno)

Jugosloven	Bosanac	Bošnjak Musliman	Hrvat	Srbin

2 / 4

Molimo Vas da na pitanja odgovorite po redoslijedu.

Pitanje 1. Ako je otac Rumun a majka Madjarica, koja je nacionalnost djeteta?

Rumun(ka) Madjar(ica) Nisam siguran(na)

Pitanje 2. Otac je Rumun, majka je Madjarica, a svi ostali u porodici su Madjari i dijete nikad nije vidjelo Rumuna, osim oca. Dijete će naučiti madjarske običaje i jezik. Koja je nacionalnost ovog djeteta?

Rumun(ka) Madjar(ica) Nisam siguran(na)

Pitanje 3. Rumunski par ima dijete koje ne žele. Oni su ga dali na usvajanje madjarskom paru kada je dijete bilo samo šest mjeseci staro. U okolini madjarske porodice samo se nalaze Madjari i dijete raste bez kontakta sa Rumuni. Još dok je bio beba, prilikom usvajanja, on ništa ne zna i misli da su njegovi biološki otac i majka zapravo madjarski par koji ga je usvojio. On raste učeći madjarske običaje i jezik. Koja je nacionalnost ovog djeteta?

Rumun(ka) Madjar(ica) Nisam siguran(na)

3 / 4

Pitanje 4. Da li bi vaši [tvoji] odgovori bili isti da su umjesto madjarske i rumunjske u pitanju bošnjačka, hrvatska, ili srpska etnička grupa? (Opcija)

Da Ne Nisam siguran/sigurana

Demografski podaci

Pol (zaokružite jedno): Muško Žensko Godine: Opština (boravište)

Nacionalna pripadnost (zaokružite jedno):

Bosanac Bošnjak Hrvat Srbin

Zanimanje (zaokružite jedno):

Student Stručnjak Radnik/Zanatlija

Preduzetnik Poljoprivrednik Ostalo (precizirajte)

Komentar:

4 / 4

Appendix C

Survey Questionnaire

Summary Statistics

Summary Statistics

Demographics Section of Survey – Page Four

Gender by Entity

	Republika Srpska	Federation	BiH
Male	65	69	134
Female	42	40	82
Total	**107**	**109**	**216**

National Group by Gender

	Male	Female	Total
Bosnian	26	10	36
Bosniak	35	17	52
Croat	19	10	29
Serb	52	40	92
No response	2	5	7
Total	**134**	**82**	**216**

Age Groupings by Gender

	Male	%	Female	%	Total
No	52	24	24	11	76
19-29	32	14.8	29	13.4	61
30-39	24	11	18	8.3	42
40-49	9	4.2	4	1.9	13
50-59	14	6.5	5	2.3	19
60+	3	1.4	2	.9	5
Totals	**134**	**62%**	**82**	**38%**	**216**

National Affiliation by Entity

	Republika Srpska	Federation	BiH
Bosnian	4	32	36
Bosniak	13	39	52
Croat	5	24	29
Serb	83	9	92
No answer	2	5	7
Total	**107**	**109**	**216**

Occupation by Entity

	Republika Srpska	Federation	BiH
Student	29	11	40
Professional	26	33	59
Worker/Tradesman	36	41	77
Businessman	7	9	16
Farmer	0	1	1
Other	9	14	23
Total	**107**	**109**	**216**

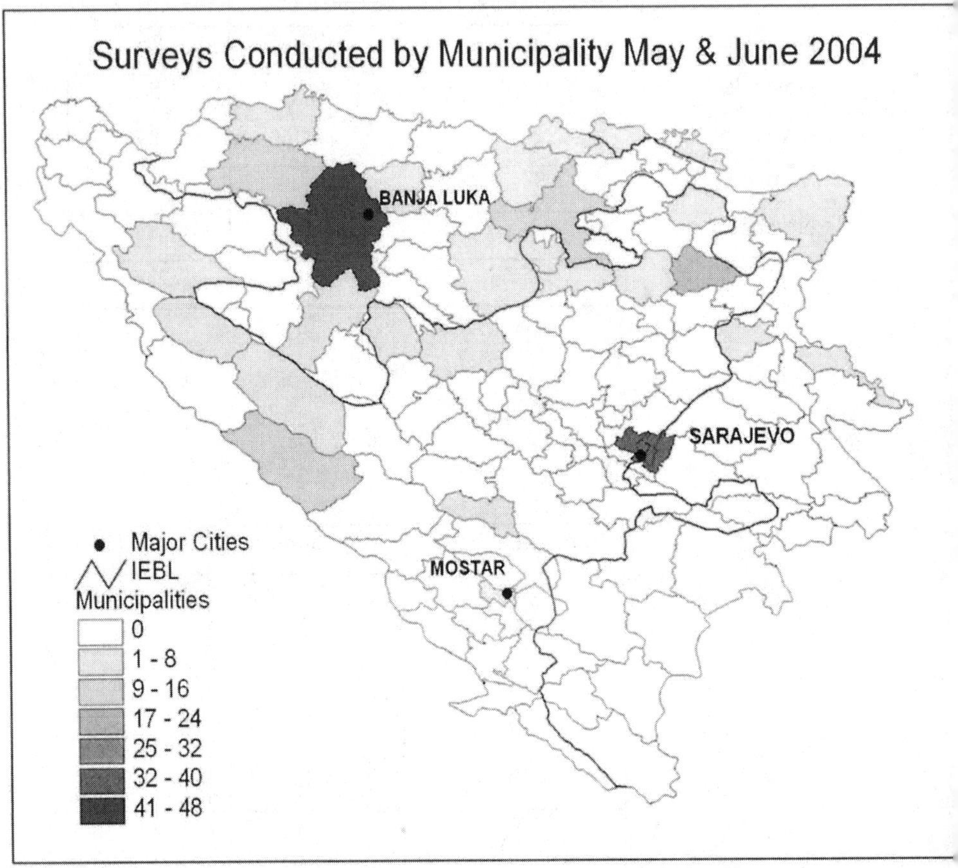
Surveys Conducted by Municipality May & June 2004
BANJA LUKA
SARAJEVO
MOSTAR
Major Cities
IEBL
Municipalities
0
1 - 8
9 - 16
17 - 24
25 - 32
32 - 40
41 - 48

Survey Location by Municipality

Municipality	Entity	# of Respondents
Banja Luka	RS	48
Bijelina	RS	3
Bosanski Petrovac	Federation	1
Bratunac	RS	2
Derventa	RS	3
Doboj	RS	16
Drvar	Federation	7
Glamoć	Federation	4
Jablanica	Federation	1
Jajce	Federation	4
Kozarac	RS	6
Laktaši	RS	6
Livno	Federation	11
Lukavac	Federation	6
Maglaj	Federation	4
Mostar	Federation	5
Mrkonic Grad	RS	4
Odžak	Federation	4
Orašje	Federation	2
Paprać	RS	2
Prijedor	RS	9
Sarajevo	Federation	35
Srpski Brod	RS	2
Tešanj	Federation	3
Teslić	RS	3
Travnik	Federation	4
Tuzla	Federation	20
Zepče	Federation	1
Total		**216**
Republika Srpska		104
Federation		112
Total		**216**

Appendix D

Survey Questionnaires

English Translation of Written Comments

The English translations of elaborations and comments made by the respondents in the Questionnaires are assembled here below. The questionnaires are coded and match the table in Annex XYZ

Questionnaire # 2 - Comments Section

I think that the citizens of RS are convinced that the line of separation is essential for RS and in that sense is my answer too. I personally do not think that the line is essential and I think it should be removed!

Questionnaire # 5 - Comments Section

You should focus onto more essential things in life; for instance on economy, living standard, etc…

Questionnaire # 7 - Comments Section

That I do not agree with the borders of Dayton Agreement because I consider them to be unnecessary and they should be eliminated. As a person that at this time lives in Sarajevo, I am faced with uneasy feeling every time I am traveling through RS. Sometimes it seems to me, that through Dayton, that the Bosnian Serbs won this war, thanks to the drafters (designers) of Dayton borders.

Questionnaire # 8 - Throughout and Comments Section

Entity lines are the biggest mistake of Dayton Agreement. The nationalities in Bosnia and Herzegovina cannot comprehend the negative influence of entities on all peoples of B&H.

A person is supposed to live in a spirit of his culture, but also to respect a culture of other nationalities.

Q1, pg. 3 Depends on the upbringing [of] received from his/her parents.

Questionnaire # 12 - Comments Section

The answers should be more precise, more numerous, particularly the third question on page 3.

Questionnaire # 16 - Comments Section

For questions 1 and 2, where I put "not sure", actually I think a person should choose [according] to his/her own liking. That is actually being done in Bosnia.

Questionnaire # 18 - Comments Section

By all means discontinue Republika Srpska and form a unified Bosnia and Herzegovina. Further on [more], you know what you should be doing.

Questionnaire # 21 - Comments Section

With everything so far, and with these questions were the attempts to confuse the people, and get the wrong (up to this point) answers to the question as to who caused the war in B&H (Yugoslavia).

Questionnaire # 22 - Comments Section

I think that this is not real! If you want to know, we are not stupid, and you did not have to put "Romanians and Hungarians!"

Questionnaire # 23 - Comments Section

A mere psychological attempt to confuse, in order to come to conclusions and answers as to who caused the military conflicts on the territory of B&H, i.e. to find out which nationality is responsible for everything that had happened!

Questionnaire # 24 - Comments Section

You were incautious!

Questionnaire # 30 - Comments Section

I think we should be again without borders and together we would still be stronger in everything.

Questionnaire # 31 - Comments Section

I think we should be without borders.

Questionnaire # 34 - Comments Section

Lots of luck.

Questionnaire # 42 - Comments Section

It saddens me that he does not talk [speak] Serbian.

Questionnaire # 50 - Comments Section

One who has not lived his life under "these sorry conditions," would not agree with me!

Questionnaire # 60 - Comments Section

I have not answered questions I to IV because I am not connected with another nation and I respect all nationalities.

Questionnaire # 63 – Comment on page 3.

Q1, pg 3. The child should decide on his own when it [he] reaches maturity or be of a nationality of the country he lives in (for example: in America (US) all are Americans).

Questionnaire # 64 - Comments Section

Demographics: Expert on religion (priest).

Questionnaire # 77 - Comments Section

For me, this was a first poll [questionnaire] in writing "and particularly verbally" in which I was able to express any thoughts. Thank you!

Questionnaire # 80 - Comments Section

Unusually beautiful and wise, for the first time being asked questions, thank you for your intention to help us.

Questionnaire # 84 - Comments Section

I think that this questionnaire is a good move in order that even we, the ordinary people, are finally able to express our opinion. Perhaps it is not very much different from those given by big shots, but it is only because at this moment the situation is such that a great misunderstanding and intolerance is present on both sides. We all want to be happy, content, free, young; but the truth is that we are petty and narrow minded. I grew up during the war. I know no other way of life, but this one. I am content, despite all! But it can always be better! I want possibilities, but I do not have them here. The people here, who want something different or new, are being disdained and defined as deviant. That is the way I grew up, and I know no other ways. I do not know where my place is. The divided us with those "lines of division," yet we all have the same desires and hopes A belief in a better life.

Questionnaire # 85 - Comments Section

I do not wish to comment.

Questionnaire # 88 - Comments Section

As soon as possible to a [new] state or (three) entities.

Questionnaire # 90 - Comments Section

The comment is superfluous, because these kinds of questions can be asked only by persons who do not live in these regions, and therefore do not know the nature of (its) their problems.

Questionnaire # 92 - Comments Section

A comment is not necessary.

Questionnaire # 93 - Comments Section

The questions are too sensitive [delicate] for this region !!! *(Mrkonic Grad, Serb).*

Questionnaire # 95 - Comments Section

There is a possibility that the questions (considering the tendency of the newly created countries in this and wider regions, to enter the European Union and to build societies that would be based on modern democratic principles), are a little "late." These questions are of current interest for a considerable part of the population from these regions I suspect.

Questionnaire # 102 - Comments Section

As far as B&H is concerned, there are many questions to be answered and many problems solved for its citizens, e.g. jobs, housing, schools in some cities, etc.

Questionnaire # 103 - Comments Section

There are many more questions that are to be answered in order to make all sides content.

Questionnaire # 104 - Comments Section

This questionnaire is not a best solution.

Questionnaire # 106 - Comments Section

I consider B&H a sovereign, undivided state that should be without entities; that is, if there are entities there will always be divisions among peoples and I know that if there would ever be more war, it would be caused by [the] mere existence of entities. *(Bosnjak, Bosanski Petrovac)*

Questionnaire # 107 – Page 2 and Comments Section

Q1, pg 2 – "that it is essential for people living in RS."
"that it is essential for the prosperity and for the economic development.

Q2, pg 2 – From the very acceptance, it tends to eliminate the lines of division (the Bosniak side of Federal B&H).

Q3, pg 2 – One government in Sarajevo should be formed, but [do] not eliminate the entities.

I think that too few questions were asked in order to draw some sort of relevant conclusion. My opinion is that some other questions should have been added; from the sphere of politics, history, economy, psychology, etc.

Questionnaire # 108 - Page 2 elaboration

Q5, pg 2 – "very simple question in comparison to the complexity of the issue."
Comment was in English.

Questionnaire # 113 - Comments Section

I think that the child has the right to know who his parents are and that he can choose his nationality and his religion.

Questionnaire # 116 - Comments Section

Elimination of entities and ethnic lines of divisions is unavoidable, as well as the elimination of the term Republika Srpska. I this term stays, it means that other nationalities in it have no place. (Mr. Holbrooke's biggest political mistake).

Questionnaire # 118 - Comments Section

Yes, the world powers are motivated by the principle of "divide and rule," as they have done in [the] former Yugoslavia, only because of different [political?] systems, and now they are doing that in Iraq, because of religion, while democracy is for the rich.

Questionnaire # 119 - Comments Section

It would be good to do the questionnaires within given nationalities.

Questionnaire # 130 – Page 3 and Comments Section

Q1, pg 3 – It depends on how he feels.

Let everybody have the same rights, as well as the right to have their own state.

Questionnaire # 147 - Comments Section

Good questions in the second part. I am very much apolitical and I do not think very much about B&H as a state.

Questionnaire # 149 – Demographics Section

Doctor (*demographics*)

Questionnaire # 155 - Comments Section

More precise and more clear questions are necessary.

Questionnaire # 156 - Comments Section

Signature, nothing else.

Questionnaire # 157 – Page 3 and Comments Section

Q1, pg 3 – I suppose one has to be a man [*context of human*].

I think it should be as it was before the war. But it is hard; somebody succeeded to tear down our values and now it does not make any difference to us.

Questionnaire # 158 – Throughout Questionnaire

Q6, pg 2 – I felt better.

Q1, pg 3 – As it [the child] wants.

Q2, pg 3 – As a child, Hungarian; and when he grows up he can choose and decide.

Really, you are pathetic; with these papers you are not going to succeed in making things better for us. Offer us employment and more or less normal pay as well as living conditions. And as for the nationalities and roads [paths?]; postpone those questions for some later opportunities [occasions]… Thank you, kindly!!

Questionnaire # 159 – Page 3 and Comments Section

Q1, pg 3 – half-half

Q2, pg 3 – It depends on [the] child.

I think there should be [exist] a third entity too.

Questionnaire # 161 - Comments Section

#5 Kosovo is not an independent state.

A child's nationality depends on the place of his birth as well as on the nationality of his father, until he becomes of age; when he can make his own choice.

Questionnaire # 163 - Comments Section

Question 5. Are you for the introduction of a third entity: If the two existing entities are not eliminated, then I am for the [its] introduction.

Very interesting, both 163 and 165 added a fictitious 5th question on page 4 and answered it.

Questionnaire # 164 - Comments Section

Question 5. Are you for the introduction of a third entity: Yes.

Questionnaire # 165 - Comments Section

Third Entity. Yes !

Questionnaire # 166 - Comments Section

They [comments] are not necessary.

Questionnaire # 167 - Comments Section

Bosnia is an unsolvable problem.

Questionnaire # 175 - Comments Section

To achieve a doctoral degree on this subject is a huge undertaking, because we ourselves do not know what we "want" !

Questionnaire # 184 – Throughout Questionnaire

Q3, pg 2 – "only as such can we go "forward"

Q4, pg 2 – "It all depends on conservative people who are looking into the past"

Q5, pg 2 – "Kosovo was a region, and R. Srpska is a part of B&H created in Dayton.

Q6, pg 2 – "But also a Bosnian."

Q2, pg 3 – If the patriarchal principles are still valid, then it is so; if the equality is in force, then the parents are to make a mutual decision.

Q3, pg 3 – The problem will arise in case the parents request a return of the child, but my opinion is that the child should be given a nationality of those who adopted him, or perhaps point out the problem and solve it mutually.

Q4, pg 4 – I (tried to put) myself in such a situation, and Bosnia is also full of problems of this nature.

Pretty interesting questionnaire, but these problematic questions will be asked in the following years.

Questionnaire # 185 – Page 3 and Comments Section

Bottom of page 3 – The comparison is not a best one, but following the logic, these [this?] would be determined in the same manner.

In demographics section – noted "**BOSHERKA**" for nationality; a combination of Bosnian & Herzegovinian. UNIQUE.

It is paradoxical that B&H is the only country in which Bosnians and Herzegovinians do not live, but Serbs, Croats, Bosniacs. There is no America without Americans; France without the French; similarly there will be no B&H without Bosnians and Herzegovinians. (continued – next page) The Dayton Peace Agreement has stopped the war, but it has now been surpassed. The changes to it are necessary. The signers of the agreement are now at The Hague. B&H is recognized as a sovereign country, but without the present (current) internal borders. Therefore, these internal borders [IEBL] should not exist, but perhaps only economic regions.

B&H is a small country. We do not need such a large number of Governments (Entity level, Brcko District, cantons, regions...). It is an expensive government. We want one government for Bosnia and Herzegovina, as a modern state.

Questionnaire # 187 - Comments Section

The future of B&H is in the community with the rest of European countries, and first of all in the EU. The Daytonian Bosnia and Herzegovina, with lines of separation, should immediately cease to exist. B&H is a multinational, European and complete state. The international community should realize that the nationalities of B&H are Europeans, and as such, they belong to Europe.

Questionnaire # 211 – Throughout questionnaire

Q6, pg 2 – Yugoslav, of Moslem faith.

Q3, pg 3 – By its birth, the child is of Romanian nationality. Considering the adoption of the child and that it grows in a Hungarian surrounding, it can be of Hungarian nationality, up to a point when he becomes of age.

I consider these questions to be insufficiently and imprecisely defined. The children are automatically of the Father's nationality. Also, someone can live in any country and yet (to) feel that one is a part of a third country, namely it is his personal right to declare.

Questionnaire # 212 – Throughout questionnaire

Q1, pg 2 – "Personal perception of RS's standpoint."

Q6, pg 2 – "It is impossible to circle one response, since that would mean a negation of national/governmental/territorial identity."

Q3, pg 3 – "It is impossible to answer the questions formulated in this manner. The answer depends on numerous other circumstances."

Appendix E

SPSS Data Output

Ethnic ID * Q1 IEBL & RS Cross tabulation

Count

		Q1 IEBL & RS					Total
		strongly agree	agree	unsure	disagree	strongly disagree	
Ethnic ID	bosnian	2	7	3	12	12	36
	bosniak	5	9	8	8	22	52
	croat	5	5	6	9	3	28
	serb	42	24	11	11	4	92
Total		54	45	28	40	41	208

Case Processing Summary

	Cases					
	Valid		Missing		Total	
	N	Percent	N	Percent	N	Percent
Ethnic ID * Q1 IEBL & RS	208	96.3%	8	3.7%	216	100.0%

Chi-Square Tests

	Value	df	Asymp. Sig. (2-sided)
Pearson Chi-Square	67.560(a)	12	.000
Likelihood Ratio	70.239	12	.000
Linear-by-Linear Association	49.632	1	.000
N of Valid Cases	208		

a 2 cells (10.0%) have expected count less than 5. The minimum expected count is 3.77.

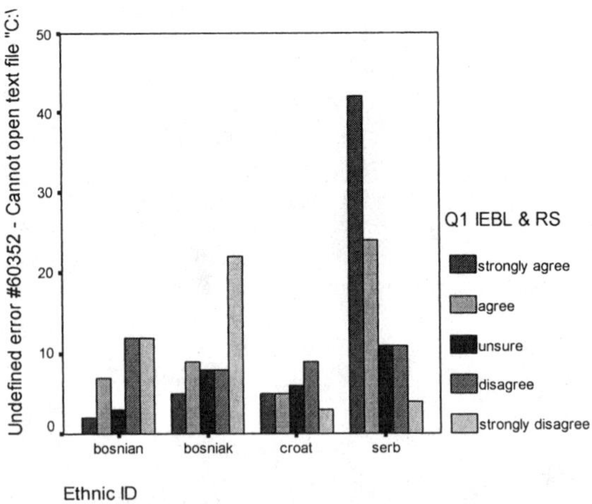

SPSS Output – Statement Nr. 1 "The IEBL is important to the RS."

Ethnic ID * Q2 IEBL & Fed Cross tabulation

Count

		Q2 IEBL & Fed					Total
		strongly agree	agree	unsure	disagree	strongly disagree	
Ethnic ID	bosnian	0	1	2	17	15	35
	bosniak	3	4	8	14	23	52
	croat	1	5	7	11	4	28
	serb	28	27	17	14	5	91
Total		32	37	34	56	47	206

Case Processing Summary

	Cases					
	Valid		Missing		Total	
	N	Percent	N	Percent	N	Percent
Ethnic ID * Q2 IEBL & Fed	206	95.4%	10	4.6%	216	100.0%

Chi-Square Tests

	Value	df	Asymp. Sig. (2-sided)
Pearson Chi-Square	84.778(a)	12	.000
Likelihood Ratio	93.640	12	.000
Linear-by-Linear Association	69.494	1	.000
N of Valid Cases	206		

a 2 cells (10.0%) have expected count less than 5. The minimum expected count is 4.35.

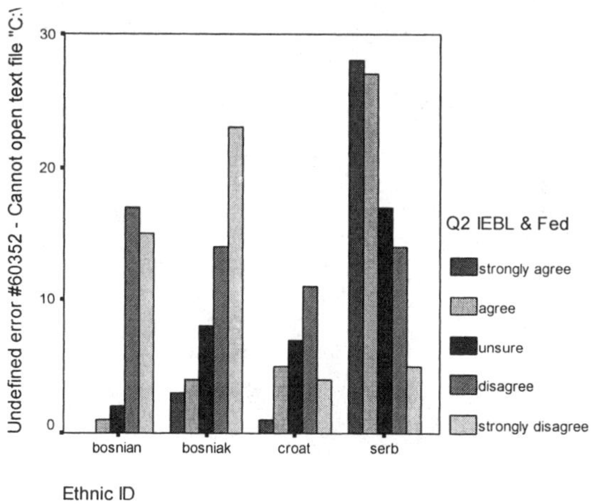

SPSS Output – Statement Nr. 2 "The IEBL is important to the Federation."

Ethnic ID * Q3 Cross tabulation

Count

		Q3					Total
		strongly agree	agree	unsure	disagree	strongly disagree	
Ethnic ID	bosnian	21	14	0	1	0	36
	bosniak	33	16	2	1	0	52
	croat	3	12	5	6	3	29
	serb	2	9	10	33	38	92
Total		59	51	17	41	41	209

Case Processing Summary

	Cases					
	Valid		Missing		Total	
	N	Percent	N	Percent	N	Percent
Ethnic ID * Q3	209	96.8%	7	3.2%	216	100.0%

Chi-Square Tests

	Value	df	Asymp. Sig. (2-sided)
Pearson Chi-Square	149.682(a)	12	.000
Likelihood Ratio	179.335	12	.000
Linear-by-Linear Association	119.501	1	.000
N of Valid Cases	209		

a 3 cells (15.0%) have expected count less than 5. The minimum expected count is 2.36.

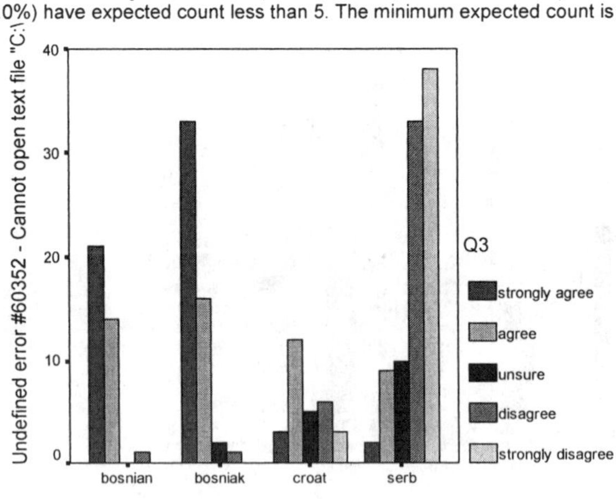

Ethnic ID

SPSS Output – Statement Nr. 3 "Both the IEBL and entities should be dissolved and a strong government and state based in Sarajevo be created in Bosnia."

Ethnic ID * Q4 Cross tabulation

Count

		Q4					Total
		strongly agree	agree	unsure	disagree	strongly disagree	
Ethnic ID	bosnian	1	6	13	12	4	36
	bosniak	3	6	17	14	11	51
	croat	3	7	5	9	5	29
	serb	22	26	26	16	2	92
Total		29	45	61	51	22	208

Case Processing Summary

	Cases					
	Valid		Missing		Total	
	N	Percent	N	Percent	N	Percent
Ethnic ID * Q4	208	96.3%	8	3.7%	216	100.0%

Chi-Square Tests

	Value	df	Asymp. Sig. (2-sided)
Pearson Chi-Square	36.329(a)	12	.000
Likelihood Ratio	39.466	12	.000
Linear-by-Linear Association	24.067	1	.000
N of Valid Cases	208		

a 3 cells (15.0%) have expected count less than 5. The minimum expected count is 3.07.

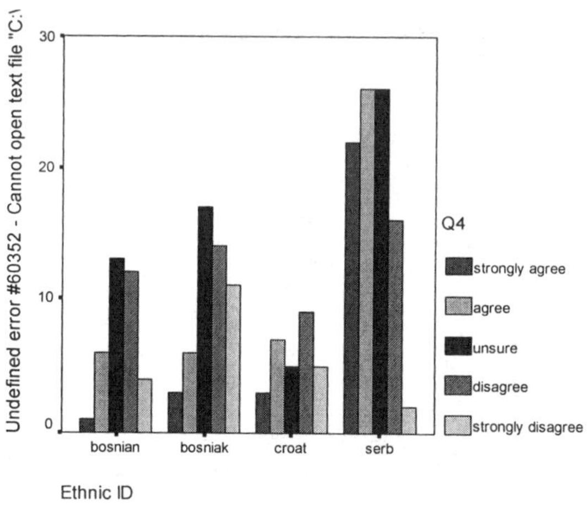

SPSS Output – Statement Nr. 4 "There could be renewed hostilities if HR Paddy Ashdown succeeded in removing the IEBL and disbanding the entity governments and creating a strong central government in Sarajevo."

Ethnic ID * Q5 Kosovo Cross tabulation

Count

		Q5 Kosovo					Total
		strongly agree	agree	unsure	disagree	strongly disagree	
Ethnic ID	bosnian	0	4	2	11	19	36
	bosniak	0	2	4	14	30	50
	croat	2	7	3	9	8	29
	serb	43	32	8	6	2	91
Total		45	45	17	40	59	206

Case Processing Summary

	Cases					
	Valid		Missing		Total	
	N	Percent	N	Percent	N	Percent
Ethnic ID * Q5 Kosovo	206	95.4%	10	4.6%	216	100.0%

Chi-Square Tests

	Value	df	Asymp. Sig. (2-sided)
Pearson Chi-Square	126.439(a)	12	.000
Likelihood Ratio	154.378	12	.000
Linear-by-Linear Association	104.230	1	.000
N of Valid Cases	206		

a 3 cells (15.0%) have expected count less than 5. The minimum expected count is 2.39.

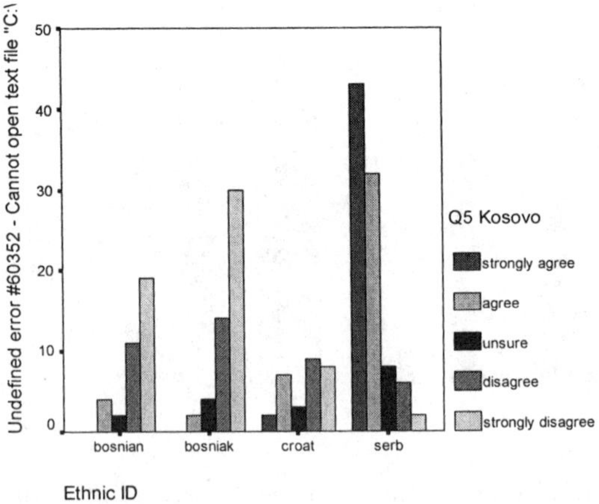

SPSS Output – Statement Nr. 5 "If Kosovo is permitted to become an independent state the Republika Srpska has the same right to sovereignty."

Ethnic ID * Q6 Ethnicity Cross tabulation

Count

		Q6 Ethnicity					Total
		Jugoslav	bosniak	bosnian	croat	serb	
Ethnic ID	bosnian	16	20	0	0	0	36
	bosniak	16	16	20	0	0	52
	croat	6	3	0	19	0	28
	serb	58	2	0	0	32	92
Total		96	41	20	19	32	208

Case Processing Summary

	Cases					
	Valid		Missing		Total	
	N	Percent	N	Percent	N	Percent
Ethnic ID * Q6 Ethnicity	208	96.3%	8	3.7%	216	100.0%

Chi-Square Tests

	Value	df	Asymp. Sig. (2-sided)
Pearson Chi-Square	276.771(a)	12	.000
Likelihood Ratio	239.867	12	.000
Linear-by-Linear Association	8.850	1	.003
N of Valid Cases	208		

a 6 cells (30.0%) have expected count less than 5. The minimum expected count is 2.56.

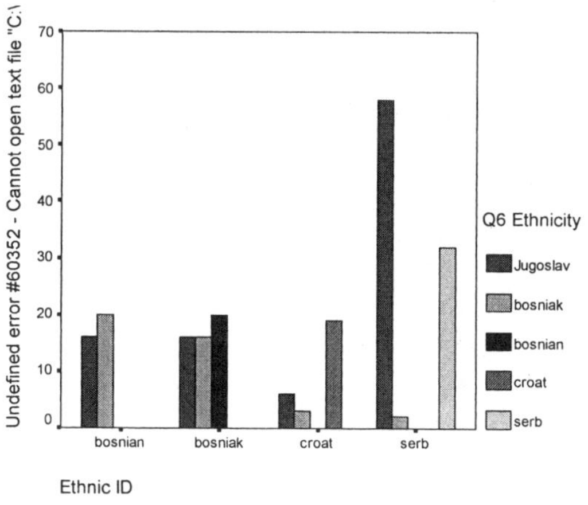

SPSS Output – Statement Nr. 6 "Before the war came to Bosnia, did you feel yourself to be."

BIBLIOGRAPHY

Agnew, John, Ed. Political Geography: A Reader. London: Arnold, 1997.

Allcock, John B. Explaining Yugoslavia. New York: Columbia UP, 2000.

Anderson, Benedict. Imagined Communities. London: Verso, 1983.

Anderson, Walter N. Land Warfare Paper No. 33, Peace with Honor: Enduring Truths, Lessons Learned and Implications for a Durable Peace in Bosnia. Washington DC: Association of the US Army, Institute of Land Warfare, 1999.

Armstrong, John A. Nations before Nationalism. Chapel Hill, NC: University of North Carolina Press, 1982.

Augelli, John P. "Nationalization of Dominican Borderlands." Geographical Review, Vol. 70, Issue. 1(Jan. 1980), pp. 19-35.

Barth, Fredrik. Ethnic Groups and Boundaries. Boston: Little, Brown, and Co., 1969.

Billig, Michael. Banal Nationalism. London: Sage, 1995.

Bodansky, Yossef, "Osama Bin Laden focuses on the Balkans." Defense & Foreign Affairs Strategic Policy, September 19, 2003.

Bonus, Rick. Locating Filipino Americans. Philadelphia: Temple UP, 2000.

Borneman, John, ed. Death of the Father: An Anthropology of the End in Political Authority. New York: Berghahn Books, 2004.

Bose, Sumantra. Bosnia after Dayton: Nationalist Partition and International Intervention. New York: Oxford UP, 2002.

Boyd, Charles. "Making Bosnia Work." Foreign Affairs, Vol. 77, No. 1, pp. 42-55.

Bradshaw, Matt and Elaine Stratford. "Qualitative Research Design and Rigour." Qualitative Research Methods in Human Geography. Ed. Iain Hay. Singapore: Oxford UP, 2000, 37-49.

Breuilly, John. "Approaches to Nationalism." Mapping the Nation. Ed. Gopal Balakrishnan. London: Verso Books, 1996, 146-174.

Bringa, Tone. Being Muslim the Bosnian Way. Princeton: Princeton UP, 1995.

---------------. "Islam and the Quest for in post-Communist Bosnia and Herzegovina," Islam and Bosnia: Conflict Resolution and Foreign Policy in Multi-Ethnic States. Ed. Maya Shatzmiller. Montreal: McGill-Queen's UP, 2002, 24-34.

---------------. "Averted Gaze: Genocide in Bosnia-Herzegovina, 1992-1995," Annihilating Difference: The Anthropology of Genocide. Ed. Alexander L. Hinton. Berkeley: University of California Press, 2002, 194-225.

---------------. "The Peaceful Death of Tito and the Violent End of Yugoslavia," Death of the Father: An Anthropology of the End in Political Authority. Ed. John Borneman. New York: Berghahn Books, 2004, 148-200.

Burg, Steven and Paul Shoup. The War in Bosnia and Herzegovina: Ethnic Conflict and International Intervention. Armonk, NY: M.E. Sharpe, 2000.

Central Intelligence Agency, Office of Russian and European Analysis. Balkan Battlegrounds: A Military History of the Yugoslav Conflict, 1990-1995 Volumes I & II. Washington, DC, 2002.

Cirafici, John L. "SFOR in Bosnia in 1997: A Watershed Year." Parameters, Spring 1999, 80-91.

Conversi, Danielle. "Reassessing Current Theories of Nationalism: Nationalism as Boundary Maintenance and Creation." Nationalism and Ethnic Politics. Vol. 1 (1), 1995, 73-85.

Copley, Gregory. "Srebrenica Casualty Numbers Challenged by Experts as Politicized and Ethnically Divisive," International Strategic Studies Association: Balkan & Eastern Mediterranean Policy Council Release, September 18, 2003.

Cornell, Stephen and Douglas Hartmann. Ethnicity and Race: Making Identities in a Changing World. Thousand Oaks, CA: Pine Forge Press, 1998.

Corwin, Philip. Dubious Mandate: A Memoir of the UN in Bosnia, Summer 1995. Durham: Duke UP, 1999.

Cosgrove, Denis E. Social Formation and Symbolic Landscape. Madison: U of Wisconsin Press, 1998.

Cresswell,John W. Qualitative Inquiry and Research Design. Thousand Oaks, CA.: Sage Publications, 1998.

Cozic, Charles P. Nationalism and Ethnic Conflict. San Diego: Greenhaven Press, 1994.

Cucolo, Tony. "Grunt Diplomacy: In the Beginning There Were Only Soldiers." Parameters, Spring 1999, 110-126.

Darby, Wendy Joy. Landscape and Identity. Oxford: Berg, 2000.

Denitch, Bogdan. Ethnic Nationalism: The Tragic Death of Yugoslavia. 2nd Edition. Minneapolis: U of Minnesota Press, 1996.

Dodds, Klaus. Geopolitics in a Changing World. Singapore: Prentice Hall, 2000.

Doyon, Roy and Hawkins, Michael. Constructing an Albanian Kosovar Identity: Heritage and Memory in the Landscape. Paper presented at the Fall 2002 SEADAAG in Richmond, Virginia.

Dragnich, Alex N. Serbia and Yugoslavia. Boulder: East European Monographs, 1998.

Dunn, Kevin. "Interviewing." Qualitative Research Methods in Human Geography. Singapore, Oxford UP, 2000.

Edensor, Tim. National Identity, Popular Culture and Everyday Life. Oxford: Berg, 2002.

Eller, Jack and Reed Coughlan. "The Poverty of Primordialism: The Demystification of Ethnic Attachments." Ethnic and Racial Studies, 16:2, 1993.

Eskelinen, Heikki, Ilkka Liikanen, and Jukka Oksa, Eds. Curtains of Iron and Gold: Reconstructing Borders and Scales of Interaction. Brookfield, Vt: Ashgate, 1999.

Fine, John. "The Various Faiths in the History of Bosnia: Middle Ages to the Present," Islam and Bosnia: Conflict Resolution and Foreign Policy in Multi-Ethnic States. Ed. Maya Shatzmiller. Montreal: McGill-Queen's UP, 2002, 3-23.

Foote, Kenneth E. Shadowed Ground: America's Landscapes of Violence and Tragedy. Austin: Texas UP, 2003.

----------------, Hugill, P., Mathewson, K., Smith, J. eds. Re-Reading Cultural Geography. Austin: University of Texas Press, 1994.

Fowler, Floyd J. Standardized Survey Interviewing. Newbury Park: Sage, 1990.

-----------------, Survey Research Methods. Beverly Hills: Sage, 1987.

Gee, James P. An Introduction to Discourse Analysis. New York: Routledge, 1999.

Geertz, Clifford, ed. Old Societies and New States. London: The Free Press of Glencoe, 1963.

-------------------. "Primordial and Civic Ties." Nationalism. New York: OUP, 1994.

Gellner, Ernest. Nations and Nationalism. Ithaca: Cornell University Press, 1983.

Gerolymatos, Andre. The Balkan Wars. New York: Basic Books, 2002.

Gilliland, Mary Kay. "Nationalism and Ethnogenesis in the Former Yugoslavia." Ethnic Identity: Creation, Conflict, and Accomodation. Walnut Creek, CA: Altamira Press, 1995.

Gil-White, Francisco J. "How thick is blood? The plot thickens…: if ethnic actors are primordialists, what remains of the circumstantialist/primordialist controversy?" Ethnic and Racial Studies, Vol 22, No. 5, September 1999, pp. 789-820.

Glenny, Misha. The Balkans: Nationalism, War and the Great Powers, 1804-1999. New York: Viking Press, 1999.

-----------------. The Fall of Yugoslavia: The Third Balkan War. 3rd Edition. New York: Penguin , 1996.

Gottman, Jean. The Significance of Territory. Charlottesville, VA: UP of Virginia, 1973

Graham, Brian, Asworth, G.J., and Tunbridge, J.E. A Geography of Heritage: Power, Culture & Economy. London: Arnold, 2000.

Grosby, Steven. "Territoriality: the transcendental, primordial feature of modern societies." Nations and Nationalism, 1 (2), 1995, pp.143-62.

Groth, Paul and Todd Bressi, eds. Understanding Ordinary Landscapes. Ann Arbor, Yale University Press, 1997.

Hall, John. "Nationalisms, Classified and Explained." Notions of Nationalism. Ed. Sukumar Periwal. New York: Central European UP, 1995. 8-33.

Hamourtziadou, Lily. "The Bosniaks: from nation to threat." Journal of Southern Europe and the Balkans, Vol 4, No. 2, 2002, pp. 141-156.

Hartshorne, Richard. "The Functional Approach in Political Geography." The Structure of Political Geography. Eds, Kasperson, R. and Minghi, J. Chicago: Aldine Publishing, 1969, 34-49.

Hastings, Adrian. The construction of nationhood : ethnicity, religion, and nationalism. Cambridge: Cambridge UP, 1997.

Hatzpoulos, Pavlos. "'All that is, is nationalist': Western imaginings of the Balkans since the Yugoslav wars." Journal of Southern Europe and the Balkans, Vol 5, No. 1, 2003, pp. 25-38.

Hay. Iain. Qualitative Research Methods in Human Geography. Singapore: Oxford UP, 2000.

----------. Communicating in Geography and the Environmental Sciences (2nd Ed). South Melbourne: Oxford UP, 2002.

Hinton, Alexander L. ed. Annihilating Difference: The Anthropology of Genocide. Berkeley: University of California Press, 2002.

Hobsbawm, Eric J. Nations and Nationalism since 1780. Cambridge: Cambridge UP, 1992.

--------------------. Bandits. Dell, New York, 1969.

Hoepken, Wolfgang. "Yugoslavia's Communists and the Bosnian Muslims." Muslim Communities Reemerge: Historical Perspectives on Nationality, Politics, and Opposistion in the Former Soviet Union and Yugoslavia. Eds. Kappeler, Andreas, Simon, Gerhard, and Georg Brunner. Durham, SC: Duke UP, 1994, 214-247.

Hoggart, Keith, Lees, Loretta and Davies, Anna. Researching Human Geography. London: Arnold, 2002.

Holdsworth, Deryck W. "Landscape and Archives as Texts." Understanding Ordinary Landscapes, edited by Paul Groth and Todd Bressi, 1997.

Honig, Jan W. and Norbert Both. Srebrenica: Record of a War Crime. New York: Penguin Books, 1997.

Hooson, David, ed. Geography and National Identity. Oxford: Blackwell Press, 1994.

Hutchinson, John and Anthony D. Smith, Eds. Nationalism. New York: OUP, 1994.

-----------, eds. Ethnicity. New York: Oxford UP, 1996.

International Crisis Group Balkans Report No. 146, "Bosnia's Nationalist Governments: Paddy Ashdown and the Paradoxes of State Building." Brussels, July 2003.

Ivanovic, Ilija. Witness to Jasenovac's Hell. Mt. Pleasant, TX.: Dallas Publishing Company, 2002.

Jackson, James B. Discovering the Vernacular Landscape. New Haven: Yale UP, 1984.

Jackson, Robert H. Quasi-States:Sovereignty, International Relations, and the Third World. Cambridge: Cambridge UP, 1990.

Jelavich, Barbara. History of the Balkans: Twentieth Century. Cambridge: Cambridge UP, 1983.

--------------------. History of the Balkans: Eighteenth and Nineteenth Centuries. Cambridge: Cambridge UP, 1983.

Johnson, Nuala. "Cast in Stone: Monuments, Geography, and Nationalism," Political Geography; A Reader, edited by John Agnew, 1997.

Jukrainen, Pirjo. "Borders Change – So Do Space, Identity, and Community." Curtains of Iron and Gold. Brookfield, Vt: Ashgate, 1999.

Kaplan, David H. "Two Nations in Search of a State: Canada's Ambivalent Spatial Identities." Annals of the Association of American Geographers, vol. 84(4), 1994, pp. 585-606.

--------. "Nationalism at a micro-scale: Educational segregation in Montreal." Political Geography, Vol. 11, No. 3, May 1992, pp. 259-282.

Kaplan, David and Jouni Häkli, eds. Boundaries and Place. Lanham, MD: Roman & Littlefield, 2002.

Kappeler, Andreas, Simon, Gerhard, and Georg Brunner, eds. Muslim Communities Reemerge: Historical Perspectives on Nationality, Politics, and Opposistion in the Former Soviet Union and Yugoslavia. Durham, SC: Duke UP, 1994.

Kasperson, Roger and Julian Minghi, eds. The Structure of Political Geography. Chicago Aldine Publishing, 1969.

Kaufman, Stuart J. Modern Hatreds: The Symbolic Politics of Ethnic War. Ithaca, NY: Cornell UP, 2001.

Kearns, Robin. "Being There: Research through Observing and Participating." Qualitative Research Methods in Human Geography. Singapore, Oxford UP, 2000, 103-121.

Kedourie, Elie. "Nationalism and Self-Determination." Nationalism. New York: OUP, 1994.

Knaus, and Felix Martin. "Travails of the European Raj." Journal of Democracy, Vol.14(3), July 2003, 60-74.

Koshar, Rudy. From Monuments to Traces: Artifacts of German Memory 1870-1990. Berkeley: U of California Press, 2000.

Laffan, R.G.D. The Serbs: The Guardians of the Gate. Dorset Press, New York, 1989.

Lange, David A. "The Role of the Political Adviser in Peacekeeping Operations." Parameters, Spring 1999, 92-109.

Lewis, Pierce, "Axioms for Reading the Landscape." The Interpretation of Ordinary Landscapes. New York: Oxford UP, 1979.

Lowenthal, David. "European Landscape Transformations: The Rural Residue." Understanding Ordinary Landscapes. New Haven: Yale UP, 1997.

Magaš, Branka. "On Bosnianness." Nations and Nationalism, Vol. 9(1), 2003, 19-23.

-----------------. The Destruction of Yugoslavia: Tracking the Breakup 1980-92. London: Verso Books, 1993.

MacKenzie, Lewis. Peacekeeper: The Road to Sarajevo. Vancouver: Douglas & McIntyre, 1993.

Malcolm, Noel. Bosnia: A Short History. London: MacMillan, 1994.

Mayo, James. "War Memorials as Political Memory." The Geographical Review, Vol. 78, No. 1, January 1988, 62-75.

Mazower, Mark. The Balkans: A Short History. New York: Modern Library, 2002.

Meinig, D.W., Ed. The Interpretation of Ordinary Landscapes: Geographical Essays. New York: Oxford UP, 1979.

Mellor, R.E.H. Nation State and Territory. London: Routledge, 1989.

Mitchell, Don. "Sticks and Stones: The Work of Landscape." Professional Geographer, Vol. 48(1), 1996, 94-96.

Muir, Richard. Approaches to Landscape. London: MacMillan Press, 1999.

----------------. Political Geography. London: MacMillan Press, 1997.

Murphy, Alexander B. "National Claims to Territory in the Modern State System: Geographical Considerations." Geopolitics, Vol. 7, No. 2 (Autumn 2002), pp. 193-214.

Nation, Craig. War in the Balkans, 1991-2002. Carlisle, PA.: US Army War College, Strategic Studies Institute, 2003.

O'Tuathail, Gearoid. "Between a Holocaust and a Quagmire." Critical Geopolitics. Minneapolis: University of Minnesota Press, 1996.

Paasi, Anssi. Territories, Boundaries, and Consciousness. New York: Wiley, 1996.

---------------. "The Political Geography of Boundaries at the End of the Millenium: Challenges of the De-territorializing World." Curtains of Iron and Gold. Brookfield, Vt: Ashgate, 1999.

Paddison, Ronan. The Fragmented State. New York: St. Martin's Press, 1983.

Papacosma, S. Victor. "The Balkans and a Transforming NATO." The New Balkans: Disintegration and Reconstruction. Eds. Kourvetaris, George, Roudometof, Victor, et al. Boulder: East European Monographs, 2002.

Parenti, Michael. To Kill A Nation: The Attack on Yugoslavia. London: Verso Books, 2000.

Patton, Michael Q. Qualitative Research & Evaluation Methods 3rd Ed. Thousand Oaks, CA: Sage Publications, 2002.

Pavlovich, Paul The Serbians: The Story of a People. Serbian Heritage Books, Don Mills, Ontario, Canada 1988.

Pavlowitch, Stevan K. Tito: Yugoslavia's Great Dictator, A Reassessment. London: C. Hurst & Company, 1992.

Peet, Richard. "Discursive Idealism in the 'Landscape-as-Text' School," Professional Geographer, Vol. 48(1), 1996, 96-98.

Perica, Vjekoslav. Balkan Idols: Religion and Nationalism in Yugoslav States. New York: Oxford UP, 2002.

Periwal, Sukumar, ed. Notions of Nationalism. New York: Central European UP, 1995.

Peterson, Robert A. Constructing Effective Questionnaires. Thousand Oaks, CA : Sage Publications, 2000.

Petrovich, Michael B. A History of Modern Serbia 1804-1918. New York: Harcourt Brace Jovanovich, 1976.

Popovic, Alexandre. "Islamic Movements in Yugoslavia." Muslim Communities Reemerge: Historical Perspectives on Nationality, Politics, and Opposistion in the Former Soviet Union and Yugoslavia. Eds. Kappeler, Andreas, Simon, Gerhard, and Georg Brunner. Durham, SC: Duke UP, 1994, 322- 340.

Prescott, J.R.V. Boundaries and Frontiers. Totowa, NJ: Rowman and Littlefield, 1978.

---------. Political Frontiers and Boundaries. London: Allen & Unwin Ltd, 1987.

Ramet, Sabrina P. "Primordial Ethnicity or Modern Nationalism: The Case of Yugoslavia's Muslims, Reconsidered." Muslim Communities Reemerge: Historical Perspectives on Nationality, Politics, and Opposistion in the Former Soviet Union and Yugoslavia. Eds. Kappeler, Andreas, Simon, Gerhard, and Georg Brunner. Durham, SC: Duke UP, 1994, 111-138.

Robinson, Guy, Engelstoft, Sten, and Pobric, Alma. "Remaking Sarajevo: Bosnian Nationalism after the Dayton Accord." Political Geography, 20 (2001) pp. 957-980.

--------. Nationality and Identity in Post-Dayton Accord Bosnia-Herzegovina. Paper prepared for presentation in 2004.

Rohde, David. End Game the Betrayal and Fall of Srebrenica: Europe's Worst Massacre Since World War II. Boulder: Westview Press, 1997.

Romanucci-Ross, Lola and George DeVos, eds. Ethnic Identity: Creation, Conflict, and Accomodation. Walnut Creek, CA: Altamira Press, 1995.

Rose, Gillian. Visual Methodologies. London: SAGE, 2001.

Rose, Michael. Fighting For Peace. London: The Harvill Press, 1998.

Rumley, D. and Julian Minghi, Eds. The Geography of Border Landscapes. London: Routledge, 1991.

Sack, Robert. Human Territoriality: A Theory. Cambridge: CUP, 1986.

Shatzmiller, Maya, ed. Islam and Bosnia: Conflict Resolution and Foreign Policy in Multi-Ethnic States. Montreal: McGill-Queen's UP, 2002.

Semonite, Todd T. "The Military Engineer as a Critical Peace Operations Multiplier." Strategy Research Project, US Army War College, Carlisle Barracks, Penn., 1999.

Seton-Watson, Hugh. Nations and States. Boulder: Westview Press, 1977.

Sells, Michael. "Crosses of Blood: Sacred Space, Religion, and Violence in Bosnia -Hercegovina." Sociology of Religion, 64:3 (2003) pp. 309-331.

Sheskin, Ira M. Survey Research for Geographers. Association of American Geographers Resource Publication, 1985.

Shrader, Charles. The Muslim Croat Civil War in Central Bosnia: A Military History, 1992-1994. College Station: Texas A&M UP, 2003.

Silber, Laura and Allan Little. Yugoslavia: Death of a Nation. New York: Penguin Books, 1997.

Smith, Anthony D. Nationalism and Modernism. London: Routledge, 1998.

----------------------. "When is a Nation?" Geopolitics, Vol.7, No. 2 (Autumn 2002) 5-32.

Stack, John F., ed. The Primordial Challenge: Ethnicity in the Contemporary World. Westport, CT: Greenwood Press, 1986.

Stavrianos, L.S. The Balkans Since 1453. New York: NY University Press, 1965.

Storey, David. Territory: The Claiming of Space. Singapore: Prentice Hall, 2001.

Strauss, Anselm and Corbin, Juliet. Basics of Qualitative Research: Grounded Theory, Procedures and Techniques. Newbury Park: Sage Publications, 1990.

Sugar, Peter and Ivo Lederer, eds. Nationalism in Eastern Europe. Seattle: University of Washington Press, 1994 edition.

Temperley, Harold W.V., The History of Serbia. Howard Fertig, New York, 1969.

Trifkovic, Srdja. Ustaša: Croatian Separatism and European Politics, 1929-1945. Aiken, SC: The Lord Byron Foundation for Balkan Studies, 1998.

Tyner, James. "Nightmarish Landscapes: The Orwellian World of Malcolm X." Race, Ethnicity and Place Conference. Howard University, Washington DC, September, 2004.

Umek, Dragan. "New Territorial Entities in the Balkan Peninsula; The Case of Bosnia and Herzegovina." Europe Between Political Geography and Geopolitics: Proceedings of the international meeting organized by the Geographical Section of the Department of Political Sciences (University of Trieste) and the International Geographical Union, Rome, 10-13 December 1997. Eds. Marco Antonisch, Vladimir Kolossov, and M. Paola Pagnini. Rome: Societa' Geografica Italiana, 2001. 829-837.

Velkonja, Joseph. "The Quest for Slovene Identity." Geography and National Identity. Ed. David Hooson. Oxford: Blackwell Press, 1994.

Velikonja, Mitja. Religious Separation & Political Intolerance in Bosnia-Herzegovina. College Station, TX: Texas A&M UP, 2003.

West, Rebecca. Black Lamb and Grey Falcon: A Journey Through Yugoslavia. London: MacMillan, 1942.

West, Richard. Tito and the Rise and Fall of Yugoslavia. New York: Carroll & Graf Publishers, 1995.

White, George W. Nationalism and Territory: Constructing Group Identity in Southeastern Europe. Lanham: Rowman & Littlefield, 2000.

Winchester, Hilary, Kong, Lily and Dunn, Kevin. Landscapes; Ways of Imagining the World. Essex, UK: Pearson Education Limited, 2003.

Woodward, Susan. Balkan Tragedy: Chaos and Dissolution After the Cold War. Washington DC: The Brookings Institution, 1995.

List of Acronyms

ABH - *Armija Bosne i Hercegovine* (Army of Bosnia and Herzegovina)

AVNOJ - *Antifašsističko viječe narodnog oslobodjenja Jugoslavije* (Antifascist Council for National Liberation of Yugoslavia)

BiH - *Bosna i Herzegovina* (Bosnia and Herzegovina)

BSA - Bosnian Serb Army

CIA - Central Intelligence Agency

DOD - Department of Defense

DPA - Dayton Peace Accords

EU - European Union

EUCOM - European Command, US Department of Defense

EUFOR - European Union Forces

HDZ - *Hrvatska demokratska zajednica* (Croatian Democratic Community)

HOS - *Hrvatske odbrambene snage* (Croat Defense Forces – the military wing of the Party of the Right)

HR - High Representative, Lord Paddy Ashdown

HVO - *Hrvatsko vjece odbrane* (Croatian Defense Council)

C - International Community

EBL - Inter-Entity Boundary Line

FOR - Implementation Forces (NATO)

OCC - International Orthodox Christian Charities

CRC - International Committee of the Red Cross

NA - *Jugoslovenska Narodna Armija* (Yugoslav People's Army)

MOD - Ministry of Defense

NATO - North Atlantic Treaty Organization

NGO - Non-governmental organization

ODC - Office of Defense Cooperation, European Command

OHR - Office of the High Representative

OSCE - Organization for Security and Cooperation in Europe

RS - *Republika Srpska*

SDA - *Stranka demokratske akcije* (Party of Democratic Action)

SDS - *Srpska demokratska stranka* (Serbian Democratic Party)

SFOR - Stabilization Forces (NATO)

SPSS - Statistical Package for Social Sciences

UDBA - *Uprava Državne Bezbjednost* (Department of State Security - the secret police)

UN - United Nations

UNHCR - United Nations High Commission for Refugees

UNPA - United Nations Protected Area

UNPROFOR - UN Protection Forces

US - United States

VRS - *Vojska Republike Srpske* (Army of the Serb Republic or Bosnian Serb Army)

WW I - World War One

WW II - World War Two